TEACHING SCIENCE FICTION:
Education for Tomorrow

TEACHING SCIENCE FICTION: Education for Tomorrow

Edited by JACK WILLIAMSON

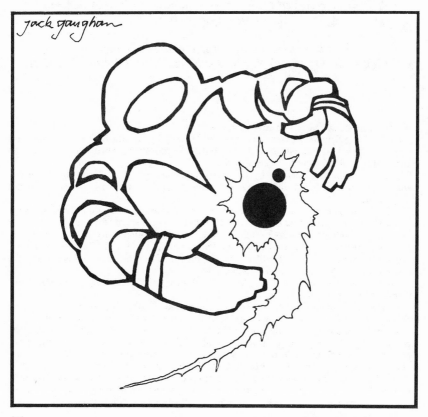

jack gaughan

Ōwlswick Press   Philadelphia

A few of these essays have appeared elsewhere:

"On Teaching Science Fiction" (as "Escape Routes") by Ursula K. LeGuin; copyright © 1974 by Universal Publishing and Distributing Corporation; reprinted by permission of the author and her agent, Virginia Kidd.

"Science Fiction and Society" by Isaac Asimov; copyright © 1974 by the American Medical Association. Reprinted from *Prism* (January 1974) by permission of the author and the AMA.

"Bridging the Gap between Technology and the Humanities" by Robin Wilson; copyright © 1973 by *Engineering Education;* reprinted by permission of the author.

"Twentieth Century Science-Fiction Writers" and "A Bibliography of Twentieth Century Science Fiction" by Alexei and Cory Panshin; copyright © 1976, 1980 by Alexei and Cory Panshin; reprinted from *Masters of Space and Time: the Story of Science Fiction* by permission of the authors and Pocket Books.

"Women and Science Fiction" by Susan Wood; copyright © 1978 by Algol Magazine; reprinted by permission of the author.

"Something Happens" by Kate Wilhelm; copyright © 1971 by Robin Scott Wilson; reprinted from *Clarion,* edited by Robin Scott Wilson, by permission of the author.

"The Infinity Connection" by Jack Williamson; passages revised from *Teaching SF,* copyright © 1971 by Jack Williamson, and "Will Academe Kill Science Fiction?", copyright © 1978 by Davis Publications, Inc., from *Isaac Asimov's Science Fiction Magazine,* March-April 1978, copyright © 1978 by Davis Publications, Inc.

"The Tinsel Screen: Science Fiction and the Movies" by James Gunn; revised from "On the Tinsel Screen: Science Fiction and the Movies" from *Isaac Asimov's Science Fiction Magazine,* February 1980; copyright © 1980 by Davis Publications, Inc.

ISBN 0-913896-15-2 **LC 79-92642**

To Isaac Asimov,
Educator

CONTENTS

I: THE TOPIC

II: THE TEACHERS

III. THE TOOLS

PREFACE:
SCIENCE FICTION—
A PERSONAL VIEW

BY CARL SAGAN

Winner of the Pulitzer Prize for The Dragons of Eden, *Carl Sagan is David Duncan Professor of Astronomy and Space Sciences and director of the Laboratory for Planetary Studies at Cornell University. A leader in establising the high surface temperatures of Venus and in understanding the seasonal changes on Mars, he is responsible for the Voyager interstellar record, a message about ourselves sent to other civilizations in space. A recent book is* Broca's Brain. *Another project is* Cosmos, *a thirteen-part TV series on science aired on PBS and around the world.*

Coming from a scientist of such renown, this rich appreciation of science fiction may seem surprising, but he confesses that his earliest interest in space science was awakened by science fiction.

By the time I was ten I had decided—in almost total ignorance of the difficulty of the problem—that the universe was full up. There were too many places for this to be the only inhabited planet. And, from the variety of life on Earth (trees looked pretty different from most of my friends), I figured life elsewhere would look mighty strange. I tried hard to imagine what that life would be like, but despite my best efforts I always produced a kind of terrestrial chimera, a blend of existing plants and animals.

About this time a friend introduced me to the Mars novels of Edgar Rice Burroughs. I had not thought much about Mars before, but here, presented before me in the adventures of John Carter, was an inhabited extraterrestrial world breath-takingly fleshed out: ancient sea bottoms, great canal pumping stations and a variety of beings, some of them exotic. There were, for example, the ten-legged beasts of burden, the thoats.

These novels were exhilarating to read. At first. But slowly doubts began to gnaw. The plot surprise in the first John Carter novel which I read hinged on his forgetting that the year is longer on Mars than on Earth. But it seemed to me that if you go to another planet one of the first things you check into is the length of the day and the year.

(Incidentally, I can recall no mention by Carter of the remarkable fact that the Martian day is almost as long as the terrestrial day. It was as if he *expected* the familiar comforts of his home planet somewhere else.) Then there were incidental remarks made which were at first stunning but on sober reflection disappointing. For example, Burroughs casually comments that on Mars there are two more primary colors than on Earth. Many long minutes did I spend with my eyes closed, fiercely concentrating on a new primary color. But it would always be a murky brown or a plum. How could there be another primary color on Mars, much less two? What was a primary color? Was it something to do with physics or something to do with physiology? I decided that Burroughs might not have known what he was talking about, but he certainly made his readers think. And in those many chapters where there was not much to think about there were satisfyingly malignant enemies and rousing swordsmanship—more than enough to keep the interest of a city-bound ten-year-old in a Brooklyn summer.

The following summer, by sheerest accident, I stumbled across a magazine called *Astounding Science Fiction* in the neighborhood candy store. A glance at the cover and a quick riffle through the interior showed me it was what I had been looking for. With some effort I managed to scrape together the purchase price, opened it at random, sat down on a bench not twenty feet from the candy store and read my first modern science-fiction short story, "Pete Can Fix It" by Raymond F. Jones, a gentle time-travel story of post-nuclear-war holocaust. I had known about the atom bomb—I remember an excited friend explaining to me that it was made of atoms—but this was the first I had seen about the social implications of the development of nuclear weapons. It got you thinking. The little device, though, that Pete the garage mechanic put on automobiles so passengers might make a brief cautionary trip into the wasteland of the future—what was that little device? How was it made? How could you get into the future and then come back? If Raymond F. Jones knew, he wasn't telling.

I found I was hooked. Each month I eagerly awaited the arrival of *Astounding*. I read Verne and Wells, read cover to cover the first two science-fiction anthologies that I was able to find, and made scorecards, similar to those I was fond of making for baseball, on the quality of the stories I read. Many of the stories ranked high in asking interesting questions but low in answering them.

There is still a part of me that is ten years old. But by and large I'm older. My critical faculties and perhaps even my literary tastes have improved. I can no longer manage credulous acceptance as well as I used to. In Larry Niven's "Neutron Star" the plot hinges on the astonishing tidal forces exerted by a strong gravitational field. But we are asked to believe that hundreds or thousands of years from now, at a time of casual interstellar spaceflight, such tidal forces, well-under-

CARL SAGAN

stood today, are unknown. We are asked to believe that the first probe of a neutron star is done by a manned rather than by an unmanned spacecraft. We are asked too much. In a novel of ideas the ideas have to work.

I had the same kind of disquieting feelings many years earlier on reading Verne's description of weightlessness on a lunar voyage occurring only at the point in space where Earth's and the Moon's gravitational pulls cancelled; and in Wells's invention of the antigravity mineral, cavorite: why should a vein of cavorite still be on the Earth at all? In Douglas Trumbull's technically proficient science-fiction film *Silent Running* the trees in a vast spaceborne closed ecological system on its way to Saturn are dying. After weeks of painstaking study and agonizing searches through botany texts, the solution is found: plants, it turns out, need sunlight. Trumbull's characters are able to build interplanetary cities but have forgotten the inverse square law? I was willing to overlook the portrayal of the rings of Saturn as pastel-colored gasses, but not this.

I have the same trouble with "Star Trek," which I know has a wide following and which some thoughtful friends tell me I should view allegorically and not literally. But when astronauts from Earth set down on some far distant planet and find the human beings there in the midst of a conflict between two nuclear superpowers which call themselves the Yangs and the Coms, or their phonetic equivalents, the suspension of disbelief crumbles. In a global terrestrial society centuries in the future the ship's officers are embarrassingly Anglo-American. In fact only two of twelve or fifteen interstellar vessels are given non-English names, *Kongo* and *Potemkin (Potemkin* and not *Aurora*?). And the idea of a successful cross between a "Vulcan" and a terrestrial simply ignores what we know of molecular biology. (As I have remarked elsewhere, such a cross is about as likely as the successful mating of a man and a petunia.) I have similar problems with films in which spiders thirty feet tall are menacing the cities of Earth: since insects and arachnids breathe by diffusion, such marauders would asphyxiate before they could savage their first city.

What has happened to me, I suppose, is that the same thirst for wonder is there that was there when I was ten. But I have learned a little bit about how the world is really put together. I find that science fiction has led me to science. I find science more subtle, more intricate and more awesome than much of science fiction. It has the additional virtue of being true. Think of some of the scientific finds of the last few decades: that the continents are moving on a vast conveyer belt with the mountains produced by collisions of continental plates; that Mars is covered with ancient dry rivers; that chimpanzees can learn languages of many hundreds of words, understand abstract concepts, and construct new grammatical usages; that all life on Earth runs off a particular molecule containing all the hereditary information and able to make identical copies of itself; that there are particles which pass effortlessly through the entire Earth so that we see as many of them coming up through our feet as down from the sky; that in the constellation Cygnus there is a double star, one of whose components has such a high gravitational acceleration that light cannot escape from it: it may be blazing with radiation on the inside but it is invisible from the outside. In the face of all this, many of the standard ideas of science fiction seem to me to pale by comparison.

But the best of science fiction remains very good indeed. There are stories which are so tautly constructed, so rich in accommodating details of an unfamiliar society that they sweep me along before I have even a chance to be critical. Such stories include Robert Heinlein's *The Door Into Summer*; Alfred Bester's *The Stars My Destination* and *The Demolished Man*; Jack Finney's *Time and Again*; Frank Herbert's *Dune*; and Walter M. Miller's *A Canticle for Leibowitz*. You can ruminate over the ideas in these books. Heinlein's asides on the feasibility and social utility of household robots wear exceedingly well over the intervening years. The insights into terrestrial ecology provided by hypothetical extraterrestrial ecologies as in *Dune* perform, I think, an important social service. "He Who Shrank" by Henry Hasse presents an entrancing cosmological speculation which is being seriously revived today, the idea of an infinite regress of universes—in which each of our elementary particles is a universe one level down, and in which we are an elementary particle in the next universe up.

A rare few science-fiction novels combine extraordinarily well a deep human sensitivity with a standard science-fiction theme. I am thinking, for example, of Algis Budrys's *Rogue Moon*, and of many of the works of Theodore Sturgeon—but particularly "To Here and the Easel," a stunning portrayal of schizophrenia as perceived from the inside, as well as a provocative introduction to Ariosto's *Orlando Furioso*. Asimov's story "Breathes There a Man" provided a poignant insight into the emotional stress and sense of isolation of many of the best theoretical scientists. Arthur Clarke's "The Nine Billion Names of God" introduced many Western readers to an intriguing speculation on Oriental religions.

One of the great benefits of science fiction is that it can convey bits and pieces, hints and phrases, of knowledge unknown or inaccessible to the reader. Isaac Asimov's robots were "positronic," because the positron had recently been discovered. Asimov never provided any explanation of how positrons run robots, but his readers had now heard of positrons. Jack Williamson's robots were run off ruthenium, rhodium, and palladium, the next Group VIII metals after iron, nickel, and cobalt in the periodic table. An analog with ferromagnetism was suggested. I suppose that there are science-fictional robots today which are quarkish or charming and will provide some brief verbal entree into the excitement of contemporary elementary particle physics. L.

CARL SAGAN

Sprague de Camp's *Lest Darkness Fall* is an excellent introduction to Rome at the time of the Gothic invasion, and Asimov's *Foundation* series, although this is not explained in the books, offers a very useful summary of some of the dynamics of the far-flung imperial Roman Empire. Time-travel stories—for example, the three remarkable efforts by Heinlein, "All You Zombies," "By His Bootstraps," and *The Door Into Summer*—force the reader into contemplations of the nature of causality and the arrow of time. They are stories you ponder over as the water is running out of the bathtub or as you walk though the woods in an early winter snowfall.

Another great value of modern science fiction is some of the art forms it elicits. A fuzzy imagining in the mind's eye of what the surface of another planet might look like is one thing, but examining a meticulous painting of the same scene by Chesley Bonestell in his prime is quite another. The sense of astronomical wonder is splendidly conveyed by the best of contemporary SF artists, among them Don Davis, Jon Lomberg, Rick Sternbach, and Robert McCall. And in the breathtaking poems of Diane Ackerman can be glimpsed the prospect of a mature astronomical poetry fully conversant with conventional science-fiction themes.

Science-fiction ideas are also widespread today in somewhat different guises. For one, we have science-fiction writers such as Isaac Asimov and Arthur C. Clarke providing cogent and brilliant summaries in non-fictional forms of many aspects of science and society. Some contemporary scientists are introduced to a vaster public by science fiction. For example, in the thoughtful novel *The Listeners* by James Gunn, we find the following comment made fifty years from now about my colleague, the astronomer Frank Drake: "Drake! What did he know?" We also find straight science fiction disguised as fact in a vast proliferation of pseudo-scientific writings, belief systems and organizations. One science-fiction writer, L. Ron Hubbard, founded a successful cult called Scientology, invented, according to one account, overnight on a bet. Classic science-fiction ideas are now institutionalized in unidentified flying objects and ancient astronaut belief systems—although one has difficulty not concluding that Stanley G. Weinbaum (in "The Valley of Dreams") did it better as well as earlier than Erich Von Daniken. R. DeWitt Miller in his story "Within the Pyramid" manages to anticipate both Von Daniken and Velikovsky, and to provide a more coherent hypothesis on the supposed extraterrestrial origin of pyramids than can be found in all the writings on ancient astronauts and pyramidology. In *Wine of the Dreamers* by John D. MacDonald (a science-fiction writer now transmogrified into one of the most interesting contemporary writers of detective fiction), we find: "and there are traces, in Earth mythology . . . of great ships and chariots that crossed the sky." The story "Farewell to the Master" by Harry Bates was converted into a motion picture, *The Day the Earth Stood Still*, which abandoned the essential plot element, that on the extraterrestrial spacecraft it was the robot and not the human who was in command. The movie, with its depiction of a flying saucer buzzing Washington, is thought by some sober invesigators to have played a role in the 1952 Washington, D.C., UFO "flap" which followed closely the film's release. Many popular novels today of the espionage variety, in the shallowness of their characterizations and the gimmickiness of their plots, are virtually indistinguishable from pulp science fiction of the thirties and forties.

The interweaving of science and science fiction sometimes produces curious results. It is not always clear whether life imitates art or vice versa. For example, in Kurt Vonnegut, Jr.'s superb epistemological novel *The Sirens of Titan*, a not altogether inclement environment is postulated on Saturn's largest moon. When in the last few years some planetary scientists, myself among them, presented evidence that Titan has a dense atmosphere and perhaps higher temperatures than expected, many people commented to me on the prescience of Kurt Vonnegut. But Vonnegut was a physics major at Cornell University and naturally knowledgeable about the latest findings in astronomy. (Many of the best science-fiction writers have science or engineering backgrounds; for example, Poul Anderson, Isaac Asimov, Arthur Clarke and Robert Heinlein.) In 1944, an atmosphere of methane was discovered on Titan, the first satellite in the solar system known to have an atmosphere. In this, as in many similar cases, art imitates life.

In fact, the trouble has been that our understanding of the other planets has been changing faster than the science-fictional representations of them. A clement twilight zone on a synchronously rotating Mercury, a swamp-and-jungle Venus, and a canal-infested Mars, while all classic science-fiction devices, are all in fact based upon earlier misapprehensions by planetary astronomers. The misapprehensions were faithfully transcribed into science-fiction stories which were read by the youngsters who were to become the next generation of planetary astronomers—thereby simultaneously capturing the interest of the youngsters and making it more difficult to correct the misapprehensions of the oldsters. But as our knowledge of the planets has changed, the environments in the corresponding science-fiction stories have also changed. It is quite rare to find a science-fiction story written today which involves algae farms on the surface of Venus. (Incidentally, the UFO contact mythologizers are slower to change, and we can still find accounts of flying saucers from a Venus which is populated by beautiful human beings in long white robes inhabiting a kind of Cytherean Garden of Eden. The 900-degree Fahrenheit temperatures of Venus give us one way of checking such stories.) Likewise, the idea of a "space warp" is a hoary science-fiction standby but it did not arise in science fiction. It arose from Einstein's Theory of General Relativity.

CARL SAGAN

The connection between science-fictional depictions of Mars and the actual exploration of Mars is so close that, subsequent to the Mariner 9 mission to Mars, we were able to name a few Martian craters after deceased science-fiction personalities. Thus there are on Mars craters named after H.G. Wells, Edgar Rice Burroughs, Stanley G. Weinbaum and John W. Campbell, Jr. These names have been officially approved by the International Astronomical Union. No doubt other science-fiction personalities will be added soon after they die. (*Mars and the Mind of Man*, a book written by two science-fiction authors and three scientists—Ray Bradbury, Arthur C. Clarke, Bruce Murray, Carl Sagan, and Walter Sullivan—and devoted to the interface between science and science fiction in studies of Mars, was published by Harper & Row in 1973. Bradbury's contribution I find extraordinarily moving.)

The great interest of youngsters in science fiction is reflected in a demand for science-fiction courses in high schools and colleges. My experience is that such courses can be fine educational experiences or disasters, depending on how they are done. Courses in which the readings are selected by the students provide no opportunity for the students to read what they have not already read. Courses in which there is no attempt to extend the science-fiction plot line to encompass the appropriate science miss a great educational opportunity. But properly planned science-fiction courses, in which science or politics is an integral component, would seem to me to have a long and useful life in school curricula.

The greatest human significance of science fiction may be as experiments on the future, as explorations of alternative destinies, as attempts to minimize future shock. This is part of the reason that science fiction has so wide an appeal among young people: it is *they* who will live in the future. It is my firm view that no society on Earth today is well-adapted to the Earth of one or two hundred years from now (if we are wise enough or lucky enough to survive that long). We desperately need an exploration of alternative futures, both experimental and conceptual. The novels and stories of Eric Frank Russell were very much to this point. We were able to see conceivable alternative economic systems, or the great efficiency of a unified passive resistance to an occupying power. (In modern science fiction can also be found useful suggestions for making a revolution in a computerized technological society, as in Heinlein's *The Moon Is a Harsh Mistress*.)

Such ideas, when encountered young, can influence adult behavior. Many scientists, deeply involved in the exploration of the solar system (myself among them), were first turned in that direction by science fiction. And the fact that some of that science fiction was not of the highest quality is irrelevant. Ten-year-olds do not read the scientific literature.

I do not know if time travel into the past is possible. The causality problems which it would imply make me very skeptical. But there are those who are thinking about it. What are called closed time-like lines, routes in space-time permitting unrestricted time travel, appear in some solutions to the general relativistic field equations. A recent claim, perhaps mistaken, is that closed time-like lines appear in the vicinity of a large, rapidly rotating cylinder. I wonder to what extent general relativists working on such problems have been influenced by science fiction. Likewise, science-fictional encounters with alternative cultural futures may play an important role in actualizing fundamental social change.

In all the history of the world there has never before been a time in which so many significant changes have occurred. Accommodation to change, the thoughtful pursuit of alternative futures, is the key to the survival of civilization and perhaps of mankind. Ours is also the time of the first generation which has grown up with science-fiction ideas. I know many young people who would of course be interested, but in no way astounded, were we to receive a message from an extraterrestrial civilization. They have already accommodated to that future. I think it is not an exaggeration to say that, if we survive, science fiction will have made a vital contribution to the continuation and evolution of our civilization.

CARL SAGAN

INTRODUCTION: THE INFINITY CONNECTION

BY JACK WILLIAMSON

Dropping out of college to write science fiction, Jack Williamson made a living at it for nearly thirty years, back when that wasn't easy. He returned to academe and became an English professor at Eastern New Mexico University, where he established one of the first science-fiction courses. Besides such novels as The Legion of Space, The Humanoids, *and* Brother to Demons, Brother to Gods, *his works include* H. G. Wells: Critic of Progress, *a study of Wells's early science fiction. He has received the Grand Master Award from the Science Fiction Writers of America and the Pilgrim Award from the Science Fiction Research Association, Retired from teaching now, he still lives and works in New Mexico. A new novel is* The Humanoid Touch. *He is President of the Science Fiction Writers of America.*

This book is for science-fiction teachers, a young but vigorously expanding academic species. When I began writing such fiction, back in 1928, the genre was confined to a single pulp magazine, unwelcome in libraries and unknown in the classroom—unless now and then concealed inside a geography book.

Earlier, the imaginative works of Poe and Verne and Wells had been respectable enough. The exile to the pulps dates from about the time of World War I and began to end soon after World War II, when a few fans started reprinting their favorite pulp classics in hard covers, leading the major book publishers to discover an opening market.

The current academic welcome is only twenty years old. Fans have usually caught the virus young. Most get over it, but a few of us never do. In the late fifties, the fans-turned-scholars in the Modern Language Association set up a science fiction seminar. This led in time to the SFRA, the Science Fiction Research Association, which now has several hundred members.

Though Sam Moskowitz and others had conducted special lecture courses earlier, the classroom boom began with the class Mark Hillegas taught at Colgate in 1962. I used a news story about that to get approval for one of my own, which I taught for a dozen years. Soon they multiplied wonderfully.

Surveying them in the early seventies, I published a descriptive listing, *Teaching SF*, intended to help instructors convince curriculum committees and departmental chairmen that they really were legitimate. By 1974, when I gave up the project because it had grown out of hand, I had found some 500 courses offered at the college level in the United States and Canada. They were sweeping into the high schools too by that time, becoming a remarkably popular elective, often offered in multiple sections with hundreds of students.

Why this sudden welcome?

I can think of several reasons. First of all, science fiction has a timely sort of realism lacking from "realistic" fiction. However unreal its weird machines and alien beings may seem at first glimpse, it accepts the real fact that technology is changing our world, that tomorrow won't just repeat today.

A second reason, somewhat paradoxical, is that same surface unreality. Those fantastic creatures and strange events can serve as symbols for realities too near and too grim to be faced nakedly. Allowing us to think about the unthinkable—nuclear war, for instance—science fiction can be the magic mirror in which we look at the writhing horror of Medusa's hair and survive unharmed.

A third value springs from that one. Science fiction offers us not only freedom to think but also to say what we think. In the schoolroom, as elsewhere, the pressures to conform can be stifling. Students and instructors, like the writer and the general reader, are delighted to find its almost perfect freedom of expression. Except on TV—where it's seldom at its best—its themes don't have to please commercial sponsors. Its editors and its audience have wide interests and open minds. It can say nearly anything. Debating every possible path of future change, perhaps it help us toward the better choices.

There's a fourth appeal, perhaps the most important: science fiction is international. Since the astronauts have let us see how small and fragile our spaceship planet is, the time has clearly come to rise above all the jealous divisions of class and race, religion and nation, that cloud our common future. In story after story, at least since Wells's *War of the Worlds*, we've been shown as just one more evolving species in danger of extinction—which I think we really are.

There are dozens of definitions of science fiction, most of them satisfactory only to the person doing the defining. I like to call it fiction that explores imagined scientific possibility. This sets it off from pure fantasy, which asks us to accept premises at odds with possible reality—though, since different people at different times have different notions about what is possible, the distinction is highly subjective and often ignored. Many people want to change the name to something like "speculative fabulation." I've learned to like "science fiction."

The term itself needs comment. It was coined by Hugo Gernsback in 1929; the earlier stories I wrote for him had been "scientifiction." The Munsey pulps had published Edgar Rice Burroughs and A. Merritt as "different stories." Wells had written "scientific romances," and the novels of Verne were *Voyages extraordinaires*. Though the label "sci-fi" was invented by a science-fiction expert, Forry Ackerman, it is used chiefly by condescending outsiders and generally avoided by people in the field. The authors of these essays have used the more acceptable SF.

The history of science fiction is ably summarized in the opening section of this book, especially by Asimov, Stover, the Panshins, and Clareson. If we see it with Stover as a consequence of the research revolution, its origins are relatively recent. Brian Aldiss, in *Billion Year Spree*, makes a good case for Mary Shelley's *Frankenstein* as the seminal work. As an evolving genre, it was enlarged by Poe and Verne, developed and defined by Wells. As magazine fiction, it was popularized by Burroughs and Merritt, named by Gernsback, refined again by a greater editor, John W. Campbell, diversified vastly by a hundred brilliant writers since.

The most useful classification I have found is into the utopian and the dystopian, the optimistic and the pessimistic about the uses of reason and the shape of the future. As technology reshapes our lives, some of us welcome new knowledge and new powers. Others recoil in alarm. The readings for my own class were selected as briefs on both sides of this old and never-ending philosophic battle.

There is no standard syllabus for the science-fiction course at any level. Though hundreds of teachers have been inquiring, I'm not sure there should be. One joy of the course, as things stand now, is the freedom it offers teacher and student to select the writers that excite them and to share their excitement.

Though no course is typical, I suppose the one I taught is a fair random sample. Offered at the junior level, it generally drew more people than I really wanted for the mixed lecture-and-discussion approach. A few were veteran fans, a few more wanted to write, most were simply curious about science fiction or looking for three more hours of upper-division English. Working toward a general appreciation of the genre, we considered definitions and origins; history and types; writing techniques and markets; the uses of science fiction for entertainment, prediction, and social comment; critical standards and literary values.

Though my own definition stresses some assumed scientific possibility, that is only a small part of the effect of any particular story. Once embarked on the narrative flow, the reader is caught and carried on by the old appeals of mood and style and theme, drawn by the drama of characters in conflict. Yet that assumption of possible truth is part of the genre; any crude violation of it can shatter the spell.

The history can begin nearly anywhere, even with *Genesis* or Homer. If we start with Mary Shelley, Poe wrote not much later, in the same Gothic tradition. He influenced Verne, the first successful professional. Wells, however, was our real founding father. A student under T. H. Huxley, he had learned evolution and applied it to invent futurology; he brought to the genre an understanding of our nature and our niche in the cosmos that Poe and Verne had lacked.

Scholars and anthologists have classified science fiction in a hundred different ways. Asimov, for example, once divided it into primitive (1818-1926), adventure (1926-1938), gadget (1938-1945), and social science fiction (after 1945 and the only sort worth critical attention). Though this does fit the American magazines, I can't quite agree that Wells was primitive.

The distinction between the prophets of progress and the prophets of doom is more revealing and more useful in the classroom. Their quarrel is probably older than the art of lighting fire, but is now more urgent every day, as our whole planet must somehow balance all the increasing expectations of mushrooming populations against the limits of our resources and the hazards of environmental damage.

Swift foresaw this conflict, and the Luddites were early skirmishers. Sir Charles Snow described it twenty years ago, in his defense of the culture of science against the traditional literary academics. New battles are raging now, over every pipeline and strip mine and nuclear reactor. Some sort of crisis is surely near, and we're all vitally involved. The issue has been a central theme of science fiction, and students are likely to be drawn into fiction that expresses their own concerns.

Class readings from the dystopians can begin with the last two books of *Gulliver*—Swift is satirizing the pioneer scientists in the Royal Society. Wells, especially in *The Island of Dr. Moreau* and *The First Men in the Moon*, is writing more voyages for Gulliver. Zamyatin's *We* echoes Wells; Aldous Huxley and George Orwell echo both. This line of alarmists runs on down through my own *Humanoids*, through Fred Pohl and the "New Wave," to Harlan Ellison and others enough.

The utopians are seldom quite so effective—I think they have an accidental handicap in the fact that ill tidings are more dramatic than good news. But there is faith in man's reason and hope for his future in the *Odyssey*, in Plato's *Republic*, in Bacon's *New Atlantis*, in Bellamy's *Looking Backward*, in Heinlein's juvenile explorers of the universe and Asimov's positronic robots and Clarke's visions of human evolution from caveman to spaceman.

A writer myself, I probably gave more attention to fiction technique than most teachers would. We discussed problems of plot and character and theme and style and viewpoint, sometimes using a little paperback of my own, *People Machines*, which grew out of the class. Students completed two assignments each semester, either critical or creative.

Most wrote stories, though I also cheerfully accepted a poem, a chap-

JACK WILLIAMSON

ter of a novel, an original painting, a recorded drama, a cartoon strip, once even a futuristic costume. Few of the stories reached the professional level, but they were nearly always interesting, certainly more rewarding than the routine term paper.

The whole class shared in reading and evaluation—with communication a two-way thing, the student writer needs an audience. Now and then, when editors volunteered, we produced a class magazine, and a good many of our productions won awards in the school's literary magazine. Sometimes, now, I see an ex-student's name on the cover of a national publication. Others showed equal gifts. Fortunately, however, for us professionals, even the most able amateur is seldom hard enough driven to make the sustained effort that the likes of Bradbury and Ellison have commonly put forth to establish their names.

Considering the uses of science fiction, I think it must first of all offer entertainment. Without that, nothing else matters. Though young writers are often scornful of it, creating good escape fiction is a high and admirable art. Whatever the message, any lack of story interest can lose it. Here, I suspect, the new generations of science-fiction critics have become a hazard to the writer. Praising obscure symbolism, far-out experiments in style, and adherence to their dogmas, they too often persuade him to neglect basic dramatic values.

In a limited but significant way, science fiction is predictive —forecasting nearly everything, we can't miss forever! The limits, however, can be severe. As Wells admitted, looking back on his problems with *When the Sleeper Wakes*, fiction and futurology are difficult to mix. The first extrapolations of Darwinism into the far-off future had given him such dazzling tales as *The Time Machine*. Trying more seriously to foresee the near future, he soon gave up his narrative art to pamphleteer for social reform.

Only now and then can the writer stick to the most probable alternative futures; in search of originality and surprise, he commonly opts for the least likely. Too, the meanings of fiction are more symbolic than literal, and the writer's aims go far beyond simple prediction. Yet most science fiction is about the future. The Clarkes and the Asimovs and the Heinleins have the backgrounds and abilities to see the shape of things to come more clearly than the oracle at Delphi did. They make livelier reading than the professional futurologists, and they can certainly set off lively class discussions of all the uncertain hazards and promises of our own tomorrows. The syllabus from Dennis Livingston in Chapter 21 relates science fiction to future studies.

Everybody knows we did at least foresee space flight and atomic war and organ transplants. That's a key feature of our popular image and a major reason, I think, for our growing vogue. We've all felt technological shock, and I do think good future fiction can shield us a little from the impact, can help us learn to ride tomorrow's waves before they break over us.

As a vehicle for social comment, science fiction has an honorable tradition. Swift invented Lilliput to symbolize statements about his native England that he couldn't make openly, and such satirists as Pohl and Vonnegut find SF equally useful today. Most of this book relates in some way to science fiction and society; Leon Stover discusses science fiction and the social sciences.

In a sense, I suppose, all science fiction is social comment. Produced by writers of our time for readers of our time, its imagined futures all reflect our own concerns. Mainstream literary critics tend to see no other use for it. Kingsley Amis, in *New Maps of Hell*, sees it as social satire and not much else. Some of it is surely more.

On the question of literary value, we must appeal to Ted Sturgeon's Law: nine-tenths of anything is crap. The other tenth of science fiction is, I believe, comparable in lasting worth and interest to the best tenth of any other body of work being done today. Witness the widening international recognition of Phil Dick and Ursula Le Guin and Stanislaw Lem.

The science-fiction classics can be approached through the traditional attention to style and structure and truth, with the added advantage that many students have already learned to like them. It may be, as Mark Hillegas suggests, that some instructors aren't well-prepared even for that, though many students will come expecting something better. That's the why of this book.

In spite of all our fond claims for it, science fiction is still widely suspect, still badly stained from its pulp past. In the publishing industry, it's only one more category, shelved beside the mysteries and the westerns and the gothics. If the science-fiction label can assure a moderate profit even on an unknown author, it seems also to limit sales. With best seller status earned, such writers as Vonnegut want to get rid of the label.

Will SF become the future literary mainstream? Though people keep suggesting that, I have doubts. Certainly, as it gains popularity, more and more maintream writers try it. Often, however, they betray a fatal ignorance of science and a painful clumsiness with the science-fiction genre. Or maybe my old prejudices are showing.

There's room at least for nearly everybody. The science-fiction audience has many appetites. Burroughs's tales of Barsoom are still in wide demand, along with Vonnegut's satire and Phil Dick's challenge to apparent reality and Chip Delany's *Dhalgren*.

The classroom approaches reflect this diversity. The courses differ as much as the writers, though I think most of them can be placed somewhere on a broad spectrum that ranges from futurology to fantasy. At the futurological extreme, the emphasis is on technological and sociological extrapolation from trends observed in the real world. At the other, it is on symbolic myth or "transcendence" or stylistic value or pure escape.

The most successful teachers are motivated, I think, by a sense that science fiction has a special relevance to life in our transitional times. In a universe of disturbing change, it can become folklore or gospel. Hard science fiction, such as Wells's *When the Sleeper Wakes*, probes alternative futures through logical extensions from the known present in much the same way that good historical fiction probes the probable past. Even far-out fantasy can examine significant human values. We need the irrational to contain the unbearable. Energized from the tensions between permanence and change, science fiction combines the appeals of fantasy with its own realism.

In a series of *Analog* editorials, Ben Bova and Jim Gunn once debated whether it ought to be taught. Both are respected experts, Ben as editor and writer, Jim as writer, critic, and teacher of an outstanding course at the University of Kansas. Ben, still smarting from the way the TV industry had mauled and cheapened Harlan Ellison's ideas for *Starlost*, was afraid poor teachers would do the same sort of thing in the classroom, turning students off. Jim, speaking from a different experience, is convinced that good science fiction, in spite of a few awkward or unprepared teachers, will turn them on.

I think Jim is right. In our TV world, even college students don't always arrive as willing readers. Leading them to appreciate Shakespeare or Dostoevsky or Joyce can be hard, even impossible. I have found it far easier to involve them in science fiction, perhaps because its futures have come to seem more real and more challenging than the classic past.

In the high schools especially, with so many of the courses multi-sectional and overflowing, hundreds of thousands of kids encounter printed science fiction every year. Some few teachers, I suppose, will limit them to the tales of Hawthorne and Poe, or take them on searches for symbols and themes the writers never intended, or bog them down in arbitrary research assignments, but many another teacher is as creative and enthusiastic as our arthritic educational establishment permits. Many a bright student, no matter what the first encounter, will want to read more.

My own course has been outlined. I know of no other much like it. This book suggests a diversity of innovative approaches. The teachers I have met are originators, always trying and improving new methods of their own. Many courses are taught by teams, often, for balance, including both scientists and humanists. Mary Weinkauf, of Dakota Wesleyan, uses otherworldly and experimental music. Richard Doxtator, of Wisconsin State, gets such writers as Ray Bradbury to lecture to his classes by telephone. Robert Barthell tells in this book how he staged his own minicon, and Jim Gunn discusses what he has done with film.

The first goal, of course, is active student involvement. My own course went best when the students did the talking, discussing their reading, reporting their research, presenting their own creative projects. In other courses, students construct their own new planets, design ecologies to fit them, write futurological scenarios—the limit is their own interest and imagination.

There is, I think fortunately, no standard reading list. The literature is vast enough to choose from, and nearly every chapter in this book suggests useful titles. Alexei and Cory Panshin list important books and writers selected to illustrate the historical development of science fiction from Edgar Rice Burroughs to Roger Zelazny.

When I began my own class, there were no special texts. I used the low-priced mass paperbacks—still low-priced then!—from such houses as Ace and Avon and Ballantine and Berkley and Bantam and DAW and Dell. They are still bargains. Issued for newsstand sale, however, many of the titles drop out of print before college bookstores can stock them.

Though critics have been trying to select a canon, the lists of books in use still vary vastly. Tabulating nearly eighty reading lists a few years ago, I found some 300 titles named, half of them only once. Even the most popular were used in less than half the classes. That was before the flood of special classroom anthologies and before the mass publishers began trying to reach the schools, but the results may still be suggestive.

The dozen most popular titles were Asimov's *I, Robot*, Bradbury's *The Martian Chronicles*, Heinlein's *The Moon Is a Harsh Mistress* and *Stranger in a Strange Land*, Herbert's *Dune*, Huxley's *Brave New World*, Le Guin's *The Left Hand of Darkness*, Miller's *A Canticle for Leibowitz*, Pohl and Kornbluth's *The Space Merchants*, Silverberg's *The Science Fiction Hall of Fame, Volume I*, and Wells's *The Time Machine* and *The War of the Worlds*.

An alluring list, though no one instructor used all the titles on it. Outstanding new books have come out since it was compiled, among them Asimov's *The Gods Themselves*, Clarke's *Rendezvous with Rama*, Le Guin's *The Dispossessed*, and Bova's two volumes of *Science Fiction Hall of Fame* novelettes. I'm sure, too, that some titles are on the list, or not on it, just because they were or weren't in print at the time.

Good audiovisual aids are now available (see the chapters by Gunn, Barthell, and Barron). Such classic films as *Metropolis* can be screened for a nominal rental. Writers can be invited to the classroom—though a few command high lecture fees, many more are pleased to meet new readers anywhere. (There's a Speakers' Bureau as part of the Science Fiction Writers of America. Write Jacqueline Lichtenberg, Box 290, Monsey, NY 10952.)

Though the mushrooming growth of this book had to be stopped, I wish it could have been a little longer. Science fiction is not all prose. Dick Allen has pointed out an impressive body of SF verse that might be brought to the classroom. A poet himself, and a professor of English at Bridgeport University, he is writing *The Space Sonnets*, a book-length study of the future.

More might have been said about SF as popular culture. Though occasional academic studies of such topics as professional wrestling and pornography have lent themselves to ridicule, I feel that popular culture is a legitimate scholarly discipline, offering sound educational strategies. What we learn has to build on what we know. When students turn up without the interests or background to serve as a substructure for Chaucer or Milton or Shakespeare, the things they do know can be turned into beachheads for the campaign to widen their intellectual awareness. Besides SF, I've taught courses in the motion picture and modern mystery fiction, which the students seemed to enjoy almost as much as I did. For anyone who doesn't know, there's a vigorous Popular Culture Association, with meetings and publications in which SF is often discussed.

There might have been more about SF elsewhere. As a named category, it's American, but the name has spread over most of the world. Its roots in Europe are older, and it was never confined to a ghetto there. The Russian tradition has diverged, but it, too, comes down from Verne and Wells. Though Zamyatin and later Soviet writers have had grave problems with the Party, Russian SF somehow thrives. Major writers include Yefremov, best known for *Andromeda*, and now the brothers Boris and Arkady Strugatsky. Stanislaw Lem is popular in Poland and widely translated; his best is *Solaris*. Darko Suvin's *Other Worlds, Other Seas* includes work from other socialist nations. SF is booming in Japan, producing such writers as Sakyo Komatsu. The popularity of my own SF seems to correlate with the technological level of the readers, highest in Western Europe and Japan.

In brief outline, the opening section of this book undertakes a broad survey of "The Topic." Writers with varied orientations and intentions ask what SF is, look at its origins and evolution, its contemporary significance and its literary values. The middle section, "The Teachers," follows it into the classroom. Outstanding instructors explain their own approaches to it, in grade school, high school, and college, in disciplines ranging from English through the sciences to religion and philosophy. The concluding section, "The Tools," explores some of the resources available to the teacher: science-fiction films, the mini-con, a selected reading list, library holdings and criticism.

Though some of the essays have appeared elsewhere, more were written especially for this book. I'm deeply grateful to more people than we have space to name, for these richly varied essays and for many helpful suggestions; to Jack Chalker of Mirage Press, who originally proposed a guidebook for the SF course; to George Scithers, who is putting it into print; most of all to the hundreds of teachers who have given me information about their SF courses.

If you're new to teaching SF, you're due one warning. In any class, you are likely to encounter students who know far more about their favorite writers than you do—not a bad thing, really, as long you aren't taken by surprise. If you want more background than this book can give, you might join the Science Fiction Research Association. (Write Robert Galbreath, Secretary, SFRA, 4217 N. Woodburn St., Shorewood, WI 53211.) You should certainly subscribe to *Locus*, the SF news magazine. (Box 3938, San Francisco, CA 94119.) You might also want the *Bulletin* of the Science Fiction Writers of America. (Address Vic Milán, 4516 5th NW, Albuquerque, NM 87107.) For an actual visit to another world, you should attend a fan convention.

As science keeps pushing our mental frontiers into new infinities, beyond the quantum and the quasar and the quark, SF follows. The first news coming back is often brief and bare, abstract reports of truth sought for itself alone. SF can help us fill the outlines in, help us see and feel the human consequences. Reaching students with it, the SF teacher can help them make new intellectual and emotional connections.

THE TOPIC

ON TEACHING
SCIENCE FICTION

BY URSULA K. LE GUIN

What is science fiction? Why is it worth teaching? This first section of this book looks at such questions from varied viewpoints, beginning with answers from Ursula K. Le Guin, who has won awards for such distinguished novels as The Left Hand of Darkness *and* The Dispossessed. *The field has produced no finer writer. Her critical essays on fantasy and SF have been collected in* The Language of the Night, *edited by Susan Wood (Berkley/Putnam, 1979). Commenting here on the study and teaching of SF, she extends a tempting invitation to the teacher, the student, and the general reader.*

At the 1974 meeting of the Science Fiction Research Association, an annual event which I like to call The Bride of Frankenstein in the Groves of Academe, Alexei and Cory Panshin held forth eloquently against the teaching of science fiction in schools and colleges. It seemed a bit quixotic, since their audience consisted of teachers of science fiction, people so interested in and committed to the subject that they had come from all over the country to talk about it and learn how to do it better; since thousands of high schools give science-fiction courses now, and the stuffiest college English Departments are stooping to conquer. I don't think there's really much question, now, of keeping the professors off Aldebaran. They're there. And that face looking out of the fifth story window of the Ivory Tower, that's the Little Green Man. For myself, I accept this miscegenation happily, and am simply interested in what the offspring may be.

For undoubtedly the recent great increase in the teaching of SF is going to affect the writing of SF. Our audience has widened immensely; and for the first time, we in the SF ghetto are beginning to get criticism—not brushoffs from literary snobs, and not blasts of praise and condemnation from jealous, loyal, in-group devotees, but real criticism, by trained, intelligent people who have read widely both inside and outside the field. This could be the best thing that ever happened to SF, the confirmation of it, both to its readers and to its writers, as a powerful and responsible art form.

A ghetto is a comfortable, reassuring place to live, but it is also a crippling place to live. The essence of a ghetto, after all, is that you are *forced* to live there. To choose the ghetto when one is free to choose the greater community is an act of cowardice. Now that the walls are breaking down, I think it behooves us to step across the rubble and face the city outside. We need not lose our solidarity in doing so. Solidarity, loyalty, is not a prison, where you can't choose: it is a choice freely made. But equally we shouldn't expect to be welcomed with songs of praise by all the strangers out there. Why should we be? We're strangers to them, too. If we have weaknesses we must learn to take criticism of them; if we have strengths we must prove them.

One way we can show our strength is by helping the serious critics of SF to set up a critical apparatus, a set of standards, suited to the study and teaching of SF. Some of the criteria by which the conventional novel is discussed and judged apply to SF, and some don't. Teachers can't switch from *A Tale of Two Cities* to *The Man in the High Castle* without changing gears; if they do, one book or the other is going to be misinterpreted, mistreated. Fortunately, in two areas at least, SF has established its own standards, and has been applying them with increasing severity, in writing, in teaching writing, and in teaching SF as literature.

The first of these is the criterion of intellectual coherence and scientific plausibility.

The basic canon of fantasy, of course, is this: you get to make up the rules, but then you've got to follow them. Science fiction refines the canon: you get to make up the rules, but within limits. A science-fiction story must not flout the evidence of science, must not, as Chip Delany puts it, deny what is known to be known. Or if it does, the writer must know it, and defend the liberty taken, either with a genuine hypothesis or with a sound, convincing fake. If I give my spaceships FTL speed, I must be aware that I'm contradicting Albert Einstein, and accept the consequences—all the consequences. In this, precisely, lies the unique aesthetic delight of SF, in the intense, coherent following-through of the implications of an idea, whether it's a bit of far-out technology, or a theory in quantum mechanics, or a satirical projection of current social trends, or a whole world created by extrapolating from biology and ethnology. When such an idea is consistently worked out in material, intellectual, social, psychological, and moral terms, something solid has been done, something real: a thing which can be read, taught, and judged squarely in its own terms. The "sense of wonder" isn't a feeble perfume, it's built right into a good story, and the closer you look at the story, the stronger the sense of wonder.

A second criterion is that of stylistic competence.

You know what SF was like in the Golden Age of Science Fiction. You know. It was like this: "Oh, Professor Higgins," cooed the slender, vivacious Laura, "but do tell me how does the antipastomatter denudifier work?" Then Professor Higgins, with a kindly, absentminded smile, explains how it works for about six pages, garble garble garble. Then the Starship Captain steps in, with a tight, twisted smile on his lean, bronzed face. His steely gray eyes glint. He lights a cigarette and inhales deeply. "Oh, Captain Tommy," Laura inquires with a vivacious toss of her head, "is there anything wrong?" "Don't worry your pretty little head about it," the Captain replies, inhaling deeply. "A fleet of nine thousand Gloobian Slime Monsters off the port side, that's all." And so on. You know. American SF used to be a pulp medium, popcult, all that. Now it isn't—not all of it, anyhow. It has rejoined the SF of England and Europe, which was sparse, but which never was schlock except when it imitated us, and which was always part of the major tradition of fiction. And therefore it is to be judged, not as schlock, not as junk, but as fiction.

What I'm saying is neither self-evident nor popular. Within the SF ghetto, many people don't want their books, or their favorite writers' books, judged as literature. They want junk, and they bitterly resent aesthetic judgment of it. And outside the ghetto, there are critics who like to stand above SF, looking down upon it, and therefore want it to be junky, popcult, contemptible. There was a strong vein of this in Gerald Jonas's otherwise perceptive *New Yorker* article, and it's one of the many games Leslie Fiedler plays. Fortunately it's a game that our best SF critic, Darko Suvin, never plays. I consider it a real cop-out, an arrogance toward both the books and their readers.

There is an area where SF has most often failed to judge itself, and where it has been most harshly judged by its nonpartisans. It is an area where we badly need intelligent criticism and discussion. The oldest argument against SF is both the shallowest and the profoundest: the assertion that SF, like all fantasy, is escapist.

This statement is shallow when made by the shallow. When an insurance broker tells you that SF doesn't deal with the Real World, when a chemistry freshman informs you that Science has disproved Myth, when a censor suppresses a book because it doesn't fit the canons of Socialist Realism, and so forth, that's not criticism; it's bigotry. If it's worth answering, the best answer was given by Tolkien, author, critic, and scholar. Yes, he said, fantasy is escapist, and that is its glory. If a soldier is imprisoned by the enemy, don't we consider it his duty to escape? The moneylenders, the knownothings, the authoritarians have us all in prison; if we value the freedom of the mind and soul, if we're partisans of liberty, then it's our plain duty to escape, and to take as many people with us as possible.

But people who are not fools or bigots, people who love both art and liberty, critics as responsible as Edmund Wilson, reject science fiction flatly as a genre simply not worth discussing. Why? What makes them so sure?

The question, after all, must be asked: From what is one escaping, and to what?

Evidently, if we're escaping a world that consists of *Newsweek, Pravda,* and the stock market report, and asserting the existence of a primary, vivid world, an intenser reality where joy, tragedy, and morality exist, then we're doing a good thing, and Tolkien is right. But what if we're doing just the opposite? What if we're escaping from a complex, uncertain, frightening world of death and taxes into a nice simple cozy place where heroes don't have to pay taxes, where death happens only to villains, where Science, plus Free Enterprise, plus the Galactic Fleet in black and silver uniforms, can solve all problems, where human suffering is something that can be *cured*—like scurvy? This is no escape from the phony. This is an escape into the phony. This doesn't take us in the direction of the great myths and legends, which is always toward an intensification of the mystery of the real. This takes us the other way, toward a rejection of reality, in fact toward madness: infantile regression, or paranoid delusion, or schizoid insulation. The movement is retrograde, autistic. We have escaped by locking ourselves in jail.

And inside the padded cell the people sit and say, Gee wow have you read the latest Belch the Barbarian story? It's the greatest.

They don't care if anybody outside is listening. They don't want to know that there is an outside.

Because the most famous works of SF are socially and ethically speculative, the field has got a reputation for being inherently "relevant." Accused of escapism, it defends itself by pointing to Wells, Orwell, Huxley, Čapek, Stapledon, Zamyatin. But that won't wash: not for us. Not one of those writers was an American. My feeling is that American SF, while riding on the reputation of great European works, still clings to the pulp tradition of escapism.

That's overstated, and perhaps unfair. Recent American SF has been full of stories tackling totalitarianism, nationalism, overpopulation, pollution, prejudice, racism, sexism, militarism, and so on: all the "relevant" problems. *Again, Dangerous Visions* was a regular textbook in Problems (and my story was one of the chapters). But what worries me is that so many of these stories and books have been written in a savagely self-righteous tone, a tone that implies that there's an answer, a simple answer, and why can't all you damn fools out there see it? Well, I call this escapism: a sensationalist raising of a real question, followed by a quick evasion of the weight and pain and complexity involved in really, experientially, trying to understand and cope with that question. And by the way, I'm not talking only about the reactionary, easy-answer schools of SF, the Technocrats, Scientologists, "libertarians," and so on, but also about the chic nihilism affected by many talented American and English writers of my generation. Annihilation is the easiest answer of all. You just close all the doors.

If science fiction has a major gift to offer literature, I think it is just this: the capacity to face an open universe. Physically open, psychically open. No doors shut.

What science, from physics and astronomy to history and psychology, has given us, is the open universe: a cosmos that is not a simple, fixed hierarchy, but an immensely complex process in time. All the doors stand open, from the pre-human past through the incredible present to the terrible and hopeful future. All connections are possible. All alternatives are thinkable. It is not a comfortable, reassuring place. It's a very large house, a very drafty house. But it's the house we live in.

And science fiction seems to be the modern literary art which is capable of living in that huge and drafty house, and feeling at home there, and playing games up and down the stairs, from basement to attic.

I think that's why kids like SF, and demand to be taught it, to study it, to take it seriously. They feel this potential it has for playing games with and making sense and beauty out of our fearfully enlarged world of knowledge and perception. And that's why it gripes me when I see SF failing to do so, falling back on silly, simplistic reassurances, or whining Woe, woe, repent, or taking refuge in mere wishful thinking.

So I welcome the study and teaching of SF—so long as the teachers will criticize us, demandingly, responsibly, and make the students read us demandingly, responsibly. If SF is treated, not as junk, not as escapism, but as an intellectually, aesthetically, and ethically responsible art, a great form, it will become so: it will fulfill its promise. And the door to the future will be open.

SCIENCE FICTION AND SOCIETY

BY ISAAC ASIMOV

Isaac Asimov not only summarizes the history of science fiction in this brief essay, but also explores its place in a wide social context. As usual, he knows what he's talking about. Isaac made his start as an SF writer, extending the myth of man's galactic future in his Foundation stories and humanizing technology with his famous Three Laws of Robotics. Turning from fiction to fact, he has become a popularizer of science and culture-in-general, a respected expert on everything from the frontiers of pure science to the Bible, Shakespeare, and Milton. Particularly admirable is the gift he shows here for clarifying a complex topic with a very few simple-seeming words.

Science fiction came into being in the early nineteenth century as a literary response to a new curiosity that did not truly exist in all of man's earlier history.

Through almost all of man's history there was never any visible change in the basic manner of life as far as the individual human being was concerned. There was, indeed, change. There was a time when fire was tamed, when agriculture was developed, when the wheel was invented, when the bow and arrow was devised. These inventions, however, came at such long intervals, established themselves so gradually, spread outward from the point of origin so slowly, that the individual human being, in his own lifetime, could see no change.

There was, therefore, until modern times, no literature that dealt with the future, since there seemed nothing about the future that could not be dealt with in terms of the present. There were fantasies, to be sure, dealing with supernatural worlds of gods and demons; fantasies of faraway mythical lands such as Atlantis, or unattainable lands such as the Moon, but all was described as taking place in the present or the past.

Those changes which did take place (however slowly) were invariably the result of technological advance. This was true even in the cases where what happened seems at first glance to have no connection with technology.

Many a military victory was won by a general who knew how to use some technological advance; that's obvious.

Less obvious is the fact that the transition from the Dark Ages to the culture of the High Middle Ages after A.D. 1000 might not have taken place without the increased food supply made possible by the development of the moldboard plow which more efficiently broke up the heavy soils of northern Europe, and the invention of the horsecollar which made it possible to hitch the horse to that plow.

Again, the Protestant Reformation succeeded where previous movements of the sort had failed, because of the invention of the printing press. Martin Luther, an accomplished pamphleteer, spread his printed words across the length and breadth of Europe faster by far than those words could be suppressed.

Even the Scientific Revolution of 1559–1650 would probably have been impossible without the printing press, which spread the news of discoveries rapidly and which, for the first time, created a continent-wide scientific fraternity.

The rate of advance in technology increased steadily over the centuries as each group of advances built on those that had gone before. By 1800, the rate had increased to the point where an Industrial Revolution was taking place in Great Britain and where this Revolution was spreading outward from its point of origin with unprecedented speed. And wherever the Industrial Revolution took hold, the rate of change increased to the point where it became noticeable in the single lifetime of an individual human being.

As a result of the Industrial Revolution, people, *for the first time,* became aware of change as natural and inevitable. For the first time, they became aware that the future would be, would indeed have to be, different from the present, and that this difference would arise specifically through the application of technological advance.

At last people became curious about the future that they would never see. For the first time in history they had occasion to wonder what life would be like in their grandchildren's time.

Science fiction arose as the literary response to that curiosity.

Mind you, change is not a pleasant thing. People grow accustomed to a way of life and to break the caked custom that has built up about them is painful, even when the change might seem, to the dispassionate, to be for the better. Or as Thomas Jefferson said in his immortal Declaration, "all experience hath shewn that mankind are more disposed to suffer, while evils are sufferable, than to right themselves by abolishing the forms to which they are accustomed."

Consequently, while some looked forward to the advance of science and technology as the means by which a Utopia might be produced on the earth, others feared the consequences of change and foresaw nightmare. From the beginning, then, science fiction has swung between the two poles of optimism and pessimism.

Consider the first novel which might be defined as true science fiction, for instance—*Frankenstein,* by Mary Shelley, published in 1818 in Great Britain, the home of the Industrial Revolution. It dealt with the creation of life not by magic or the supernatural, but by the reasoned application of electrical force. And it dealt with the evil consequences thereof. As we all know, the Monster that was created destroyed Frankenstein, his creator.

The nineteenth century mood, however, rapidly became one of optimism. The developing Industrial Revolution fastened a factory system on Great Britain that was one of the nightmare horrors of history, but the middle and upper classes, who alone were articulate, benefited greatly. Great Britain's empire spread, and other nations, as they industrialized, grew in power and in (unevenly distributed) wealth.

It is not surprising, then, that the French writer, Jules Verne (the first professional science-fiction writer, in the sense that he was the first to make the major portion of his livelihood out of tales we now recognize to be science fiction), breathes optimism in his tales. His heroes probe the air and the sea-depths; they penetrate indeed to the height of the Moon and to the depth of the Earth's center, and always with a glory in achievement that carries us along with them. There are barriers to be hurdled, and the hurdling's the thing.

We must realize, of course, that no science-fiction story with thought behind it—whether as pessimistic as Shelley or as optimistic as Verne—is unrelated to the society in which it is produced. The writer's imagination, though it soar its mightiest, is tethered perforce, however long the thread, to the life the author lives and knows.

Thus, Shelley's life-through-electricity was based on the discovery of the Italian anatomist, Luigi Galvani, twenty years earlier, that an electric shock would cause dead muscles to twitch as though they were alive. And Verne's tales were written in the era, and permeated with the spirit, of the great nineteenth century inventors—Thomas Alva Edison, most of all.

Even when a man like Herbert George Wells divorced himself from the immediate effects of technology and allowed himself unlimited range of imagination, he left himself tied to his own society.

In *The Time Machine* (1895), the very first true time-travel story and his first success, Wells made use of a device that could take men through time at will, something for which the technology of his time (and of ours, too) holds out no promise. The time traveller finds a far future in which men are divided into two classes, one beautiful but decadent, the other ugly and depraved. This is an obvious reflection on the possible consequences of a class society such as the Great Britain of Wells's time still was.

In *The War of the Worlds* (1898), which was the first tale ever written dealing with interplanetary warfare, Wells was inspired by the discovery of markings on Mars, twenty years earlier, which were interpreted as canals and which gave rise to speculations concerning the

ISAAC ASIMOV

presence of an advanced civilization on Mars; one that was fighting, desperately, to survive on a dying world.

Wells's picture of Martians landing in Great Britain and remorselessly taking over the land without any regard for the native Earthmen, whom the invaders clearly pictured as inferior beings with no rights that needed to be respected, was, however, as clearly inspired by the fact that the British themselves, and to a lesser extent other European nations, had just completed the takeover of the African continent under precisely similar conditions.

Whereas Verne was almost invariably optimistic, Wells's vision of the future was tempered by pessimism, as might be expected, since the opening decade of the twentieth century was filled with the booming of war drums that were steadily growing louder. Wells's view of future wars was as fearsome as it was accurate; and it is in Wells's works, half a century before the reality, that we come across what he calls "the atomic bomb."

When World War I did come, it put an end to the almost childlike optimism of the nineteenth century. It was seen that civilized nations could make war in fashion worse than barbarians and that science—the great force that was to bring all mankind to a Utopia—could introduce unprecedented horrors in the form of advanced explosives, bombing from the air, and—worst of all—poison gas.

In 1920, immediately after the end of the war, the Czech playwright, Karel Capek, wrote *R.U.R.* ("Rossum's Universal Robots") concerning the mass production of artificial living creatures called "robots," the Czech word for "workers." By the end of the play, the robots, intended by science to bring Utopia, had brought instead the end of humanity.

In 1926, science fiction entered a new phase when Hugo Gernsback, a Luxembourg-born American, published *Amazing Stories,* the first magazine ever to be devoted to science fiction exclusively. At first, Gernsback had to reprint stories by Verne, Wells, and other writers of the past to fill his pages, but slowly he attracted American writers of a new generation, who took to the new field.

The stories, as always, were sometimes pessimistic and sometimes optimistic. On the whole, though, despite the experience of World War I, magazine science fiction opened a new era of optimism in the field. There are reasons for this.

The United States, in which the new magazine science fiction rose to prominence, had suffered least in World War I, and had carried the Industrial Revolution to its highest extreme. There seemed nothing Americans could not do in the booming twenties, and the "superscience" story originated in consequence.

The first of these, *The Skylark of Space* by Edward E. Smith, appeared in *Amazing Stories* in three parts beginning in the August, 1928, issue at the very height of the boom. In this story and in others of the sort that followed, engineers conceived new inventions, constructed and put them to use at once and in the space of a few years conquered the Galaxy.

There were many who followed Smith's lead, notably John W. Campbell, Jr., and for several years this variety of science fiction carried all before it.

But the Great Depression began at the end of 1929, and optimism shrank steadily in the world generally and in the United States in particular. The new pessimism was reflected in Aldous Huxley's *Brave New World*, published in 1932 at the depth of the Depression. In it science was portrayed as a dehumanizing agent.

Even in the adventure-centered magazines, the loss of optimism took place. One of the first of the magazine writers to feel the new mood was Campbell, who, in 1934, when the Depression in the United States had begun to yield to Franklin Delano Roosevelt's New Deal, began a new deal of his own. He abandoned superscience stories and, under the pseudonym of Don A. Stuart, started to deal with human beings at closer range and with technology at more plausible focus.

In 1938, he came into editorial control of *Astounding Stories,* the most successful of the science-fiction magazines. He at once altered its name to *Astounding Science Fiction,* and its outlook as well. Campbell, who had received an education in physics, began to search for writers who had an understanding of science and scientists and who could write believably about it. In the process, he discovered and helped develop many of the science-fiction writers who now, a generation later, still dominate the field.

The verb "to affect" is double-edged. Society, while affecting science fiction, was, in its turn, affected.

For one thing, while science-fiction magazines had relatively small circulations, the youngsters who read those magazines in the twenties and thirties were, for the most part, keen-minded, imaginative, and feverishly interested in science. They might have made up no more than a tenth of one percent of the population, but they grew up to form far more than a tenth of one percent of the scientists, engineers, and, in general, the intellectual leadership of the nation.

There was also a kind of fallout. There were comic strips such as *Buck Rogers, Flash Gordon,* and *Superman* which presented a diluted science fiction to all levels of the population. The concept of scientific advance became a dim part of the general consciousness thereby, so that when the time came, for instance, to reach the Moon, enough romance had been created around that theme to make the concept acceptable to the general population.

To be sure, in the thirties science fiction had been stigmatized by those who took refuge in haughty ignorance as childish escape literature. This escape was, in many cases, an escape to reality.

In 1933, for instance, Laurence Manning wrote *The Man Who Awoke,* which dealt with a world of the future in which life was restricted by the fact that energy could be used only in dribbles because *our* generation had burned up the world's supply of oil and coal with thoughtless wastefulness. Youngsters reading that story in 1933 would have been concerned with an energy crunch, which their "realistic" betters had to face only in 1973. The science-fiction stories of the thirties dealt with overpopulation and atom bombs, with television and computers, with mutations and organ transplantation—the kind of escape it would have been better to force on all the world.

Under John Campbell's leadership, *Astounding* began to depict societies that were plausibly and accurately extrapolated from new discoveries. As soon as uranium fission was discovered and announced in 1939, atom-bomb stories began to be written. In the March, 1944 issue of *Astounding,* Cleve Cartmill published a story called "Deadline" which dealt with the atom bomb so accurately that security agents descended on the offices of the magazine and had to be convinced how powerful the disciplined imagination was.

Even earlier than that, in the May, 1941 *Astounding,* Robert A. Heinlein published "Solution Unsatisfactory" under the pseudonym of Anson MacDonald. In that story he quite accurately foresaw the Manhattan Project and the nuclear stalemate that followed World War II—something none of the leaders of mankind succeeded in foreseeing at that time.

With the coming of the atom bomb, society could no longer look upon science fiction as childish escape literature. The science-fiction writer had seen too much to which others were blind.

It was clear by then, moreover, that the rate of change of society, sparked by technological development, had been continuing to increase throughout the nineteenth and twentieth centuries, and had now reached the point where decisions could no longer be made on the basis of present conditions only. In order to make intelligent decisions, the future would have to be foreseen.

As a consequence, what had been science fiction has now become "futurism," a respectable specialty highly thought of by those in government and industry who must, every day, make decisions by guessing the future, decisions that affect millions of people and billions of dollars.

And this has, in turn, profoundly affected science fiction.

By 1960, the Campbell era was about over, for Campbell had been too successful. The real world of the sixties proved to be so like the science-fiction world of the forties that writers in search of tales that would not be so readily overtaken by fact moved away from the hardware of technology and toward the more difficult software of the human being.

Secondly, a growing disillusion with science and scientists had begun to sweep the world in the wake of World War II, and by the sixties there was an antiscience mood among the young sufficiently deep to be reflected in science fiction.

This second effect was intensified by a third, the general decline of fiction in the wake of World War II. The rate and importance of change was so great that fiction dealing with the here-and-now seemed increasingly irrelevant. Magazine markets for fiction withered; novels appeared in smaller numbers and were, generally, less successful.

Young writers, looking about, found almost no flourishing fiction market but science fiction. As a result, the sixties saw the rise of new writers who lacked knowledge of science and even sympathy for science, but who wrote science fiction because that was all there was.

The overall result was the New Wave, as some call it, in which the most pronounced characteristic is that of stylistic experimentation, a heavy infusion of sex and violence, and, most of all, a mood of deep pessimism.

In its extreme form, the New Wave has not been successful, but it has succeeded in making its point, and in science fiction generally the deeds of the engineers sink into the background and the present-day frustrations of human beings take the stage.

To take one example out of very many, consider "When It Changed" by Joanna Russ, which won the Nebula Award as the best science-fiction short story in 1972. It pictures a planet far out in space from which the males have disappeared and on which the women have been left behind alone. They manage to devise and maintain an inter-fertile homosexual society and to find joy in it; and then, before that society can be made strong enough to defend itself, the planet is rediscovered. Men arrive—and all is changed.

It is the ultimate Women's Lib story, one that can be told only in a science-fiction milieu—but like almost all science fiction, though it seems to concern itself with human beings and worlds of the far distance and far future, it also concerns itself with the here and the now.

SCIENCE FICTION AND THE RESEARCH REVOLUTION

BY LEON STOVER

Leon Stover is a professor of anthropology at Illinois Institute of Technology. He has been teaching social science fiction there since 1965 and recently added a course in Wells's SF. His publications include two volumes on Chinese culture and civilization, which he says is his specialty, another offering a new theory of Stonehenge, and The Coming Terror: Statism and the Science Fiction of H. G. Wells.

This paper was the Distinguished Faculty Lecture delivered at IIT to the Society of the Sigma Chi, April 18, 1978. Drawn from his book, La Science Fiction Américaine, *it opens fresh historical perspectives on the origins and meanings of the genre.*

Science fiction is an American publisher's category, created for the specialty magazines. The first specialty magazines appeared in the eighteen-forties, the so-called dime novels. They established the various categories of specialized fiction now tagged on paperback book racks, such as western, romance, crime, etc. The dime novel entered a boom period in the eighteen-seventies and the prominent publisher was Frank Tousey. Number 451 of his *Wide Awake Library,* for example, entitled *The True Life of Billy the Kid,* was issued in 1881. It is a booklet of sixteen pages, measuring 8 by 12 inches, and set in very small type. The cover is printed with a crude steel-plate engraving. Price: five cents (some other "dime novels" cost up to twenty-five cents). On the inside cover are listed several hundred of the 1,353 titles published by Tousey. *The True Life of Billy the Kid,* which is altogether fiction, is an example of the western genre. Other genres in *The Wide Awake Library* are pirate stories, sea stories, city stories about high life or low life, and stories of exploration, adventure, and romance.

Another dime-novel series was *Beadle's Popular Library,* which advertised the following genres: Wild West, Border, Mining, Ranching, Secret Service, Detective, Robber, City, and Sea Life. Dime novels sold in the millions, and the industry hired hundreds of hack writers who specialized in one category or another.

The dime novel died out by the turn of the century and was replaced by the pulp magazine. Its standard format was 120 untrimmed pages of rough woodpulp paper, measuring 7 by 10 inches, with an enameled cover and interior illustrations. The price ranged from ten to twenty-five cents. At its height during the nineteen-twenties and -thirties the pulp magazine industry produced about 200 titles and sold about twenty million copies a month.

The first of the pulps was *Argosy,* an adventure story magazine, started in 1896. Street and Smith Publications, a rival of Tousey's until they absorbed it, originated three more pulp magazines: *Detective Story* (1915), *Western Story* (1919), and *Love Story* (1921). These four categories—adventure, detective, western, and love—dominated the pulps until the pulps yielded to paperback books in the nineteen-forties. The categories they carried forward have now passed into television programming.

Introduced to the pulp market at its peak was *Amazing Stories.* Its editor and publisher was Hugo Gernsback, the father of magazine science fiction. The first issue appeared in April, 1926, and sold over 100,000 copies. It soon was imitated with stories *Astounding, Astonishing, Startling* and *Thrilling.* By the fifties there were over fifty magazines in the field, quite a few more titles than there were synonymns for "amazing" in Roget's *Thesaurus.*

The reader always knew what to expect in the magazine of his choice, and his loyalty was as focussed as his favorite genre was specialized. Readers were in fact not readers but "fans," short for fanatics.

What new species of loyalty did Hugo Gernsback cultivate in science-fiction fans? What amazing things did they expect to find in *Amazing Stories,* issue after issue? The answer is, amazing inventions. Across the magazine's masthead was the slogan, "Extravagant Fiction Today. . .Cold Fact Tomorrow." For Hugo Gernsback, science fiction—or "scientifiction" as he called it up until 1929—was a trade name for invention stories.

Invention stories, however, did not originate with him. They go back, as do so many of the categories of pulp fiction, to the dime novel. In this case, to another one of Frank Tousey's dime-novel series, *The Frank Reade Library,* which ran between 1892 and 1898. Frank Reade, boy inventor and backyard gadgeteer, who cobbles up things like steam-operated manikins to do household chores and pull the family buggy, is modeled after young Tom Edison, King of Inventors, Modern Magician, and Wizard of Menlo Park. But this was before anyone had the historical perspective to see that Edison was no naïvely inventive gadgeteer working in the tradition of "Yankee ingenuity," much less a wizard working in the chancy alchemical tradition. His "invention factory" at Menlo Park was emphatically a factory, organized along the lines of group research for the purpose of turning out new products to meet evident commercial needs of the marketplace. His grasp of the problem of electric lighting, as a system to replace the system of gas lighting, shows that. The electric light bulb was no accidental flash of intuitive genius, but the product of a larger purpose; it plugged into a network of electric power lines and finally to a central power station. Edison began working on all these problems at the same time, and in 1878 his invention factory was incorporated as the Edison Electric Light Company, out of which grew the General Electric Company, formed in 1892.

It was Edison's concept of group research, not the spirit of the lone inventor, to which *Amazing Stories* was a response. Or at least a belated response. Before the first science-fiction magazine could capture a market of fans interested in the romance of industrial research, the idea itself had to be popularized and embodied in widespread practice.

If Edison was the first American to organize group research, its first missionary was Arthur D. Little, who took it upon himself (in his own words) "to preach the Gospel of Research." He travelled all over North America, preaching to manufacturing firms, chambers of commerce, and scientific associations. "Research," Little said, "is the mother of industry." At the same time, he pioneered the private consulting laboratory, set up at No. 103 Milk Street in Boston, Massachusetts, in 1886. In accordance with his will, after his death in 1935 the firm of Arthur D. Little was bequeathed to M.I.T., where he had studied chemistry and where the firm still does business, doing, in the words of his original prospectus, "investigations for the improvement of processes and the perfection of products."

In due time, the gospel of research was received at large by American industry, the pioneer industrial research laboratory being founded by General Electric in 1900, for the purpose of investigating all the various applications of electricity. After this, Du Pont Laboratories appeared in 1911 and the Kodak Research Laboratories in 1912, followed by laboratories in the United States Rubber Company in 1913, in Standard Oil of New Jersey in 1919, and in the Bell Telephone Company in 1925. By mid-century, the nation had 200 large industrial research laboratories and 2,000 others. Besides the research departments of industrial firms, there were the government laboratories pioneered by the Department of Agriculture and those in the Department of Commerce established by the Bureau of Standards. This year, 1978, the combined investment by the federal government and private industry in research will amount to over forty-four billion dollars. In 1920 (which is as far back as I can trace the figures), the amount was only eighty million dollars. The difference is a measure of the impact of what historians call the research revolution.

Magazine science fiction, then, is a response to the research revolution, to the romance of industrial research. The romance is a bit faded now, but in the early days, when research was a new gospel to be missionized, its spirit was quite literally electrifying. Out of General Electric's investigations into all the various applications of electricity came RCA, the Radio Corporation of America, formed in 1919. From a toy, radio had by the twenties become a household appliance in all mature industrial nations. Radio! Magic word it once was. It lent glamor even to the movies, with the formation in 1928 of RKO Radio Pictures. Its monument is seventy stories of RCA building in Rockefeller Center, built during the thirties, part of a complex of five buildings named Radio City and renowned to all the world for its Radio City Music Hall—now become a relic to be saved by nostalgia buffs.

Science fiction was thus a response to the romance of radio, for Hugo Gernsback evolved *Amazing Stories* out of an earlier series of magazines, starting in 1908 with *Modern Electrics,* the world's first radio magazine. This was the advertising arm of his radio store, also the world's first, which sold wireless parts to amateurs. He also broadcast programs on station WRNY (326 meters) so the amateurs would have something to listen to. This before KDKA. In fact, Gernsback acted as business manager to the Wireless Association of America during the term of its first president, Lee De Forest, inventor of the vacuum tube that made radio possible.

In 1914 *Modern Electrics* became the *Electrical Experimenter,* which in 1920 became *Science and Invention,* the ancestor of *Popular Science,* "America's favorite what's new magazine," as the ad goes.

It's a joke among science-fiction writers that in the early days of *Amazing* they couldn't get published unless they dreamed up at least three patentable inventions per story. To make sure of that, Gernsback had the stories vetted by his associate editor, Dr. T. O'Conor Sloane, Edison's aging son-in-law. Gernsback himself set the pace with his novel, serialized during 1911 in *Modern Electrics,* entitled *Ralph 124C41 + , A Romance of the Year 2660.* Ralph is no Frank Reade, boy wizard; he is the owner of a one-man consulting laboratory, an Arthur D. Little of 2660 A.D. Among Ralph's perfected products are fluorescent lights, automatic packaging machines, plastics, radar, juke boxes, liquid fertilizer, tape recorders, stainless steel, loudspeakers, television (the word is Hugo's), microfilm, vending machines dispensing hot and cold foods and liquids, solar power units, spun glass, synthetic fiber like nylon for wearing apparel, and spaceships. All of these inventions and many others exist now, in the twentieth century, and were made possible by industrial research, or what its practitioners call the R&D business. R&D stands for Research and Development—scientific research and engineering development. The phrase is doubly significant. The rise of the engineering profession owes as much to big science as the rise of science does to its industrial applications. R&D did not begin in America, but it got its name here, famed in the acronym of the RAND Corporation.

The R&D business originated in late nineteenth-century Germany with the application of coal tar chemistry to the manufacture of aniline dyes, and culminated in the Kaiser Wilhelm Institutes, formed in 1911. That was the monument to German industrial research—the Kaiser Wilhelm Institutes, a government-led research academy. How else elevate coal tar chemistry? Aniline City Music Hall?

At all events, supremacy in the R&D business passed to the Americans with the establishment of the General Electric labs, which then set the standard for industrial research laboratories all over the world. And in just about the same year the Kaiser Wilhelm Institutes were formed, R&D found its name in a small company called AMRAD, short for American Radio, and at the same time an acronym for American Research and Development Corporation. AMRAD was a venture of J.P. Morgan, founded and run by a chap who had been the wireless operator on board Morgan's yacht. It made radio apparatus for amateurs, and no doubt it supplied parts for Hugo Gernsback's radio store at 69 West Broadway in New York City. R&D got its name, as did science fiction its impulse, from the radio business.

The novel factor in the R&D equation is industrial science. Industry itself had always been a practical matter, whereas until the advent of the research revolution, scientists were merely philosophers; they studied the world but did not as yet help determine the world. With the industrialization of science, theoretical and practical men assisted each other, brought together in marriage by corporate enterprise or by government. Until then, scientists were to be found only as modestly paid professionals in the university, where they had come to roost after the Civil War. Family fortunes that had supported nonprofessional science were destroyed in the Civil War. Before that, going back to Colonial times, the scientist was a wealthy amateur, like Benjamin Franklin in silk hose and knee britches, who did experiments out of pocket for the good of general knowledge.

The figure of the mad scientist, Dr. Frankenstein of the horror movies, is a garbled memory of the elegant amateur whose original civic-mindedness has been forgotten. In Mary Shelley's novel, Dr. Frankenstein is sane enough; he scraps the prototype of his female monster following a vision of her awful offspring. He is remembered as mad probably because he bought his own test tubes. But that is what all independent amateurs did and had to do, either in Pennsylvania or Translyvania, before science was industrialized by the research revolution.

Today, Dr. Frankenstein's commanding genius would make him a great scientific mandarin presiding over group research, like Edwin Land, founder and head of the Polaroid Corporation.

BRIDGING THE GAP BETWEEN TECHNOLOGY AND THE HUMANITIES

BY ROBIN WILSON

Sir Charles Snow stirred up an academic hornets' nest a few years ago with his lecture on "The Two Cultures and the Scientific Revolution," suggesting that our world is crippled because we are divided into two camps that don't communicate, the scientific culture and the traditional academic culture. After all the uproar, it appears that he's at least partly right. Robin Wilson is a scholar with one foot in each camp. Now Associate Provost for Instruction at the Ohio State University, he has published science fiction and pioneered a remarkable new way of teaching people to write it, described in this essay.

Once, not so long ago as gods and glaciers measure time, men were satisfied with an educational taxonomy that consisted of only seven entries, the *trivium* and *quadrivium* of the medieval scholar. In 1970, the Office of Education's "Conventional Academic Subdivisions of Knowledge and Training" listed 572 entries. For half a millennium, we have been busily fractionating our knowledge of nature, of man, and of the relationship between man and nature (which, excluding the work of theologians, is all the knowledge we can aspire to), and now many of us wonder if our gains in depth and detail of knowledge have not cost us too dearly by producing a society of "educated" people, many of whom can neither fully comprehend their world nor even effectively communicate their bewilderment to one another.

Scientists and humanists alike decry a technologically based economy that seems to many to be running uncontrolled; engineers and artists can agree that human institutions seem increasingly uncertain in their response to human needs. Thoughtful men everywhere suspect that our civilization has achieved some sort of critical mass which provides it a momentum that is beyond the control of any of us acting singly or all of us acting in concert through the rusty social and political machinery at our disposal.

The problem, of course, is essentially one of communication. It is no longer simply a matter of scientists *vs.* humanists, the controversy so dear to our nineteenth-century forefathers. The intellectual gap between a nuclear physicist and a limnologist is nearly as great as that between a microbiologist and a novelist of manners; the elegant principles of magnetohydrodynamics are no more perceptible to an entomologist than to a Supreme Court Justice. For far too long, we have based our approach to knowledge on the assumption that it came in two irreconcilably different packages: the cumulative, empirical, and general knowledge we call science and the spontaneous, intuitive, and subjectively derived perceptions that have always been considered the special material of the artist and humanist. And yet, is not science at least in part intuitive and spontaneous? Isn't man's knowledge of his own condition and his expression of that knowledge at least in part cumulative and empirical? Most scholars, humanists and scientists alike, would agree that they are more unified by their common allegiance to scholarship than divided by their disciplinary fealties—an explanation, perhaps, for why that remarkably heterogeneous gathering of people called a university faculty works as well as it does.

Intellectual Ghettoes

But this community of understanding does not pertain very much to practitioners in those professions based on the fruits of scholarship. Large numbers of engineers and physicians and schoolteachers and journalists and businessmen and foresters have very little of substance to say to one another outside the artificiality of such client-purveyor relationships as they may establish. They have been intellectually ghettoized by their pursuit of professional knowledge, a process which begins very early in their college careers. Trained both in science and in letters, I have been appalled at the lack of even the most primitive understanding of science among many of my students in the humanities; they seem willing to accept the technological innovations that surround them without criticism or curiosity. "As long as the damn thing works, who cares why or how?" I have been equally appalled at the lack of understanding of art and letters shown by many students of science and engineering. "I don't know anything about art, but I know what I like." How can a student of the humanities so ill-educated participate in the great public decisions of our time, almost all of which—environmental control, economic and cultural egalitarianism, international relations—contain integral technological components? How can an engineer or scientist so ill-educated participate in the same controversies, almost all of which contain integral components of aesthetics, history, and some perception of alternate systems of values?

The higher educational establishment that has been largely responsible for our society's intellectual ghettoization has tried to do something about it, but the efforts—in comparison to the problem—are trifling. A typical engineering student is required to spend something less than fifteen per cent of his undergraduate time on the humanities and the social sciences; his studies in these areas almost inevitably consist only of sequences of two or three highly generalized "survey" courses which are seldom intellectually demanding. A student of the humanities or the social sciences is required to spend an even smaller proportion of his college career studying one of the natural or physical sciences, often in courses that have been specially diluted for him. Nowhere is he likely to find a course in engineering technology open to him. The result is a smattering of this and a smattering of that; rigor and true intellectual involvement are reserved to the field of the major. Perhaps this is the best we can do. There is much to learn and not very much time, and I do not wish to rehearse the tired controversy between the advocates of liberal as opposed to specialized education. But I wonder if, given only ten to fifteen percent of a student's time, we might not make better use of it.

What is necessary, I believe, is a series of new undergraduate courses designed to bridge the gap between technical (or scientific) and humanistic (or artistic) disciplines. These courses should *not* be generalized surveys of man's humanistic accomplishments or pallid depictions of nature's marvelous mechanisms. There is nothing in a young engineering student's mind that precludes his understanding of Kant's Categorical Imperative or the priggishness of Polonius, nothing to prevent him from writing a poem or producing aesthetic gratification from a lump of clay. No wall need come down in the mind of a student of the arts or humanities that bars him from an understanding of Young's Modulus or plate tectonics, nothing need keep him from trying his hand at circuit design or the development of a do-it-yourself sphygmomanometer. Rigorous mathematical proofs and intensive historical analyses may be beyond the scope of the new kinds of courses I propose, but basic concepts and established truths—no matter how sophisticated or demanding—are open to any man and may be taught and understood for themselves.

As a few examples of the sorts of new courses I propose, consider the following:

Science Fiction
A selection of readings from nineteenth- and twentieth-century authors who have concerned themselves with the impact of technological change on human values. Included is a laboratory workshop in which students attempt to write science fiction, giving expression in fictional form to their own conceptions about the social and human consequences of changes they expect either to help bring about or to be affected by.

ROBIN WILSON

The Technology of the Graphic and Plastic Arts

An examination of the physics of color, the chemistry of graphic media, the structural aspects of sculpture, with emphasis on how finished art interacts with and is governed by the physical media of expression. Included is a laboratory/studio in which students experiment with media in the production of original works of art.

Anatomy and Aesthetics in Product Design

An analysis of a range of manufactured objects and devices intended for direct human use which reveals trade-offs between manufacturing efficiency and comfort, utility, and appearance. Included is a design workshop in which students will redesign common consumer products and establish costs for increases in beauty, utility, and comfort.

The Economics of Energy

A consideration of the total cost of energy production and utilization—including environmental, capital, extractive, social, and transportation costs—within the context of physical and engineering limitations. Included is a workshop in planning, power-plant siting, energy transmission, consumption prediction, and potential new energy sources.

The Technology of Warfare

A historical analysis of the relationship between technological change and the imposition of national will by force of arms, from the introduction of archery to the development of the antiballistic missile. Included will be computerized war games in which classic battles are re-fought with advanced weapons and an attempt is made to measure the economic and social impact of weapons-related industries.

The Physics of Music

A study of the physical and mathematical principles of music, its generation, transmission, and reception. Included is a music-workshop in which students compose and play simple melodies on a Moog synthesizer, establishing the physical parameters of rhythm, tone, harmony, counterpoint, etc.

The reader can surely think of many more such courses, e.g.: The Anatomy and Kinematics of the Dance; Synergy and Serendipity: the Psychology of Discovery; Philosophical and Physical Theories of Time; Mensuration: From King John's Nose to the Cross-Sectional Probability of Quark Production; etc. The variations are almost infinite, but all such "bridging" courses have the following in common:

1) They focus on an area of interface between the arts or humanities

or social sciences on one hand and science or technology on the other.

2) They recognize that creativity is the common element in all valid intellectual endeavor, and they require student participation in the creative process, whether the creativity of the engineer or the creativity of the artist.

3) They are frequently problem-oriented, relevant to matters of contemporary social concern.

4) They sacrifice breadth for intensity and rigor on the assumption that to know a piece of a problem well is to learn a little bit about the whole of it.

5) They are suitable for students in any discipline in any field, and the indiscriminate mixing of such students in a single course is in itself a valuable "bridging" function.

6) They are all genuinely interdisciplinary (that much abused word) and will require either a new breed of teacher or some sort of team-teaching arrangement.

7) They all aim at putting back together the humpty-dumpty of knowledge, something all the king's horses and all the king's men have so far been unable—or unwilling—to do.

Although most of the bridging courses I have suggested remain hypothetical, one of them—science fiction writing—has been well tested. Some years ago, I was invited to join the English department of a small Pennsylvania college in order to establish a program in creative writing which was to include an intensive summer workshop. Because I believe people should write for publication and not for the attic trunk, and because science fiction presents a relatively good market for the novice writer, I established the Clarion Writers' Workshop in Fantasy and Science Fiction. Students signed up from all over the country, and to my great surprise I found that a very considerable number of them were not liberal arts students, not the English and journalism majors I had expected. Instead, in the initial workshop of about twenty people, we found an age range of 17 to 65 and a class that included three engineering students, a couple of housewives, a professor of plant pathology from the Midwest, a retired Navy surgeon, a machinist from New England, an electronics technician from California, a saddle-maker, an ex-Air Force missile technician, and a mixed bag of undergraduates whose academic interests fully reflected the curricular supermarket of American higher education. In the dozen subsequent sessions of the workshop (at Clarion State College, Tulane University, the University of Washington at Seattle, and Michigan State University), this diversity of background and interest has continued. There seems to be no shortage of people of all ages and all sorts of training who wish to engage in creative activity in an area where science and technology are juxtaposed with humanistic and artistic interests.

Now, no one goes to historical novels to learn history, nor should anyone seek scientific knowledge in science fiction. But to *write* a good historical novel requires a sound knowledge of the historical setting, and to *write* science fiction requires a sure understanding of physical nature and the impact on society of its exploitation and manipulation. The old authors of pulp science fiction who glorified in bug-eyed monsters clutching scantily clad maidens and who were capable of depicting their square-jawed heroes blithely making 180 degree turns in a spaceship travelling at some sizable fraction of the speed of light—much as I revelled in their work at fourteen—are no longer with us. Their disappearance may be a loss to fourteen-year-olds; it is no loss to students of literary art or—in the context of this discussion—to those interested in science fiction as a cultural bridge. In short, while science fiction is free to speculate about the unknown, it must start from a firm foundation of the known; it cannot—if it is to achieve the verisimilitude that is one of its characteristics—contravene what scientists know to be true. And to know what is blatantly untrue in science is to know a fair amount about what is true.

As a bridging course, then, science fiction is primarily valuable for the motivation it gives its would-be practitioners. The budding engineer or scientist who wishes to communicate his speculations about nature and her impact on mankind is led to study people and to learn the tools of the writer's craft. The student of man and society who wishes to communicate his speculations about the human condition in a technological age is led to study that technology. Two sorts of minds approach a common problem—the justification of the ways of the god technology to man—from opposite poles.

And they meet.

SCIENCE FICTION, LITERARY TRADITION, AND INTELLECTUAL HISTORY

BY THOMAS D. CLARESON

In search of a respectable pedigree for science fiction, its more enthusiastic critics commonly trace its origins back to Homer or Plato or Lucian of Samosata. Too often, they examine it in isolation, connecting it to nothing else. In this significant essay, Tom Clareson places it firmly in the major narrative traditions of Western literature. Professor of English at the College of Wooster and editor of Extrapolation, *he has edited critical series for Bowling Green Popular Press and Kent State University Press, and edited two series of microforms of early SF magazines for Greenwood Press. He received the Pilgrim Award from SFRA in 1977.*

Since the mid-sixties I have had the pleasure of dealing with science fiction in a variety of courses here at the College of Wooster. During one term (1974–75), for example, for the first time I offered "The Utopian Tradition in Western Literature" so that I could include Continental as well as British and American titles. The reading list—some ten books plus others which the student could read individually—ranged from More's *Utopia* and Bacon's *The New Atlantis* to Gabriel de Tarde's *Underground Man,* Zamyatin's *We,* and Anthony Burgess's *The Wanting Seed.* Such a selection permitted us to trace the changing dreams (and nightmares) of Western society, thereby giving us some insight into the intellectual history of the West.

Last fall in a course required of all entering freshmen, seven of us banded together to offer "The Year 2000: Speculations"; the faculty came from the departments of psychology, sociology, English, music, and computer science. We adopted as our common—our "core"—texts the anthology *Survival Printout* (Vintage Books) and B.F. Skinner's *Walden Two* and *Beyond Human Freedom and Dignity* (as it appeared in *Psychology Today* for August, 1971). Each of us was free to add whatever books and articles we wanted; among a number of non-fiction titles, I included Clifford Simak's *A Choice of Gods.* We gained a further common bond among the sections by sharing a number of films and outside speakers. The course will be offered again next fall and grew, incidentally, out of an offering originally team-taught by a professor of psychology and me in the late sixties in which we emphasized portrayals of alternate societies.

Most often, however, I have given "Modern Science Fiction and Fantasy," first planned as a "special topics" seminar primarily for seniors but now open to all students of the College. While I assume a knowledge on their part of at least some of the major Utopias, Mary Shelley's *Frankenstein,* and the works of Poe, Fitz-James O'Brien, and Verne, for example, I normally begin with H.G. Wells and Jack London and conclude the term with works by Silverberg, Gunn, Delany, and Aldiss. My emphasis is historical rather than thematic, for I want to show the diversity with which science fiction has developed since the last decades of the nineteenth century. For the same reason, I always try to include works by at least several authors who did not publish originally in the science-fiction magazines; after all, by 1917 at the latest Dorothy Scarborough, among others, recognized the existence of the "scientific romance" and accepted it as a noteworthy part of contemporary fiction. Moreover, we tend to forget how many science-fiction titles appeared in the early magazines (*Cosmopolitan,* for example, serialized Wells's novels at the turn of the century and within a decade featured Arthur B. Reeve's tales of Craig Kennedy, the scientific detective, while *The Saturday Evening Post* published Arthur Train and Robert William Wood's *The Man Who Rocked the Earth* in the autumn of 1914—to say nothing of the innumerable stories and serials in the Munsey magazines, *Pearson's,* and *The Strand,* among others). Nor in saying this do I take into account the hundreds of titles—aimed both at the juvenile and adult audiences—issued only in book form as late as the thirties.

Some may wonder, if not protest, at the inclusion of the term "Fantasy" in the course title; actually, the only fantasy that I have thus far included is that of James Branch Cabell (no, not Tolkien—as yet). I use the term primarily to give myself any leeway that I might sometime want and, more important, to underscore that science fiction is not a type of literature originating in, and confined to, the last century either in terms of theme(s) or form. I myself am not impressed with the narrow, often pedantic definitions which some critics have tried to impose upon science fiction recently in order to differentiate it, for whatever reasons, from the Utopia, the imaginary voyage, heroic fantasy, or whatnot. Indeed, to attempt to do so is, I believe, a major misjudgment which would divorce science fiction from a major literary tradition leading back through the medieval travel book and medieval romance to the heroic epics of Beowulf and Odysseus. As a result, although for almost a decade I have offered courses devoted exclusively to science fiction, I have as frequently included it in general fiction courses whatever period or periods from the eighteenth century to the present they deal with. I have found that a number of teachers, including such individuals as Robert Scholes, have advocated this practice.

In "SF: The Other Side of Realism" and the Introduction to *A Spectrum of Worlds,* I have tried to suggest that two equally strong narrative traditions exist side-by-side throughout Western literature. [Thomas D. Clareson, "SF: The Other Side of Realism," in *SF: The Other Side of Realism* (Bowling Green, Ohio: Bowling Green University Popular Press, 1971), pp. 1-28; "Introduction," *A Spectrum of Worlds* (Garden City, N. Y.: Doubleday & Company, Inc.), pp. 7-31.] On the one hand, the writer—particularly in the novel since the eighteenth century—has focussed his attention upon the familiar scenes and minutae of an everyday social and personal (psychological) world, increasingly de-emphasizing plot action in favor of intensive character study. (There are those academicians who dismiss narrative fiction as "mere story" and will not consider it a novel unless it makes a probing study of character.) In contrast, other writers have explored little-known areas of this world and since the seventeenth century, as early as Francis Godwin's *The Man in the Moone* (1638), have employed other worlds, both in space and time, as their settings. Whatever the characteristics that individualize science fiction from previous works, it obviously belongs to the latter tradition, whose authors have been less fettered by society-as-it-is either in the here-and-now or within the limitations of the historical record.

In those earlier essays, for convenience, I called the two traditions realism and fantasy and noted that, ironically, both were responses to the science of the various periods. Three examples may suffice. After the new interest in science had created the Royal Society in the eighteenth century, the same impulse to observe and classify so as to understand the order of the natural world—which led through the developing science of paleontology to the "catastrophists" and, eventually, to Darwin—helped to create the modern novel. Its authors and their small audience were fascinated by the nature and order of the society around them; in the novel, therefore, a group of characters was brought together so that their actions and conversations and thoughts (revealed especially through their letters) might be recorded in order to "observe" and judge the workings of society. As has been said so often, the changes occurring in British society in the wake of the Industrial Revolution kept the "condition of England" a matter of extreme interest to the major novelists; certainly one of the central themes of the British novel throughout the nineteenth century remained the study of the rise and fall of a character within the class-structure of the society.

Despite this emphasis upon social realism, however, throughout the period "fantasy" maintained an important place in the fiction, giving to modern science fiction perhaps its basic narrative structure, that of the "imaginary voyage." One cannot, I believe, overemphasize the

THOMAS D. CLARESON

importance of this structure to the novel: Fielding permitted Tom Jones to journey to London in order to provide a credible basis for a wider panorama of society; Defoe's Captain Singleton travelled across Africa, as well as becoming involved with pirates; and, of course, Gulliver voyaged to purely imaginary islands to give Swift a means of castigating contemporary Europe. As Philip Babcock Gove has pointed out, the "imaginary voyage" became the most popular form of fiction during the eighteenth century. That popularity grew out of the continuing interest in exploration, which was but another expression of the growing interest in the nature of the physical world. (Significantly, the legendary *terra australis incognita* has played an important part in these voyages as late as the twentieth century; indeed, by sampling these "imaginary voyages," one can easily discover the focal point that has captured the imagination of explorer and public alike at any given time.) Because of the impact of geology and archeology, the voyage remained popular throughout the nineteenth century, not changing in its essentials until H. Rider Haggard transformed it in the eighteen-eighties into the so-called "lost race" novel, which was in its turn unquestionably the most popular form of the "scientific romance" written before the nineteen-twenties.

The voyage structure ties science fiction to another literary tradition. Basically, it allows its narrator/protagonist to leave his familiar, everyday world and venture into the unknown, whether it be some unexplored area of this world or another planet either of our solar system or of some other; in recounting his adventures, he gives much attention to the exotic, mysterious, often terrible natural phenomena which he encounters (nor should one forget how many contemporary SF writers insist that they *must* give so much attention to setting that they have little time for fuller characterizations); he overcomes all obstacles, he survives, and he returns to the familiar world to tell of his strange adventures. This pattern, as several critics have noted, ties science fiction to the pastoral tradition. Indeed, in that the central issue often becomes one of survival, such worlds echo the hostile environments which the literary naturalists emphasized in the late nineteenth and twentieth centuries. The failure of the narrator/protagonist to return from his adventures provided the "imaginary voyage" with one of its most enduring (and, in a way, endearing) conventions: the discovery of a manuscript; in the nineteenth century, under the increasing demand for "fact" and "truth to nature," such a device gave an acceptable credibility to the tales, and its use has survived into the twentieth century. At times it became a device for satire, as when on the eve of Peary's discovery of the North Pole, Wallace Irwin based his report of "A New Angle on the Old Pole" (*Cosmopolitan,* 1909) on "a manuscript found in a ketchup bottle." Yet the "imaginary voyage" survived to give us the Shangri-La of James Hilton's *Lost Horizon* (1936), and its continued viability may be measured by the success of Ian Cameron's

The Lost Ones (1968), used as the basis for the Disney film, *The Island at the Top of the World,* in which a colony of Vikings is found surviving within the Arctic circle.

The literary tradition to which science fiction belongs found new expression in the Gothic, responding once again to issues within the intellectual history of the period. By the end of the eighteenth century the discussion of epistemology begun a century earlier by John Locke, the "great empirical rationalist," had led through Berkeley to the skepticism of Hume. The result was disconcerting; its implications may be seen in the paintings of the Romantic artists. The human figures are pictured alone, solitary against a backdrop of a vast, brooding nature. Moreover, the individual, isolated in his own consciousness, cannot be certain that his senses correctly perceive the nature of any external "reality," nor can he be certain that his mind functions correctly. Here, as much, if not more, than in any social or political condition, lies the beginning of that sense of alienation and estrangement which has come to dominate so much of modern literature. For this reason any attempt to identify science fiction specifically as a literature of estrangement and thereby use that criterion to separate it from the body of modern literature seems to me a misjudgment. The science-fiction protagonist is himself no more isolated or estranged from his society than were, for example, Clyde Griffiths in Dreiser's *An American Tragedy* or Coleridge's Ancient Mariner. It may be, however, that for present audiences in the last third of the twentieth century, the materials of science fiction can more vividly dramatize that estrangement; even so, the theme ties science fiction more tightly to the main body of literature than it gives the genre separate identity.

Be that as it may, the Gothic not only reawakened the demonic and irrational, but gave science fiction one of its most enduring themes: that of the monster created by Dr. Frankenstein, the scientist. In a sense the genre is doubly indebted to Mary Shelley's novel. On the one hand, of course, Dr. Frankenstein updates the theme of Faust; he is the man so devoted to science that he trespasses beyond those boundaries which man should respect, taking upon himself the Godlike power of creating life. He becomes the prototype of the "mad scientist," including such figures as the protagonist of W.H. Rhodes's "The Case of Summerfield" (1870, 1917) and the villain of Stewart Edward White's *The Sign at Six* (1912)—to say nothing of those creatures who haunted not so much the science-fiction magazines themselves as such essentially sadistic pulps as *Horror Stories* and *Terror Tales* in the thirties. On the other hand, of course, *Frankenstein* gave science fiction the prototype for its loathsome monsters of whatever shape or origin. It survives effectively as the all-enveloping computer of Harlan Ellison's "I Have No Mouth, And I Must Scream" (1967), but for the most part it is such papier-mâché as poor horror films are made of.

One of the most successful (and typical) science-fiction stories re-

THOMAS D. CLARESON

sulting from the Gothic emphasis upon the abnormal mind— madness—was Fitz-James O'Brien's "The Diamond Lens" (*The Atlantic Monthly,* 1858), the first-person narrative of "Linley, the mad microscopist." He tells of his intellectual dissatisfaction at not possessing a perfect lens, his acquisition of one, and his love for the sylphlike woman whom he discovers in a submicroscopic world within a drop of water. One day the drop of water evaporates, she and her world are destroyed, and Linley is taken to an asylum. One suspects that the Gothic endured as long as it did because in a society that increasingly emphasized material "reality," such stories could be momentarily accepted and enjoyed so long as they could then be dismissed as the aberrations of an abnormal mind. Significantly, by the end of the century, Ambrose Bierce, for example, was giving scientific explanations in terms of the knowledge and theories of his day.

The most effective portrayals of an abnormal state of mind came, of course, in the works of Edgar Allan Poe. By and large his most effective stories employ the first-person narrator so that his readers share quickly and fully the horrific experiences of his protagonist. His finest achievement occurs in *The Narrative of A. Gordon Pym,* for in that story he dramatizes the dilemma which the long debate on epistemology had produced. Whatever else the story may symbolize, its first half reveals how untrustworthy are the perceptions of the human senses; the latter half, how uncertain the supposed realities of the external world. This is the nightmare in which the reader and Pym are caught as they approach the southern polar area. Here, again, is a revelation of man's total isolation and alienation in an unreliable world; I think that one might well undertake the argument that *The Narrative of A. Gordon Pym* more than any other single work of modern fiction marks our entry into the grotesque and absurd.

As the century progressed, particularly after the shattering impact of both Darwin and Marx, the traditional values which had shaped Western society and literature were brought increasingly into question. The gloom engendered by determinism—the vision of an animal man caught in a meaningless, uncaring universe—engulfed the literary imagination. As Robert E. Spiller has pointed out, much of the central task for twentieth-century writers and critics alike has lain in the search for a new center, a new authority, which can once again give meaning to the creative act. Thus, for example, the continued emphasis upon Freudian theory by writer and critic alike, for in a sense, at least, Freud renewed the validity of the imagination. And that emphasis has continued despite the demotion given him within psychological circles. Late in the nineteenth century another possible solution was voiced by those who espoused literary realism: "the business of the novelist is to make you *understand the real world through his faithful effigy of it. . ."* [William Dean Howells, "Novel-Writing and Novel-Reading, an Impersonal Explanation," *Howells and James: A*

Double Billing, edited by William M. Gibson (NY: New York Public Library, 1958), p. 24. The emphasis is mine.] The result was the wedding of a narrative technique (mimesis) and a philosophy (naturalism) to produce an intensified social and psychological realism. Rather than a new unity, as such men as Howells, Gissing, and Zola, among others, had hoped for, the result further dramatized the fragmentation and isolation of the individual within society, attaining perhaps one of its most vivid expressions in John Dos Passos' novel, *Manhattan Transfer* (1925).

Granted that H.G. Wells, for example, warned repeatedly against naive beliefs both in the inevitability of progress and in the certainty that man is the highest possible expression of evolution and will remain forever unchanged, if, indeed, he survives as a species, in America particularly the early writers of science fiction were the optimists. That is to say, unlike their colleagues who may be identified with the "high" and traditional culture, they did not see man lost in a meaningless universe. Rather, they had a vision of an imminent "Earthly Paradise" growing out of the benefits resulting from the new technology which had transformed the United States within a single generation. By World War One, at the latest, industrialization had already become the dominant factor in all phases of American life. One need not detail again the effect upon the popular literature. Boy inventors were legion in number; man and boy alike sought the "ultimate" energy, the "ultimate" metal, and the "ultimate" weapon; wondrous machines conquered nature and gave man a freedom which he had never known before. As Robert Silverberg and Donald Wollheim, among others, have said, that vision expanded in the science-fiction magazines until it saw man *as he is now* and his technology triumphant throughout the universe. It reached its climax in the vision of "Galactic Man."

One could go on and describe the reaction which, after World War Two, emphasized dystopia—the "Earthly Hell"—and has become so important in recent science fiction. Perhaps, however, these three examples will suffice to show how closely science fiction is related to both literary tradition and intellectual history. Other points might be stressed. For example, just as literary realism, with its demands for "truth to life" and a "faithful effigy" of the "real" world, trapped itself in the cul-de-sac of the here-and-now and thereby often failed to achieve the level of symbolic statement, so, too, the early science fiction, with its emphasis upon gadgetry and, supposedly, accurate prophecy, trapped itself in a linear history which was only an extension of *now* instead of the creation of symbolic worlds giving insight into the nature and condition of man.

One last point: in advocating his theory of literary realism, Howells denounced that fiction which relied primarily, if not exclusively, upon "dramatic situation"—that is, upon plot action. Granted that the very best fiction will probably balance—fuse—action and character, one

THOMAS D. CLARESON

cannot but recall that throughout Western literature many narratives have not given primary attention to character. Beowulf seems little more than a braggart, but his actions reveal him to be the ideal king. Arthur is often little more than a shadow, while his knights are no more than vivid stereotypes; again, it is their acts—such as the search for the Grail—which make them important. And surely Cooper's Natty Bumppo—the Leatherstocking—particularly in the later tales depicting the exploits of his youth, is less important than his acts. Perhaps only in that fiction which gives its basic attention to a delineation of the familiar, everyday world can (should?) character study be the author's primary concern. Significantly, however, because of the increased emphasis upon social and psychological realism, the hero has been displaced by the anti-hero. Science fiction has been called a literature of ideas; belonging as it does to that literary tradition which creates and explores imaginary worlds, perhaps it should be recognized as a literature of action—at its best, symbolic action.

TWENTIETH-CENTURY SCIENCE-FICTION WRITERS

BY ALEXEI AND CORY PANSHIN

> *Not only is Panshin the author of a Nebula-winning novel,* Rite of Passage, *he is also the author of* Heinlein in Dimension, *the first full-length critical study of a contemporary SF writer. Alexei now writes in collaboration with his wife Cory, a former graduate student in linguistics at Harvard. In the seventies, the Panshins have published a novel and a collection of critical essays on SF, and have completed a major book,* Masters of Space and Time: The Story of Science Fiction. *Here they offer a historical survey of the most prominent writers of SF. Symbols such as A1, B11, and D28 are cross-references to their bibliography of modern science fiction and fantasy in Chapter 24.*

This historical survey is intended to give some impression of the peak periods, significant works, styles and influence of a number of modern science-fiction writers. It is organized on the basis of the first appearance of the author, and is divided into four chronological sections.

I. 1912–1934

These writers, who were born between 1875 and 1911, invented modern science fiction on the foundation laid by Edgar Allan Poe, Jules Verne and H.G. Wells. The two peak periods of this early work were 1912–21 and 1928–36.

Edgar Rice Burroughs (1875–1950)

A writer of colorful action romances, most notably four series—Tarzan; a series set on Mars; a Venus series; and the Pellucidar books, a hollow-Earth series. First publication was "Under the Moons of Mars" (*A Princess of Mars,* A2) in *All-Story Magazine,* 1912. Active into the forties. Most influential 1912–16.

John W. Campbell (1910–71)

First published 1930 in *Amazing.* Initial impact was with science-

A. & C. PANSHIN

oriented planet-busting space opera, 1930–32. His more atmospheric and philosophical stories under the name "Don A. Stuart" (1934–39), collected as *The Best of John W. Campbell* (1976), A3, were his most influential work and outshone his concurrent stories under his own name. He gave up writing to concentrate on the editorship of *Astounding* (later called *Analog*) (1937–71), in which role he had his greatest impact on modern science fiction. Stories in A1, B11, B16, and D28.

Robert E. Howard (1906–36)

First published 1924 in *Weird Tales,* his chief place of publication. Incredibly prolific. He found his stride in 1928 with vigorous fantasy-adventures, climaxing in the Conan series (1932–36). These set the mold for all subsequent sword-and-sorcery stories, have been packaged and repackaged under various titles, and have been continued by other writers, chiefly L. Sprague de Camp.

Murray Leinster (William Fitzgerald Jenkins) (1896–1975)

Science fiction was only a small part of the production of this writer of popular fiction and inventor. First SF 1919. Continued to write science fiction into the late sixties, always adapting to the standard of the time. His work was more often competent than distinguished, but notable stories include "The Mad Planet" (1920); "Sidewise in Time" (1934) and "Proxima Centauri" (1935), both in A1; "First Contact" (1945) in B16; and the Hugo-winning "Exploration Team" (1956) in D3. A recent collection is *The Best of Murray Leinster* (1978).

H.P. Lovecraft (1890–1937)

First fiction published in little magazines 1919. Most frequently appeared in *Weird Tales* from 1923 until his death. Wrote purple horror stories on a science-fiction rather than fantasy basis, chiefly within the framework of the "Cthulhu Mythos," which was amplified and continued by many other writers. Had two long stories, *At the Mountains of Madness* and "The Shadow Out of Time," in *Astounding,* 1936. August Derleth founded Arkham House publishers (1939) to rescue his work from magazine limbo. Has a higher reputation in Europe than America.

A. Merritt (1884–1943)

Active 1917–34. Widely popular and influential writer of highly colored lost-race fantasies. *The Moon Pool* (1919), A10, was reprinted in *Amazing Stories,* 1927. Other notable stories include *The Ship of Ishtar* (1924) and *Dwellers in the Mirage* (1932).

C.L. Moore (1911–   )

First published 1933 in *Weird Tales.* Notable 1933–36 for fusion of fantasy and space opera. Had Jirel of Joiry and Northwest Smith series in *Weird Tales.* Appeared in *Astounding* in middle and late thirties. From 1942 to 1957, her work appeared chiefly in collaboration with her husband, Henry Kuttner, under one or another of their many pseudonyms. Her work was strong on sensuous detail, weakest in plot, as in her collection, *The Best of C.L. Moore* (1975), A11. Story in C8A.

Clifford D. Simak (1904–   )

Early stories, 1931–32, not notable, though one appears in A1. Brought back to writing SF by John W. Campbell. Simak has been continuously active since 1938. His first influential work was collected as *City* (1952), B17; and a story from this series appears in B16. The Hugo-winning "The Big Front Yard," in C8B and D3, is typical of much of his work: humanistic, often bucolic stories of human-alien contact. Since his recent retirement as a newspaper editor, has produced frequent novels.

E.E. Smith (1890–1965)

The Skylark of Space, A13, serialized in 1928 in *Amazing Stories,* was his first story. A landmark in science fiction—the first interstellar story. Smith was a major innovator from his first appearance through 1942. He wrote crude novels on a grand scale, chiefly in two series: the Skylark stories (1928–34; 1965) and the Lensman novels (1937–50). These last were space opera with galactic scope. One of the best of these is *Gray Lensman* (1939), B18.

Olaf Stapledon (1886–1950)

Stapledon was a British lecturer in philosophy who used science fiction as a vehicle for speculation about the future of man and the universe. Most notable are his first work of fiction, *Last and First Men* (1930), and *Star Maker* (1937), collected as A14. Also of interest are *Odd John* (1935), the story of an intellectual superman, and *Sirius* (1944), the story of a dog with artificially enhanced intelligence. An omnibus containing all of these titles is available under the title *To the End of Time.*

Stanley G. Weinbaum (1900–35)

Weinbaum died within eighteen months of the publication of his first story, "A Martian Odyssey" (1934), in B16. His work is dated now, but his humorous, comparatively realistic space operas, of which "A Martian Odyssey" is one, and "The Parasite Planet" (1935), in A1, is another, were highly influential during the thirties. Weinbaum was then considered a model of sophistication. Several collections of his short stories have recently been published, including *The Best of Stanley G. Weinbaum* (1974), A15.

Jack Williamson (1908–   )

First published in *Amazing Stories* in 1928. Except for World War II, steadily active since. Most influential 1934–38 with highly romantic stories like *The Legion of Space* (1934), A17, and "The Moon Era" (1932) and "Born of the Sun" (1934), both in A1. Also notable are his novels *Darker Than You Think,* in *Unknown,* 1940, and *The Humanoids* (1948), B23. Williamson is still active, both alone and in collaboration with Frederik Pohl. Story in C8A.

§ § §

II. 1937–1942

These writers, born between 1905 and 1923, arrived during a period still remembered as the Golden Age. This group produced the major shapers of modern science fiction. Their careers were generally interrupted by World War II, and most did their best work in the years 1949–58, especially in the peak period, 1950–53.

Isaac Asimov (1920–   )

First story, 1939. With Heinlein and van Vogt, may be counted one of the central figures of modern science fiction. Asimov had some success during the forties, especially with the story "Nightfall" (1941), in B11, B16 and D28, and with his robot and his Foundation series (B1). His greatest impact was 1949–57 with the revised book versions of these series and with such new works as *The Caves of Steel* (1953), C4. His recent fiction has been comparatively infrequent, as Asimov has concentrated on works of popular science and history, but his one recent novel, *The Gods Themselves* (1972), D2, won the Hugo and Nebula awards. His work is strongest in conceptual clarity. Story in C8B.

Alfred Bester (1913–   )

Early stories 1939–42 largely minor productions. After period writing comic-book scripts and radio and TV, returned with great success 1950–59, especially with two novels, *The Demolished Man* (1952), C5, and *The Stars My Destination* (1956), C6. Recently active again with novel *The Computer Connection* (1974), and two retrospective collections of his short fiction. Bester often concentrates on favorite themes such as psi powers and time travel which give scope for pyrotechnic inventiveness and the exploration of questions of identity. Stories in B11, B16, and D28.

James Blish (1921–75)

Early stories 1940–42 in minor magazines. Most active 1948–57. His work was highly private and intensely intellectual, but occasionally struck notes of more general and emotional appeal, especially in *Jack of Eagles* (1949), B2; "Surface Tension" (1952), in B16; and "Common Time" in *Science Fiction Quarterly* in 1953. Also notable are "Earthman, Come Home" (1953) in C8B, and the Hugo-winning novel, *A Case of Conscience* (1958), C7.

Ray Bradbury (1920–   )

First collaborative story, 1941. Bradbury is primarily a writer of short stories—stylized, nostalgic fragments. Unusually for a forties writer, not influenced by John W. Campbell. His best work appeared 1946–51. Has rarely written science fantasy since. Recommended are

The Martian Chronicles, B4, and *Fahrenheit 451,* C9.

Fredric Brown (1906–72)
First story, 1941. Most active 1948–54. A former newspaper proof-reader turned writer of detective stories and science fiction. His typical work was in short story and short-short length, often blackly humorous, as in *The Best of Fredric Brown* (1977), B5. His most notable novel is *What Mad Universe* (1948), B6. Brown's strength was his unique combination of vigorous pulp action with an acute sense of the bizarre. Short stories in B11 and B16.

Hal Clement (Harry C. Stubbs) (1922–   )
First story in *Astounding,* 1942. His major work appeared in *Astounding,* 1949–57, most notably *Mission of Gravity* (1953), C12. Clement has been a high school teacher of science for many years. His stories feature scrupulously detailed un-manlike aliens and un-Earthlike worlds. He is the most one-sidedly science-oriented writer ever to write SF.

L. Sprague de Camp (1907–   )
First story 1937. Most active 1939–42 and 1949–54. Some rare fantasy but little science fiction since. His forte was humorous adventure cast as logically rigorous fantasy or as melodramatic and romantic science fiction. Besides the Harold Shea series of other-world fantasies (1940–41; 1953–54), written in collaboration with Fletcher Pratt, of which *The Compleat Enchanter* (1975), B7, collects three, other major works include *Lest Darkness Fall* (1939), B8 and *Rogue Queen* (1951). Story in B11.

Robert A. Heinlein (1907–   )
The dominant writer of modern science fiction. First story in *Astounding,* 1939. Heinlein had a crucial impact on SF 1939–42, especially with the Future History series, B13, which aimed to make SF as solidly actual as realistic fiction. His most impressive early work was *Beyond This Horizon* (1942), B12. Returned to writing 1947, in particular with a superb series of juvenile novels, of which *Have Space Suit—Will Travel* (1958), C13, is an example. His novels since 1959 have been long, strange, and private—most notably the Hugo-winning *Stranger in a Strange Land* (1961), D13. Stories in B11, B16, and C8A.

Damon Knight (1922–   )
Early stories 1941–44. Returned 1948, with peak 1951–58. Occasional fiction since. Knight's most notable fiction has been his many snappy, ironic short stories. His best novel is his first, *Hell's Pavement* (1955), C15. His pioneering SF criticism was collected as *In Search of Wonder* (1956; expanded 2nd edition, 1967). Founder of Science Fiction Writers of America. Recently most active as anthology editor and patron of young authors. Stories in B16 and D28.

C.M. Kornbluth (1923–58)
Early stories under many names, 1940–42. Returned 1949–58. Best known for collaborations with Frederik Pohl, such as the novels *The*

Space Merchants (1952), C19, and *Wolfbane* (1959), C20. His best solo novel, *The Syndic* (1953), C16, is but slightly less black and cynical than his short stories, such as "The Words of Guru" (1941); "The Little Black Bag" (1950), in B16; and "The Marching Morons" (1951), in C8A and D28.

Henry Kuttner (1914–58)

First story 1937. Largely inactive after 1953. Alone or in collaboration with his wife, C.L. Moore, Kuttner did large amounts of lively hackwork, much of it pseudonymously. Some fine, even brilliant, stories—ironic and psychological—were published under the name "Lewis Padgett" in *Astounding*, 1942–49. See the collection, *The Best of Henry Kuttner*, B14. Stories in B11 and C8A.

Fritz Leiber (1910–   )

First story 1939. Made some impression in the early forties with novels like *Conjure Wife* (1943), in *Unknown,* and *Gather, Darkness!*, serialized in *Astounding* in 1943. His mordant and decadent tales of satiric near-futures and fantasy worlds are fairly represented in *The Best of Fritz Leiber* (1974), C17. Work produced in bursts until the later fifties. Best work and many awards 1957–70. Notable is the Fafhrd and Gray Mouser sword-and-sorcery series, which has continued from 1939 to the present. Stories in B16 and D3.

Frederik Pohl (1919–   )

First collaborative story, "Heavy Planet," 1939, in B11; but early solo work not notable. Pohl has continued the habit of collaboration, most notably with C.M. Kornbluth and Jack Williamson. In the fifties, Pohl was the dominant figure in the school of science-fiction satire, as in "The Midas Plague" (1954), in C8B, and in his collaborative novels with Kornbluth, such as *The Space Merchants* (1952), C19, and *Wolfbane* (1959), C20. Award-winning editor of *If* and *Galaxy* during the sixties—a continuing editorial influence second only to Campbell in many posts since 1939. Recently, Pohl has been the author of two award-winning novels, *Man Plus* (1976) and *Gateway* (1977).

Eric Frank Russell (1905–78)

First story in *Astounding,* 1937, in style of Weinbaum. This British writer was noted for the novel *Sinister Barrier* (1939), in the first issue of *Unknown*. Active until 1959. Peak 1951–57, when his lively and optimistic melodramas such as ". . . And Then There Were None" (1951), in C8A, and *Wasp* (1957), C21, contrasted sharply with the increasingly claustrophobic satire which dominated the period. Stories in B11, one under the name Maurice G. Hugi.

Theodore Sturgeon (1918–   )

Notable first for finely wrought fantasies in *Unknown,* 1939–43. An early story, "Microcosmic God" (1941), is included in B16. Peak of activity 1951–57. Only rarely active since. Sturgeon's most influential work is the novel *More Than Human* (1953), C22, the central portion of which appears separately in C8A. Sturgeon's impact has primarily been as modern science fiction's first stylist. Story in D28.

A.E. van Vogt (1912–   )

During the forties, Van Vogt was rated second only to Heinlein, and he remains one of SF's dominant figures for his early work. His first story, "Black Destroyer" (1939), appears with two other early stories in B11. Most influential were his chaotic but thought-provoking stories of supermen with identity problems, chiefly the novels *Slan* (1940), B20, and *The World of Null-A* (1945), B21. Active until 1950. Returned in the sixties, but without his previous impact. Stories in B16 and D28.

III. 1943–1956

These many writers, born between 1909 and 1934, were overshadowed by their immediate predecessors. They had the misfortune to reach what should have been their peak during the creatively barren late fifties. Some faltered, a few adapted brilliantly, several fell into facile hackwork. Many attained their greatest stature and produced their most successful work during the peak 1965–69.

Brian W. Aldiss (1925–   )

In 1954, winner of third prize in London newspaper SF competition. First notable work 1958–61, including the Hugo-winning *The Long Afternoon of Earth* (1961), D1. Pessimistic. In the late sixties was led to attempt SF novels in the manner of the French anti-novelists and James Joyce. His historical and critical book, *Billion Year Spree* (1973), proposed a division of science fiction into literature and sub-literature. The dominant British SF writer of the last twenty years.

Poul Anderson (1926–   )

First published in 1947 in *Astounding*. Peak 1958–62, but overall the most consistent writer during the last twenty years. The delight of John Campbell's old age for stories like "Call Me Joe" (1957), in C8A; *The Man Who Counts* (1958), C3; and the Hugo-winning "The Longest Voyage" (1960), in D3. Writes science-oriented space opera, but also rational fantasy like *Three Hearts and Three Lions* (1953; 1961), C2. A romantic. A would-be tragedian. A lighter side is evident in *Earthman's Burden* (1957), C1, written in collaboration with Gordon R. Dickson. Two other Hugo-winning stories in D3.

J.G. Ballard (1930–   )

First story in British magazine *Science-Fantasy* in 1956. Most active 1961–70. His most visible work was a series of novels that destroyed the world variously with wind, water and fire, culminating with the novel *The Crystal World* (1966), in which time comes to a stop. In the later sixties appeared in several British magazines, chiefly *New Worlds*, with highly experimental, static and surrealistic set-pieces, such as "The Assassination of John Fitzgerald Kennedy Considered as a Downhill Motor Race" in *Ambit* in 1967. His present work, very private, seems something other than science fiction. Story in D28.

A. & C. PANSHIN

John Brunner (1934–   )

A British writer, first published in 1951. Very prolific from 1955. More serious and individual work after 1965, such as the Hugo-winning, Dos-Passos–influenced *Stand on Zanzibar* (1968), D4. Has now written a number of long, ambitious, pessimistic near-future melodramas.

Algis Budrys (1931–   )

A Lithuanian exile, primarily raised in America. First story 1952. Very prolific 1953–56. In the late fifties, he wrote a number of increasingly serious stories about alienation and the search for identity, culminating in the novel *Rogue Moon* (1960), a short magazine version of which appears in C8B. One isolated novel, 1967. In the middle seventies has returned to writing SF, as well as very useful SF historical criticism.

Arthur C. Clarke (1917–   )

First story, "Rescue Party" in *Astounding* in 1946, was notable. Clarke writes in two veins. One, a pedestrian near-future technical style, reflects his careers as sometime Chairman of the British Interplanetary Society, scuba diver, and popular science writer. The other, influenced by Olaf Stapledon, whom he knew as a youth, is visionary and may be seen in Clarke's notable novels, *Childhood's End* (1953), C10, and *The City and the Stars* (1956), C11. Both styles are reflected in the Kubrick-Clarke movie and book, *2001: A Space Odyssey* (1968). Clarke is the one writer of his writing generation and the one Briton to be ranked with Heinlein, Asimov, and van Vogt. In recent years has written little science fiction; but the first of several new novels in the seventies, *Rendezvous with Rama* (1973), D6, was a Hugo and Nebula winner. Stories in B17, D3, and D28.

Avram Davidson (1923–   )

First SF story 1954. Prolific writer of clever and erudite short stories 1957–61, of which the Hugo-winning "Or All the Seas with Oysters" (1958), in D3, is an example. In the early Sixties, after serving as editor of *F&SF*, he made a somewhat uncomfortable transition to the novel form, the most fascinating example of which may be *Masters of the Maze* (1965). Since 1966, has launched a number of unfinished fantasy novel series.

Philip K. Dick (1928–   )

First story 1952. Very prolific writer of short stories 1953–54. Influential 1957–64 with a number of novels questioning reality, in particular *Eye in the Sky* (1957); the Hugo-winning *The Man in the High Castle* (1962), D9; and *The Three Stigmata of Palmer Eldritch* (1964), D10. In more recent novels, he has continued to weave his webs of radical insecurity. Story in D28.

Gordon R. Dickson (1923–   )

First story 1950. Collaborated with his friend Poul Anderson on a series of humorous stories collected as *Earthman's Burden* (1957), C1.

A steady, sound but unspectacular writer, especially visible since 1959. His story, "Soldier, Ask Not" (1964), in D3, was a Hugo winner. Beginning with the novel *Dorsai!*, serialized in *Astounding* in 1959, Dickson has been working on a vast tapestry of melodrama concerning the coming appearance of intuitional supermen.

Harlan Ellison (1934–   )

First story 1956. Prolific 1956–59. Primarily a writer of violent and emotional short stories. Three of these, " 'Repent, Harlequin!' Said the Ticktockman" (1965); "I Have No Mouth, and I Must Scream" (1967); and "The Beast That Shouted Love at the Heart of the World" (1968), are Hugo winners and appear in D3. Editor of two influential anthologies, *Dangerous Visions* (1967) and *Again, Dangerous Visions* (1972), wherein he encouraged controversial, taboo-breaking and experimental science fiction. Story in D28.

Philip José Farmer (1918–   )

Made an initial impact 1952–54 with stories of alien sexuality, most notably his first story, *The Lovers* (1952; 1961). Active again in the sixties with the Riverworld series, whose publication was postponed from the early fifties. The re-revised book version of some of these won a Hugo award as *To Your Scattered Bodies Go* (1971), D12. His Joycean "Riders of the Purple Wage" (1967), in D3, was also a Hugo winner. Many novels in the sixties and seventies, including a number of fictions and fictional biographies involving characters like Doc Savage and Tarzan. One such exercise in secondary realities, *Venus on the Half-Shell* (1975), published under the name of Vonnegut's SF-writing character, Kilgore Trout, was financially successful. Story in D28.

Charles L. Harness (1915–   )

Active 1948–53, and occasionally since. A patent attorney who writes didactic and highly eccentric melodramas of identity, revenge and altering reality. Notable are *Flight Into Yesterday* (1949; 1953), B10; "The New Reality" (1950), which is printed with "The Rose" (1953) in *The Rose* (1965); and *The Ring of Ritornel* (1968). A novel, *Wolfhead*, was published in 1978.

Frank Herbert (1920–   )

The first SF story by this man of many careers appeared in 1952. Two widely spaced notable novels, awkward but powerful—a psychological drama, *The Dragon in the Sea* (1955), C14, and the monumental melodrama of ecology and fanaticism, *Dune* (1965), D14. Frequent novels since 1965, but none with comparable impact until *The Children of Dune* (1976), which appeared on general bestseller lists.

Walter M. Miller, Jr. (1923–   )

First story 1951. Attracted attention for novelettes like "Dark Benediction" (1951), the Hugo-winning "The Darfsteller" (1954), in D3, and "Conditionally Human" (1952), all in the collection *Conditionally Human* (1962). These were a vigorous attempt to use science fiction to inquire into the human condition, compromised somewhat by pulp

SF trappings. His major work, the Hugo-winning novel *A Canticle for Leibowitz* (1959), C18, balances science fiction and Roman Catholicism. It was incompletely revised from magazine appearances, 1955–57. No new fiction since 1957.

Andre Norton (Alice Mary Norton) (c. 1915–   )

This writer of children's books and former librarian first was published in the thirties. Her first SF novel was *Star Man's Son* (1952). She has been a steady producer of highly competent but non-innovative juvenile and paperback science fiction and fantasy novels, now numbering well over forty.

Edgar Pangborn (1909–76)

First story, the notable "Angel's Egg," in *Galaxy,* 1951. A musician, late come to writing SF. His work was slow, gentle, and lyrical. Stories occasional, more frequent 1960–65. His best novels were *A Mirror for Observers* (1954) and *Davy* (1964), D20, the latter one of a loose series set in a post-atomic disaster America, as was his novel, *Company of Glory* (1974).

James H. Schmitz (1911–   )

Isolated first story in *Unknown* (1943). Active from 1949, with peak 1961–65. Recently less active. His most noted story is "The Witches of Karres" (1949), in C8B. Many stories and novels have been melodramas about psionically gifted females with animal allies, set against a common galactic future background, an example being *The Demon Breed* (1968).

Robert Sheckley (1928–   )

First published 1952. Many bright, clever and comic stories, the earliest and happiest flowering of which is contained in *Untouched by Human Hands* (1954). After 1958, less prolific. A few novels in the sixties, including the reality-trip and farce *Mindswap* (1966), D23. Like Philip Dick, another writer of the same age, also first published in 1952, Sheckley finds no reality worth taking seriously. Dick panics. Sheckley attempts to laugh, as in his most recent novel, *Options* (1975).

Robert Silverberg (1934–   )

First story 1954. Super-prolific hackwork 1956–59. Largely abandoned science fiction to write hundreds of books under many names. Returned to attempt more serious work in science fiction in 1965. After 1968, his haunted and despairing stories won awards and sharply raised his reputation. Notable stories include the Hugo-winning "Nightwings" (1968), in D3, and the Nebula-winning novel, *A Time of Changes* (1971), D24. Declared farewell to SF writing with novel, *Shadrach in the Furnace* (1976). Story in D28.

Cordwainer Smith (Paul Linebarger) (1913–66)

Linebarger was a soldier, psychologist, and political scientist. His first story under the name Cordwainer Smith was the notable "Scanners Live in Vain" (1950), in B16 and D25. Second story 1955. Active 1957–66. Bulk of best work 1960–63. The center of Smith's work—austere, mystical and private—is a protracted moment of agony as played out by sub-men and superhumans in a legendary future. His short stories are gathered and placed in order in *The Best of Cordwainer Smith* (1975), D25. A fascinating imperfect novel is *Norstrilia* (1964; 1968; 1975), D26.

William Tenn (Philip Klass) (1920–   )

First story 1946. Tenn's forte was irony. He wrote many blackly humorous stories, including "Child's Play" (1947), in Tenn's collection *The Seven Sexes* (1968), and "Null-P" (1950), in Tenn's *The Wooden Star* (1968). Most active 1951–56. Only occasionally active since 1959, save for a burst of publishing activity in 1968, which included Tenn's only novel, *Of Men and Monsters*.

Jack Vance (1916–   )

First story 1945. His work has appeared in bursts, 1950–53, 1957–58, 1961–66, and since 1969. His most notable early work was the strange, magical, and romantic story cycle, *The Dying Earth* (1950), B22. Vance's work tends to be cool, didactic, romantic, and remote. Among his better stories are "The Moon Moth" (1961), in C8B, and the Hugo-winning short novels, "The Dragon Masters" (1962) and "The Last Castle" (1966), both in D3. In recent years, Vance has been embarked on a number of novel series.

Kurt Vonnegut, Jr. (1922–   )

During the fifties, Vonnegut was a frequent contributor of short stories to the slick magazines, including some SF. A few satirical short stories in the SF magazines, such as "Harrison Bergeron" in *F&SF* (1961). Vonnegut's most notable work has been his novels, the most conventional of which was his first, *Player Piano* (1952), C24. His most original work was the black satire, *The Sirens of Titan* (1959), C25. Vonnegut's recent books have been bestsellers, marginally fiction, marginally SF, increasingly autobiographical.

IV. 1958–1964

These writers, born between 1914 and 1942, were among the ornaments of the peak period, 1965–69. Much of their work is in reaction and rebellion against the strictures of Golden Age science fiction. As a group, they are notable for their serious literary ambitions. Comment on their work is necessarily fragmentary and subjective since their careers are thus far only half-formed.

Samuel R. Delany (1942–   )

The first notable black writer of science fiction. Delany's first novel was published in 1962. Eight novels, 1962–68, including two Nebula winners, *Babel-17* (1966), D7, and *The Einstein Intersection* (1967). From 1967, short fiction in magazines and anthologies, including two more award winners, collected in *Driftglass* (1971), D8. Poetic, ambitious, self-indulgent, sometimes pretentious. From 1968, Delany was

A. & C. PANSHIN

largely silent while working on the 900-page novel, *Dhalgren* (1975). Stories in D3 and D28.

Thomas M. Disch (1940–   )
First story 1962. Most active 1964–67 and since 1971. An author of bleak surrealistic parables like "Descending" (1964), in D28, and "The Squirrel Cage" in *New Worlds* in 1966. Disch's novels, also bleak and nihilistic, are stronger as writing than as exercises of imagination. They include *Camp Concentration* (1967), D11, and *334* (1974).

R.A. Lafferty (1914–   )
First science fiction published 1960. An electrical engineer who took up writing at an unusually late age, Lafferty eventually found the science fiction field most open to his individual and eccentric fictions. Many short stories, particularly 1965–67 and since 1970. One collection of his work is *Nine Hundred Grandmothers* (1970). His most successful novel, which could only be the work of a highly imaginative, conservative, Roman Catholic, American Irishman, is *Fourth Mansions* (1969), D15.

Ursula K. Le Guin (1929–   )
First published 1962. Author of nine increasingly serious novels since 1966. Le Guin has been influenced by the anthropological interests of her parents and by Taoist thought. Her stories are clear and chilly. *The Farthest Shore* (1972), last of three connected juvenile fantasy novels, won the National Book Award. *The Left Hand of Darkness* (1969), D17, won both the Nebula and Hugo awards. Her most recent major novel is *The Dispossessed* (1974), D16, also a double award winner. Story in D28.

Larry Niven (1938–   )
First story 1964. The least literary and most science-oriented writer of his generation. Most active 1965–67, but a steady presence. Three Hugo awards for short fiction, including "Neutron Star" (1966), in D3. Most of his work is scientific and melodramatic space opera in a common future setting, with emphasis on ingenuity. His novel *Ringworld* (1970), D19, won both the Hugo and Nebula awards. In 1974, Niven published *The Mote in God's Eye,* the first of several long popular collaborations with Jerry Pournelle.

Alexei Panshin (1940–   )
First SF story 1963, later part of Nebula-winning first novel, *Rite of Passage* (1968), D21. Peak period of production 1968–69. Fiction is both earnest and playful and concerned with questions of maturity, as in collection *Farewell to Yesterday's Tomorrow* (1975; 1976). Fan writer Hugo 1967 for critical work published as *Heinlein in Dimension* (1968). Fiction and criticism, such as the critical collection *SF in Dimension* (1976), now written in collaboration with wife, Cory.

Joanna Russ (1937–   )
First story 1959. Never prolific, but a larger flurry of short stories 1971–72. A college teacher of English, in recent years highly concerned

with the issue of women's liberation. This concern is reflected in the Nebula-winning short story, "When It Changed" (1972), in *Again, Dangerous Visions*. A notable novel is *And Chaos Died* (1970), D22. Several recent novels.

Thomas Burnett Swann (1928–76)

An American teacher of college English and poet. First science-fiction story 1958. Had a burst of stories in 1964–65. Most of his stories were delicate, pastel fantasies in ancient Mediterranean settings. Typical of his work were the novel *Day of the Minotaur* (1964–65), and the story collection *The Dolphin and the Deep* (1968). His best novel may be *Wolfwinter* (1972).

Roger Zelazny (1937–   )

With Delany, Zelazny must be counted the most immediately impressive of the new writers of the sixties. First story 1962. First attention won by his many novelettes, through 1966, like "A Rose for Ecclesiastes" (1963), in B16, and also collected with three others in *Four for Tomorrow* (1967), D29. Another notable novelette, "For a Breath I Tarry" (1966), is in D28. A poetic, extravagant and charming writer. Best novel is the Hugo-winning *Lord of Light* (1967), D30. His work in the seventies, mainly novels, has been less successful.

WOMEN
AND SCIENCE FICTION

BY SUSAN WOOD

Pulp SF was written mostly by and for young men, but all that has changed. Susan Wood turns a revealing light on the old stereotypes and the outstanding writers, sometimes men as well as women, who have begun to break them. She has set up and taught SF courses across Canada: at Carleton University; the University of Regina; and the University of British Columbia, where she is now an assistant professor. As editor and critic, she has won three Hugos. She writes: "The original version of this paper was prepared for a seminar titled 'Power and Imagination: Fantasy, Science Fiction, and Mystery' delivered at the University of California, Berkeley, in July, 1977. The version which appears here is an edited one, with a few minor corrections. The author is happy to acknowledge that the paper is rapidly becoming outdated; good writers are creating fully human people in science fiction, and are stimulating us to think in new ways."

"Women have their great and proper place, even in a man's universe," conceded the crusty old spaceship captain who narrated "Priestess of the Flame" by Sewell Peaslee Wright (*Astounding,* June 1932).

"Women, when handled in moderation and with extreme decency, fit nicely into scientifiction *at times,*" wrote Isaac Asimov in the letter column of the November, 1939 issue of *Startling Stories.* He was nineteen.

"There are plenty of images of women in science fiction."

"There are almost no women," observed Joanna Russ in "The Image of Women in Science Fiction," an article first published in 1971, which stimulated much discussion when it was reprinted in *Vertex* in 1974. Russ was criticizing SF on what are, by now, familiar grounds: its failure to develop characterization, and its failure to provide genuine social extrapolation, notably of changes in human relationships and sex roles. Russ and other critics have, in turn, been attacked on everything from their examples to their premises that men and women should not only be legally equal, but should have equivalent roles in society. Nevertheless, people are starting to question the stereotypes of a popular literature which has always been male-oriented and male-dominated. As a result, there are more stories about real women, and real men, emerging in the SF field. And there are plenty of articles about their absence.

Most of these articles follow a pattern typified by Russ's discussion, and by Pamela Sargent's excellent long introduction to *Women of Wonder* (Vintage, 1975), a landmark collection of SF stories by women, about women, and the place to start looking for those elusive creatures. The typical article begins by identifying SF as a man's universe, or an adolescent male universe, in which woman's great and proper place was on the cover of a pulp magazine, dressed in as little as possible and being menaced by a bug-eyed monster. Inside, the lovely woman was much less visible for, as Anne McCaffrey so succinctly puts it, "Science fiction . . . is more cerebral than gonadal." In the pulp era (roughly from the birth of *Amazing Stories* in 1926 through to the mid-forties), gadget stories of pseudo-science sometimes featured a rare female, usually a scientist's daughter to whom scientific principles could be explained in simple terms, and with whom the steely-jawed young hero could exchange a closing kiss if "love interest" were deemed necessary to liven up the jargon. Hugo Gernsback's novel *Ralph 124C41 +* contains interminable examples of woman-as-recipient-of-expository-lump, a technique brought to its highest pitch, of course, by Heinlein. More numerous, however, and rather more fun (if only for the horrible examples) were the science-fiction adventures, or "space operas." Women in these got to fill two roles. They could either be blonde Victims, shrieking "eek" at monsters and being rescued by the hero; or they could be dark, sultry Temptresses, eternally trying to seduce the hero away from his rescue mission. The latter had rather more fun, but ended up heartbroken when the hero abandoned them—and usually dead, as well. It is tempting to feel superior to such formula fiction, only until we realize that the stereotypes haven't changed since the Priestess of the Flame vamped around over forty years ago.

If the half-naked women have vanished from the magazine covers, it's only to reappear inside as overt sex objects. The February 1974 issue of *Vertex* which carried the Russ article, for example, also contained "Nobody Lives Around Here," a minor effort by a major new author, Gregory Benford. The illustration features, yes, a naked black woman and two clothed white police, and the opening paragraphs describe in detail how a gang member is using the sobbing girl: "She was a groupie, really, always following our squads around with that hungry look in her eyes. She just liked to hump the boys, I guess . . ." The leader tells his subordinate to " 'Finish it off and form up,' " and the real action begins: street fighting, burning, killing—mostly by men, though a grandmother who gets rid of her aggressions by chopping up a fireman with an axe is included for shock value. Finally, when a man in the squad starts questioning their violence-as-therapy games, the leader concludes that "His woman was pushing him," and decides to have a state "psycher" examine her. Benford is, of course, criticizing contemporary society, not admiring male violence; but I wonder how many readers sympathized with his satisfied narrator? And those stereotypes of young victim/sex object, nagging wife, and death-dealing old lady are remarkably persistent.

In fact, SF continually confronts us with evidence that it has advanced very little in characterization and social extrapolation, as evident in the portrayal of women, in the fifty-one years since Gernsback founded *Amazing Stories*. My own ★click★ of consciousness came in 1972, after I had been reading what the library clerk coldly informed me were "boys' books" for some fifteen years, happily substituting my female self for their male protagonists. In the December, 1972 issue of *The Magazine of Fantasy and Science Fiction*, I read "The Garbage Invasion," a Retief novelette by Keith Laumer. This one, unusually enough, featured a woman, "Anne Taylor, who was tall and beautiful and held the title: Field Curator of Flora and Fauna, assigned to the unpopulated world, Delicia." She is *in charge* of the world; Retief is assisting her as "Acting Wildlife Officer" during a crisis. So what happens? She spends all her time calling the crisis "perfectly horrid," and worrying that an arriving shuttlecraft may "tear up the lawn and mash my flower-beds." When Retief's superior arrives, this woman, who is described by Retief himself as filling "a position . . . of considerable responsibility" with "commendable efficiency," is summarily dismissed with an order to " 'mix us a couple of tall cool ones and . . . punch in a nice dinner to celebrate Mr. Magnan's visit.' " At this point, I threw the magazine across the room, and so missed the ending, which has Anne knocking out Magnan with her purse—" 'struck by the wild beauty of the place,' " as Retief archly comments. As Sam Lundwall has observed, "The woman in science fiction remains what she was, a compulsory appendage."

There were a few women writers of space opera—Leigh Brackett and C.L. Moore, most notably—but they tended to accept its conventions. Things began to change in the forties and early fifties, that era which, in North America, saw the development of a social ethos designed to get the little woman out of the munitions factory and into that all-electric kitchen in suburban New Jersey where she could consume all day. As early as 1938, Lester del Rey's "Helen O'Loy" had given readers another image of woman: futuristic housewife. Between 1947 and 1949, Margaret St. Clair published a series of stories about Oona and Jick Ritterbush, a suburban married couple of the future who faced quite ordinary *Ladies' Home Journal*-style adventures with a rotating house and thirty boxes of "Super Whost," the "chronometrized carbohydrate." In 1948, John W. Campbell commissioned Judith Merril's first science-fiction story, asking her to provide "the woman's point of view" on scientific developments. The story, "That Only a Mother," deals with the effects of radiation in terms of a mother's blind love for her mutant daughter. The galactic housewives of 2050, happily dusting the robochef in the living unit while hubby tends the yeast farms, might represent a failure of social extrapolation, but they were, perhaps, a little more believable as human beings than all the princesses and priestesses. Perhaps.

A number of women writers entered the field during the fifties and early sixties. Joanna Russ notes, however, that while they tended to place more emphasis on character development than had the earlier, mostly male writers, they still tended to "see the relations between the sexes as those of present-day, white, middle-class suburbia," a world which might be satirized but which was rarely questioned. But how can we know the future? How can we make guesses about it, except on the basis of our life today? Thus, for example, Jerry Pournelle assumes "that there is a nature of man, that part of that nature consists of innate differences between the sexes, and that social orders which conform with that nature and those assumptions survive better than those that do not." On these assumptions, and on the basis of his observations of women, he defends such portraits as that of Lady Sally in *The Mote in God's Eye,* a blonde doctoral student in anthropology who doesn't understand the alien Moties, is concerned mostly about her upcoming wedding and the attendant parties, and, as the only woman in the "male-oriented society" of a spaceship misses "what she thought of as girl talk. Marriage and babies and housekeeping and scandals: they were part of civilized life." One reader of Pournelle's article, George Fergus, was moved to write a twenty-page response discussing sex roles and cultural conditioning, assembling evidence from the few studies we have about behavior. Pournelle's response was to reaffirm his belief that "there are profound temperamental differences between the human sexes; that these are biologically determined; and that they are the result of a very long period of evolution." Thus "we should be very careful about making radical changes in family structures and reversing sex roles." The debate, and the changes, continue. Meantime writers such as James Tiptree, Jr. are creating powerful fictions out of the idea that men and women are aliens to each other, while other writers such as John Varley explore the possibilities of worlds in which highly developed medical techniques allow people to swap organs, or even bodies, conceiving and siring children as the dual-sexed Gethenians of *The Left Hand of Darkness* can do. In the meantime, too, women such as Ursula Le Guin, Joanna Russ, Kate Wilhelm, Vonda McIntyre, Pamela Sargent and Suzy McKee Charnas, to name a few, are creating a few new imaginative roles for the woman who rebels against being told, like the brilliant engineer in *Podkayne of Mars,* that she's failing in her duty if she doesn't stay home with the children: " 'building bridges and space stations and such gadgets

SUSAN WOOD

is all very well . . . but . . . a woman has more important work to do.' "
In the process, they're creating a few new roles for men, too.

Thus any criticism of science fiction's failure to depict believable
woman characters really brings up two points. One is primarily literary: the need for science fiction to replace all the cardboard characters, he-men as well as she-devils, with functioning people. (It is
interesting to note that Gordon R. Dickson, in an essay on "Plausibility
in SF," deals with how to establish setting, background and scientific
facts but never mentions the development of plausible characters.) The
other is primarily social: the need for SF to actually do what it pretends
to do; that is, envision genuinely new cultures and societies. This need
is explicit in Russ's appeal for SF which will at least show men and
women participating in everyday work life (as they do now) with some
suggestion of sexual equality. We find it, especially, in Ursula Le
Guin's criticism that: "In general, American SF has assumed a permanent hierarchy of superiors and inferiors, with rich, ambitious, aggressive males at the top, then a great gap, and then at the bottom
the poor, the uneducated, the faceless masses, and all the women. . . .
It is a perfect baboon patriarchy, with the Alpha Male on top, being
respectfully groomed, from time to time, by his inferiors."

Sam Moskowitz, in his introduction to *When Women Rule,* conjectures that women's demands for equality have influenced the development of the Amazon theme in the twentieth century, and that these
stories in turn reflect fear, on the part of women as well as men, that
"this 'equality' . . . will end in domination" by the women. He continues: "The implication is almost that a male and a female are two
completely different species instead of two indispensable sexes of the
same animal." Unwittingly, he identifies another of the major roles
women can play in SF: that of aliens. In James Gunn's "The Miso-
gynist," (*Galaxy,* November 1952), the premise that women really are
evil aliens is developed as a joke, though like many sexual jokes the
stance fails to hide a strong undercurrent of fear and hostility; those
women with their cold feet in bed are really out to kill men! In Philip
José Farmer's "The Lovers," (*Startling Stories,* August 1952), the story
credited with first introducing mature sexuality as a theme in SF, the
woman is literally an alien, an extraterrestrial insect who dies when
her human lover tricks her into becoming pregnant. In "When I Was
Miss Dow" by Sonya Dorman (*Galaxy,* June 1966), the "woman" is also
an alien, shape-changed to spy on a Terran scientist; trapped in a
female body, she learns human emotions, but also the limitations of
the female role.

The most powerful examination of this theme, of course, is "The
Women Men Don't See" by James Tiptree, Jr. (*F&SF,* December 1973).
A woman and her daughter choose to leave earth with an unknown
alien, rather than live as aliens in male society. As Ruth Parsons

explains to the protesting liberal-male narrator: " 'Women have no rights, Don, except what men allow us. . . . What women do is survive. We live by ones and twos in the chinks of your world-machine,' " not even hoping for changes. Tiptree, who originally thought of the women as aliens, later commented in the *Khatru* symposium that "Of course it is not women who are aliens. Men are." As is common in much contemporary SF, the fictional situation serves as a metaphor for the author's vision of contemporary society, in which the cultural differences between men and women seem insurmountable. Tiptree is a pseudonym for Alice B. Sheldon, a psychologist who also writes under the name Raccoona Sheldon. Her story "The Screwfly Solution" (*Analog,* June 1977) is a powerful examination of men's alienation from and fear of women, and the ugly cultural myths of woman's inferiority that underlie civilized societies.

Woman as heroine, woman as hero, woman as alien: we do have plenty of images of women in SF. Many of them, however, are degrading to all people, and most of them are one-dimensional, the lowest common denominator of social stereotypes that are already passé. There *are* some real women, some real people who move convincingly off the page—my two current favorites are Odo of Ursula K. Le Guin's "The Day Before the Revolution" (*Galaxy,* August 1974), and Zoe Breedlove of Michael Bishop's "Old Folks at Home" in *Universe 8,* who enters into an unusual, and unusually happy, group marriage between seven elderly survivors in a joyless future city. But while it's easy enough for readers to demand that SF show real people in a convincing future, it's rather harder for writers to find ways to escape the compelling stereotypes.

It might even be valuable to reexamine the stereotypes, if only to really understand their limitations. Then push the limitations. Alldera of Charnas's *Walk to the End of the World* is literally woman-as-object, totally degraded by her society; the novel, and its sequel, *Motherlines,* tell the story of her physical escape, and her gradual growth as a person beyond the limitations of her slave mentality. Unfortunately, stereotyped characters and situations are not only easier to write, they are also easier to get accepted by editors in commercial publishing houses. Charnas reports that one woman editor rejected *Motherlines,* which has an all-woman cast of characters, in the following terms: " 'You know, if this story were all about *men* it would be a terrific story. I'm worried about my market. *The Female Man* had male characters in it, so men would pick it up and at least open it. But men get *very angry . . .' "* Charnas adds, "You finish it, it's not hard: 'to be left out.' "

It would be even more valuable to examine the archetypes behind the stereotypes. The aspects of the Triple Goddess still offer marvelously rich material for the imagination. The woman-as-nurturer image, in particular, is extremely powerful; for example, in the majority of stories in *Women of Wonder,* the female protagonist functions in some sort of nurturing role, either directly as a mother or indirectly as a space doctor, an empath, the person who takes care of others. But why not depict a nurturing male? There are examples in our society, but the only ones I can think of in science fiction, offhand, are Jason, the teacher in Terry Carr's *Cirque* (Bobbs-Merrill, 1977) and Coyote in Paul Novitski's "Nuclear Fission," in *Universe 9.* John Varley's "Options," also in *Universe 9,* may well be the best and most powerful story in the field to examine the implications of sex and gender, and explore the meanings of "male," "female" and "person." His novels, *The Ophiuchi Hotline* (Dial, 1977) and *Titan* (Berkley/Putnam, 1979) both feature strong women, supportive men, and all the human varieties between; his "Eight Worlds" stories, set in a universe in which cloning, sex-changes and genetic manipulation have enabled people to switch sex at will, also explore new social possibilities. A similar test of the power and validity of archetypes and social roles is found in Elizabeth A. Lynn's fantasy novel, *The Northern Girl* (Berkley Putnam, 1980), the third volume of her fantasy trilogy *The Chronicles of Tornor.* Lynn has taken a number of archetypal figures (the warrior, the wise elder, the young person setting out on a quest) and a number of social roles (the politician, the teacher) and embodied them all as women. The result is not only a powerful story, but a good deal of stimulus to actually think about social roles, sex roles, and cultural archetypes.

Are the archetypes familiar to North Americans valid for people of other cultures? Many SF and fantasy writers are turning for inspiration to such "alien" cultures as those of North American Indians. Richard Lupoff went to Japanese culture for Kishimo, the woman warrior of *Sword of the Demon* (Harper and Row, 1977). If the first generation of SF writers were primarily adventure-story hacks, and the second generation were the science-trained men like Asimov, Heinlein and Clarke, then perhaps the third generation, women and men, can be cultural anthropologists and sociologists, genuinely examining new forms of social organizations in the only fiction that allows us to play god. Between observing people on busses and in the supermarket, and drawing on all the cultural resources available as alternates to North American society here-and-now, surely a good writer ought to be able to stimulate her imagination beyond the Princess, the Priestess and the Galactic Kitchen Sink. As to how, that's summed up by a speaker in Monique Wittig's Amazon novel, *Les Guérillères* (1969; Viking, 1971):

> There was a time when you were not a slave, remember that. You walked alone, full of laughter, you bathed bare-bellied. You say you have lost all recollection of it, remember. The wild roses flower in the woods. Your hand is torn on the bushes gathering the mulberries and strawberries you refresh yourself with. You

run to catch the young hares that you flay with stones from the rocks to cut them up and eat them all hot and bleeding. . . . You say there are no words to describe this time, you say it does not exist. But remember. Make an effort to remember. Or, failing that, invent.

Other relevant literary/social material:

Fiedler, Leslie. *Love and Death in the American Novel.* New York: Criterion, 1960.

Firestone, Shulamith. *The Dialectic of Sex.* New York: William Morrow, 1970.

Friend, Beverly. "Virgin Territory: Women and Sex in Science Fiction," *Extrapolation,* Dec., 1972, pp. 49–58.

Graves, Robert. *The White Goddess.* Revised edition. London: Faber, 1964.

Greer, Germaine. *The Female Eunuch.* London: Palladin, 1971.

Hardwick, Elizabeth. *Seduction and Betrayal: Women and Literature.* New York: Random House, 1974.

Koppelman Cornillon, Susan, ed. *Images of Women in Fiction: Feminist Perspectives.* Revised edition. Bowling Green: Popular Press, 1973.

Rule, Jane. *Lesbian Images.* New York: Doubleday, 1975.

THE TEACHERS

SCIENCE FICTION IN THE PRIMARY SCHOOL?

BY BARRY B. LONGYEAR

From its first beachhead in the colleges, science fiction has spread to the high schools and now to the grade schools. Barry B. Longyear offers telling evidence of its teaching value there. Children do come to school creative. Too often, creativity is killed. Here's one way to keep it alive—and also a wonderfully simple and clear how-to-do-it guide to the short story for nearly anybody. Now a full-time writer, Barry lives in Maine with his wife and three cats. Since his first fiction sale in 1978, he has placed stories with most of the SF magazines and three novels with Berkley/Putnam.

In the essays that follow, other able teachers guide us though a whole galaxy of classes.

There are many demands upon the attention of the primary school student. There are sports, outings with friends, slumber parties, dances, movies, comic books and the ever-present television set. Against this, exercises on grammar and punctuation, and themes and book reports are as dry as a mouth full of cold ashes. For many students, the English period is something to be endured, much like a prisoner putting in his time until the bars part and he is free once again. This attitude leads to such things as shooting broken paper clips at other students, drawing pictures, gossiping, and sleeping in class. Not only does this eliminate the value of the experience to the student, it can and does make the teaching of English a less than enjoyable chore.

Frequently the teacher will point to the movies, comic books, and TV set as the villains that are attempting to prevent the communication of English skills to his or her students. Four years ago, however, a sixth grade English teacher introduced me to her program, which turns these "villains" into friends. Her students learn their English skills by using them through writing stories. Part of her program includes hooking every writer who comes within twenty miles of her classroom to come in and talk to her students about writing and how that particular writer does it. I was (and still am) one of her writers, and I have seen Beverly Bisbee's program grow to the point where students of hers are writing well enough to become published.

All fiction, including movies, TV, comic books, and magazines, re-quires writing at some point. And to write, and write well, virtually all necessary English skills must be employed. Getting students to write, however, is another matter, and this is where science fiction comes in. For most students, science fiction has high interest value. To prove this to yourself, take a vote in class on whether to write a science-fiction story or write a book report.

But writing a story is not something that can be done in ignorance of the rules of English or the rules of storytelling, and these are the things the teacher will be grading and correcting and giving instruction in *along the way*. It is learning while doing, not to mention while doing something that interests the student. Spelling is no longer lists to be memorized from a book and then tested. Spelling errors are things to be picked out and shown to the student from his or her story. This applies as well to punctuation and grammar. If Johnny fouled up in his use of punctuation, the opportunity has thus presented itself to point out the error, why it is an error, and why it harms the story. Then, to Johnny, the rule is no longer another senseless thing he must memorize; he can see why, how, and where it works. More than that, he will gain experience in the application of the rule through use.

There are, in addition, the rules of storytelling, and making those rules understandable to primary-level students. While I was working with Mrs. Bisbee, and after reading hundreds of her students' stories, I devised the following outline which is now part of the text material for each student. It was written for sixth graders, but fifth graders have also used it with success, and new writers in their twenties and thirties who have asked me for advice on writing have found it very useful.

What Every Young Writer Should Know

A Story Just as a machine has parts, a story has parts; and just as all of the parts must be in the machine and put together properly for the machine to work, the parts of a story must be all there and put together properly for the story to work.

The Parts of a Story

The Hook The hook is at the beginning of the story. The opening words of a story must be designed to grab and hold the reader's attention and make the reader want to read more. If the opening is dull or boring, it can kill a story no matter how good the rest of it is. The most common mistake is wandering around at the beginning of a story setting up the situation. The best beginnings get right into the action.

"Through my blur of tears, I could see the cold, dark bars of the cell.

It was a nightmare. I couldn't be in jail—I just couldn't! I turned and saw a heavy, cruel man sitting on the cell's only bed. He held up a huge hand, made a fist, and grinned. I could see the scars on his knuckles. 'I've killed a lot of men with this. . . .' "

Compare the opening above with the one below:

"The sky was blue with small tufts of clouds as I walked toward the shore. The street was wide and crowded with cars as I made my way toward the large, brown building. . . ."

The two openings above are the beginnings to two different versions of the same story. Which one do you think is the more effective "hook"? Why?

Backfill   The "hook" that places the character in jail begins with the hero in a dire situation. Now the reader needs to know *why* he is in that situation. This is done by "backfilling," and it can be done several ways:

First, it can be done by the character just saying it in the narrative: "A couple of rolls of film! All I did was shoplift a couple of rolls of film. It's nothing! All the kids do it and nothing happens to them."

Another form of backfill is the *flashback:* "I thought back to yesterday in the drug store. The film was just sitting there on the counter. No one was around. Who would know if I just picked it up and stuck it in my pocket? I reached out my hand. . . ."

Another way to backfill is through conversation. "The huge convict leered at me, then laughed. 'What're you in for, little boy? Steal a lollypop?' "

The purpose of backfilling is to explain to the reader why the hero is in the situation that he is in.

Buildup   This is the body of the story. Once your hero is faced with his problem, he must be put through trying times trying to solve it. The boy in jail for shoplifting wants to get out; that's his problem. The troubles he is faced with in trying to get out make up the "buildup." For it to be a successful buildup, each problem he faces must be more difficult than the last.

There are two more parts to the buildup. The first is called "The Bright Moment." It looks as though the hero has finally gotten out of his mess—all of his problems appear solved. Then comes "The Dark Moment." Just when the hero thinks he is out of his mess, everything falls apart and he is in worse trouble than when the story opened.

The Ending   Throughout a story, a character has been presented with a problem that he tries to solve through his own efforts. An "up" ending is one in which the problem is solved; a "down" ending is one in which it is not solved. In any event, the ending has to be the believable result of the events that took place in the story.

§ § §
Putting the Story Together

The Plot   The basic plot of all fiction is this: Face your character with a problem, get your character into trouble with it, then have your character solve the problem through his own efforts. In other words, get your character to the tree, get him up the tree, then get him down.

Timing   The rate at which you present the parts of a story is important to keep the reader interested. Usually, get the character to the tree fast, have him struggle among the branches, then, when you have him down from the tree, end the story.

Characterization   These are the qualities that you—the writer—give to the characters in your story. You tell the reader what kind of person a character is by showing what that character thinks, acts, does, and says. An appealing character must have a worthwhile goal that he or she is struggling to achieve.

Change   As a result of the things that happen during the course of the story, the character must change—the character must learn something about himself, discover something that changes his views about something, or fall in love. Stories in which the characters do not change are much like machines that are turned on and run, but don't do anything.

Believability   While reading it, the reader has to believe it, and it takes skill to make robots, werewolves, dragons, ghosts, magic, and vampires believable. They are made believable by doing two things: first, while you are writing, you have to believe in them yourself; second, you must prepare the reader. Following is an example of *not* preparing the reader:
"One day while I was leaving school, I saw Count Dracula fighting with Frankenstein's Monster. . . ." (This is *not* believable.)
Now what follows is an example of preparing the reader:
"It was when I got up to hand my paper in. I came up behind Tommy and he looked very pale. He kept pulling his collar up to cover his neck, and I looked and saw two red marks on his neck. Suddenly he turned around and looked up at me. His eyes were dark and glassy. 'What are you looking at?'
"I swallowed and shrugged. 'Nothing. I don't want anything.'
"He smiled, his lips very red. 'What are you doing after school today?' His tongue went over his lips and I shuddered."

Feelings   If you don't care what you are writing about, you can do everything else right and the story won't "work": it will be dull, un-

BARRY B. LONGYEAR

feeling, unbelievable, and uninteresting. Every story that works has part of its author in it, and that part is feeling—emotion. For example, to write about terror, you have to feel the terror when you put the words on the paper. Look at the two examples below:

"The escaped convict held the knife at my mother's throat. Boy, were we scared. But I bet Mom was more scared than I was." (Do you believe the author of that was scared?)

"The polished glare of the knife the killer held at my mother's throat flashed into my eyes as I fell to my knees and wrapped my arms around the man's legs. 'Please. Please don't hurt her.' I wiped the tears from my eyes and looked up at him. He grinned and I opened my mouth to scream as he pointed the knife at me. . . ."

Put it all together and you have a story.

The outline above contains the basic elements of writing a "mainstream" story: stories about current events, characters, and settings. The different forms of "category fiction" require additional explanation to the student. Some of the more common categories are listed below:

Science fiction
Western
Fantasy
Mystery
Romance
Adventure
Occult
Historical
Horror

In many cases, obviously, the lines dividing one category from another are obscure or nonexistent. Practically every western is a western–adventure, just as there are science-fiction–adventure and science-fiction–mystery stories. In the classes I have worked with, however, the most popular choices among the students are as follows:

Science fiction & Fantasy (45–60 percent)
Mystery (25–30 percent)
Mainstream (5–15 percent)
Adventure (5–15 percent)

The teacher should be able to explain the differences between the various categories. For example, science-fiction stories are not simply tales set in the future, nor are they stories that have a lot of "science" in them. Mysteries are not stories where someone simply gets murdered and the murderer gets caught. Fantasy stories are not tales in which no rules apply (for even "no rules apply" is a rule).

What makes a story "science fiction" is treated elsewhere in this volume. However, what makes science fiction different from fantasy is that all of the strange and wondrous things happening in the tale must be explained to the point of plausibility (yes, the hero can make himself disappear, but there's this machine over there, see, and it . . .). The essential element of fantasy is that magic works, and does not need to be explained. In fantasy, however, the magic, as mentioned before, must have rules—that is, it must be consistent within itself. Each category of fiction has its musts. Westerns must be set in the American West during the nineteenth century; any time before, or set anywhere else, is historical fiction, and so forth.

The teacher I worked with gives her students complete freedom as to the types of story they write. In addition, she does not supply her students with "ideas." As all writers do, her students must pull all of that stuff out of their heads, and then put it on paper. With four to six stories per semester, and each story going through as many as three drafts, the opportunity to point out and have corrected errors in spelling, punctuation, and grammar is presented. In addition, errors in storytelling technique can be demonstrated, and this has an especially important effect on the student. Some students will learn to love writing sufficiently to keep at it through the morass of themes, book reports, and research papers they will have to endure throughout their remaining years in school. However, all of the students will come to understand the parts of a story and how they are put together. From this, they gain a greater appreciation of the stories they read or see on television, and they will be able to distinguish a good story from a bad one. The blue ribbon for the teacher, of course, is that the student has almost painlessly been taught all of these English skills that before seemed so boring.

Science Fiction in the Primary School Science Class

English teachers became English teachers, usually, because they liked English. For the same reason, science teachers became science teachers. Just as it is difficult for me to understand why anyone would rather do anything else with his or her life than write, it is at first surprising, then discouraging, for the science teacher to discover that many students consider science a crashing bore. This is where science fiction can come to the rescue.

Science fiction, first, is in many cases written by scientists. In any event, there will be scientific questions raised in every science-fiction story. Making such stories part of the students' class experience, first, increases student interest, and, second, serves as a means of leading in to the particular area of science being studied. For example, if the general science teacher were about to begin on an introduction to biology, a science-fiction story with a biological theme could be assigned to be read. The "science" in the story can then be picked out and discussed. Not only will this cast the students' usual text material in a new light, it will also help to nurture that "what if" quality necessary to the student scientist.

BARRY B. LONGYEAR

Where to Get Writers

Since full-time writers are usually busy people who cannot be bothered with things such as addressing a primary school class, it might be wondered just where the teacher can come up with writers. First, it should be remembered that there is nothing that writers like to talk about more than writing, particularly their own. There are exceptions, of course; and if your hunting is done among established, "big name" authors, the pickings may be pretty slim. However, there are numerous first and second story writers, and if you hunt among them, your chances will be vastly improved. All published writers can be contacted through their publishers. A cautionary note: Since the usual primary school budget makes no allowance for shipping writers across the country, concentrate on writers who live locally. There are no writers living local to your school? There is still hope.

In every hamlet across this nation there are one or more persons crouching over typewriters, writing what they hope will be their first sale. There is a great deal of knowledge about storytelling that one must have before being able to turn out professional, salable material. I suspect that most of these beginners would be thrilled to share their knowledge before your class. First, for someone who has taken on an extremely lonely occupation, there is the chance at last to talk about writing and his or her interests. Second, before that first sale, the beginning writer is crawling with crushing doubts. Such a person might even be willing to pay *you* for the ego-propping opportunity to be introduced to anyone as "a writer." Third, the experience for the beginning writer is invaluable. The beginning writer will learn much more about his craft than he will be able to teach, which just might be enough to put him over the top. I know, because that's where I started out.

I was wrestling with a first novel when a certain sixth grade teacher invited me to talk to her students about science-fiction writing. To teach my chosen craft to a bunch of eleven-year-olds, I had a lot to learn. But I enjoyed the first time so much, I appeared before that class five or six times that year (in between other writers). It was after one of those experiences that I went home and wrote the story that eventually became my first sale. Even though I am now a full-time writer, I still do my stints with that class. I enjoy watching the students' imaginations soar once they understand the basics of storytelling, and they are still teaching me a great deal. Explain this to that shy friend who is sweating over a typewriter trying to write, then just try and keep him *out* of your classroom.

SCIENCE FICTION
IN THE HIGH SCHOOL

BY ELIZABETH CALKINS AND BARRY McGHAN

*Elizabeth Calkins and Barry McGhan once taught to-
gether in an urban Michigan high school. When the
curriculum was revised to include a one-semester
"theme" course in science fiction, Mrs. Calkins volunteered to teach the course if Mr. McGhan—a math
teacher and a long-time SF buff—would provide advice
and assistance. This chapter, as well as their book,*
Teaching Tomorrow, *came out of this collaboration.
Their well-tested advice in this essay runs all the way
from selecting objectives to awarding the final grade.*

At the outset we wish to make it clear that our primary interest
in SF is utilitarian: it is a tool for achieving certain educational purposes not solely related to SF. However, a good craftsman cares for his
tools and we urge that teachers who use SF—for their own purposes,
or for ours, or to round out someone else's curriculum—become familiar
enough with it to care for it properly.

The possible subject-matter orientations to teaching science fiction
which are discussed elsewhere in this book can be as varied in the
high school as they are at the college level. While our experiences with
teaching SF in high school have been in English and social science
classes, we will discuss somewhat more general relationships between
science fiction and the high school student's nature and real needs.

The first and most important use for SF is to meet students' reading
needs. Some of these needs (increased vocabulary and comprehension,
greater speed and accuracy) are met or pursued in most English classrooms. However, reading is such a fundamental set of skills that all
teachers, no matter what their special subject matter interest, must
be concerned with helping students to master it. (The things we have
to say about reading and SF are not concerned with the special problems of teaching reading to teenagers with severe reading problems,
and we will not delve into the extensive literature of this area.) SF is
one of several categories of fiction upon which students can hone their
skills. We think it is one of the most suitable categories since it contains
a large number of books and its scope is wider and more varied than
some others. Furthermore, science-fiction stories seem to have a popular appeal lacking in other categories of reading material that are
appropriate for public schools. For example, in the widely read *Hooked*

on Books: Program and Proof, author Daniel Fader notes that SF books were the most popular type among the delinquent youngsters with whom he worked. Also, SF has been connected with studies of popular culture, has been termed "street fiction" by SF writer Harlan Ellison, and has certainly seen a robust development over the years without formal educational attention and perhaps in spite of academic disapproval.

Let us digress to say that our own experiences make us cautious about stating how popular SF is with high school students. For example, quite a few come to our classes with little knowledge of what printed SF stories are like, though they are familiar with the visual (per)versions of SF stories usually presented on TV and in the movies (which do not, for the most part, deal with the social extrapolation and criticism often found in SF writing). Some students have even come to us thinking that the class was a science course. Furthermore, although we know of no serious sociological studies of the typical SF reader, our hunch is that regular SF readers are preponderantly white, middle-class, and male, hardly a group that we would say indicates wide popular appeal. (The annual reader poll of the popular fanzine *Locus* showed that in 1974, 82 percent of its readers were male, 71 percent had at least a bachelor's degree, and only about 10 percent listed themselves as blue collar/clerical/agricultural workers. However, *Locus's* editor notes that his readers may be different from the general SF reader (identified by publishers as a teenager who reads SF for four or five years), and we have no information on the socioeconomic status of this wider group, whatever it is.) In any case, if SF is really street fiction, our streets must be peopled with less able readers than Mr. Ellison finds in his; or perhaps the books we are familiar with are more challenging than those to which he refers.

While we could cite a number of dismal statistics attesting to schools' lack of success in teaching reading, our opinions are mostly based on the pedagogical realities we have experienced in our classrooms. We quite frankly feel that there is nothing particularly unusual about our teaching situations or our students, and we believe that the difficulties of teaching students to read are not often understood—or overcome. We have found, for example, that emphasis on teaching reading generally ignores the problem of helping students consciously apply devices to grasp second levels of meaning. Readability formulas don't measure the existence of subsurface levels of meaning; comprehension tests don't measure the development of skill in understanding them. Most often, students respond merely to the literal aspect of the stories they read, completely missing the symbolic meanings, allusions, and allegory which writers intend their readers to grasp. As far as schools are concerned, students seem to be expected to get the point of the story, not through instruction, but by a kind of osmosis.

We feel that science fiction is a particularly effective vehicle to *teach* levels of meaning and that the primary aim of science fiction in the high school should be to help the student learn to "escape from the literal."

The reason SF is especially good for developing comprehension of subsurface levels of meaning is partly because of its relatively simple structure: it contains fewer literary elements than other fiction commonly used in high school. We do not mean that SF is simple or that it is suited for simple-minded people—far from it. It is simpler than other categories of literature because the out-of-this-world settings of most SF stories require the author to devote considerable attention to developing the world of the book (its *weltanschauung,* if you will). This necessity, for example, causes him to focus on the outer social action and conflict of his characters rather than on their inner personal life, and this focus in turn somewhat limits character development so that major characters are often stable, recognizable stereotypes. Furthermore, the author's attempt to develop the book's world in the reader's mind is often carried out through a kind of symbolism which is commonly used in SF as a shorthand for conveying concepts, and thus presents the student with many instances of its use. The kind of symbolism we are talking about can be found, for example, at the beginning of Pohl and Kornbluth's *Space Merchants,* where there is a reference to Madison Avenue. Many students fail to recognize the allusion and are therefore unaware of the intended frame of reference. Similarly, in one of Simak's *City* stories there is a reference to a "chamber of commerce mentality." It is surprising how many times the student has no way of following the author's meaning because he missed a reference the author assumed was general knowledge. Identification of such key phrases should be provided when a student is asked to deal with the development of the world of the book which usually follows. Sometimes, the student lacks the linguistic sophistication to see the recognizable roots of a word which contain the clue to its meaning. For instance, in Asimov's *The Stars Like Dust* the reference to "Tyranni" may be obscure either because the student doesn't know the root word to begin with, or perhaps because he doesn't apply his knowledge of the root to the seemingly new term. (Students sometimes seem to feel they don't know a word if they can't pronounce it.) By taking the skein of such references and teaching them, the beginning SF reader can be helped to move toward an understanding of the more general, manifest symbolic themes of SF stories.

Another important reason for using science fiction with high school students, related to the author's concentration on developing a worldview, is that it can help them to develop a coherent view of *their* world. We believe that through experiences with the author's concept of the world explicated in his story, students can begin to develop and articulate notions of the world about them. The teen-age years seem to be the time in people's lives when they are most consciously concerned with who they are, what the world is like, and where they can and cannot go in it. By reading, discussing, and writing about the worlds projected in SF stories (which are often extrapolations of elements of today's world), they can grasp the idea that their world has elements which shape it, too. And, since most SF stories are in one way or another about the future, students have the chance to learn that a future can follow from their "now," even though the projected future may be undesirable and/or not at all like the real one will be.

Another goal of using science fiction in high school is to introduce students to the study of a genre. In fact, it seems to us that SF is the only category of fiction in which high school students can read enough material to get at least a "seat of the pants" feeling for what a genre is. We think a feeling of confidence is generated by the ability to recognize a genre and feel familiar with its conventions, and the knowledgeable SF students we encounter seem to exhibit this confidence about their field with greater frequency than students in other courses.

Having stated in general terms why science fiction should be used with high school students—to develop comprehension of subsurface levels of meaning, awaken a sense of world concept, and introduce the study of a literary genre in an informal way—we now turn to a more detailed explanation of how we work with students.

We teach in a large urban industrial area in the Midwest. At this writing, the black/white racial distribution of the school population is about 50–50. Although many students come from blue-collar families there is a considerable range of social backgrounds in the student population; about 34 percent of the students go on for some college work. The average reading level of our tenth graders falls about 1.5 years below grade level (not unusual for urban districts).

As far as materials are concerned, at least for an introductory English class, we recommend that novels rather than short stories be used. At the very beginning a short story may provide a useful introduction to some of the background and techniques of SF, but we are strongly in favor of using full-length novels for the bulk of the course. In the first place, many high school students need to read more novels. They need to learn to read the longer pieces in order to experience the immersion in the story which can only happen in a developed novel, and they need the discipline of sticking to it so that an aesthetic experience can develop. Moreover, only novel-length fiction has sufficient scope to permit the development of the techniques of reading and analysis which we believe are a necessary part of an SF course. Plot, character, setting, and theme cannot be sufficiently developed in the scope of a short story.

If a subject matter course other than English is offered, then an anthology or other collection of short stories may be appropriate. However, even in these cases we think that serious consideration should be given to using some novel-length material. Most high school students are not so knowledgeable about physical and social science ideas that they will feel deprived by the lack of enriched material found in anthologies. In novels they can get at the basic ideas the teacher desires, and much more as well.

The novels that we feel are most appropriate come, with some exceptions, from the period between 1945 and 1965. There are several reasons why novels published during this rather standard and traditional era of SF writing are most suitable. For one thing, it is in this era that some of the most influential writers did their most important work. Also, these books have been tested by time and the critics and have found wide acceptance in the field, even among those who periodically "go to the lists" over current issues. Furthermore, insofar as we are concerned with identifying and dealing with science fiction as a specific genre, it seems that the more central and obvious the choices, the better. Students often confuse SF with horror, witchcraft, deviltry, mythology, and fantasy stories, and, while we recognize that there is no boundary which neatly encircles all of SF-dom, we do feel that there is a kind of group consciousness which more or less defines the field and to which students need a quick introduction. Such writers as Heinlein, Clarke, and Asimov provide a starting point. Also, the important books of this period seem to have a better record for staying in print, i.e., available for class use. However, the final selection of books to use—whether standard or experimental—must be made by the teacher who knows what the specific goals of the course are.

The only additional information we can offer about SF books here has to do with their readability. From a list of 200 recommended novels in our book *Teaching Tomorrow* augmented by an additional thirty recent titles, we selected a random sample of twelve books. We estimated their readability with a computer program using the Flesch formula, which uses sentence length and number of syllables to estimate reading difficulty. The mean grade level of the sample was 11.0. We also checked the readability of three SF books with strong juvenile appeal and three "experimental" books. (The sample of twelve included *Rogue Moon, No Blade of Grass, Rogue Queen, Nerves, Too Many Magicians, The Moon Is a Harsh Mistress, The Black Cloud, Fourth Mansions, Journey Beyond Tomorrow, The Long Loud Silence, Cat's Cradle,* and *The Lathe of Heaven.* The juveniles included *Crossroads of Time, A Princess of Mars,* and *Lucky Starr and the Big Sun of Mercury.* The experimental authors' books included *Nova, The Book of Skulls,* and *Terminal Beach.* Three passages were selected at random, one from each third of the book. The highest grade level equivalent readability found was judged to be the minimum reading level necessary to master the book.) The mean grade level of the former trio was 10.4, the latter 12.4. We cannot claim any statistical inferences about all SF books as a result of this analysis, but the results—though only measuring the most mechanical and superficial aspects of writing—do tend to follow

CALKINS & McGHAN

the pattern one might expect, with juveniles slightly easier than "average" and the experimental books somewhat harder than average. When one considers that these readability formulas come nowhere near assessing the amount and kind of extended meaning present, it seems easy to believe that the increased complexity of recent writing would make some of these works even more difficult for high school students to comprehend. Obviously these findings are of a most preliminary kind and much more work would be necessary to pin down even the surface reading difficulty of SF novels. We do not feel that any class or type of book should be automatically excluded from use with high school students, but we urge that the selections be made cautiously, with adequate consideration of both purpose and reading level.

Having made the choice of a novel, the teacher must help the mostly inexperienced high school reader get started. The problem with science-fiction stories is that there is a great deal to pay attention to at the beginning of the book. The author must not only introduce the characters and rapidly establish a dramatic situation, but he must also begin, as we have said, to limn a world that may have very little relation to our own. And so, the reader is asked not just to suspend disbelief but to have faith that he will eventually begin to see and understand the nature of the book's world from the clues the writer provides. To understand the problem for the high school reader, look at the opening of Heinlein's *The Puppet Masters*. The young reader is asked to construct a society in which there exists a super-secret spy organization unknown even to the CIA; to place the action far enough into the future so that the technology of instantaneous cosmetic surgery is possible; and to construct, on the basis of part of a sentence ". . . on the Northside launching platform, high above New Brooklyn and overlooking Manhattan Crater," a history of the world which has had an atomic disaster severe enough to have created a "Manhattan Crater" but from which the world has recovered to the point of supporting an advanced technology. For the high school student who has little concept of the passage of time (beyond the fact that fifth hour seems a year away) or knowledge of the location of Manhattan, the effectiveness of these clues is lost.

We feel that before the students can master the development of the world of the book, they need to develop some skills in note-taking. For instance, in some books the time-frame is a central factor in the story. Yet, students do not always follow the story's transition from time A to time B. Taking notes will focus their attention on such details and help them to keep their place so that they know what is going on. Taking notes also helps the students to be selective and conscious about the input of data from the page, to identify words and sentences that are difficult to understand, and to translate the understandings they have gained into written material. Moreover, the process of note-taking allows the teacher to audit each student's reading and permits daily student/teacher interaction.

In every possible way the classroom experience should lead the students to see that they cannot take a test successfully, or produce a satisfactory theme, without the mass of data found in their notes. At the beginning, many samples of note-taking should be put before the class, to give the students clues for things to look for and to establish a pattern for the way the notes should appear. Typically, students will complain that they do not know what to put down in their notes (because they do not know what material is significant). But, as they work along taking notes and having short and long tests for which they use their notes, they have a chance to discover what is relevant and what kind of data do count. The note-taking we recommend requires recording of times, places, events, and in general keeping track of pertinent data so that the reader consciously knows where the story is in space and time as he reads. The data should be put down in list form as much as possible under headings that categorize the information. For instance, in the second chapter of *The Puppet Masters* "triangulation" is mentioned in reference to a photograph taken from Space Station Beta. In the same chapter there is a reference to "harem guards." If his notes have been taken in list form, it is possible for the student to insert explanations of those terms along the margin of the page.

To take notes in this way, the reader must learn to forego a sentence pattern and concentrate on the data which must be extricated from the passages and then organized. The student should feel free to abbreviate, use short forms, and slang. If he records an item, it tends to demonstrate that he has understood the material. Needless to say, many students will attempt to hold to old patterns. They won't want to break up the reading experience to take notes; they will copy from the text; they will be uncomfortable with lists and abbreviations. Some students claim, with some justification, that interrupting the reading to take notes "spoils the pleasure of the story." However, for many students the reading process that has gone on previously is a superficial experience with the written word undertaken merely to pass the time. Our approach to a novel helps the students develop a special attitude toward the story, and reading becomes a process in which the students are actors rather than spectators. We have found that when the student is expected to improve his reading technique and is held responsible for understanding the content, note-taking is actually quite useful. We feel there is no point in discussing other levels of meaning until the student knows what the literal level says; then his attention can be turned to such special problems as analogies, allusions, and extended meanings. In the long run, most students do acquire a certain amount of skill and technique in the process of note-taking.

Although some SF devotees may feel that such attention to detail may turn students off SF, we believe that students' objections to the method of instruction will not be transferred to the materials of instruction (which in the instances of SF seem intrinsically interesting and resistant to causing boredom), and that if our methods lead students to overcome the difficulties they have in reading, they will then be able to read more SF with more pleasure after they leave us.

As the world of the book emerges in the early chapters, it is helpful to interrupt the note-taking to spend some time identifying and discussing the nature and characteristics of that world. It may be impossible to deal with every esoteric reference. However, if specific reading assignments are made, so that the class is responsible for the discussion of certain pages on particular days, it is possible to deal with those references which are absolutely necessary to following the story. If they are not deliberately discussed, the student sometimes gets only a rather jumbled and incoherent picture. The time in which the world (or terra or whatever it may be called) exists, its general ecological condition (population size, climatic peculiarities, technological development, etc.), its social and political unity or lack of it, the type of government and its relationship to other worlds, and so on, should all be identified for the student.

For example, in "Seventh Victim" by Sheckley, legalized murder has been substituted for too-expensive wars. The opening scene presents a clothing executive receiving confirmation of his request to commit murder. From this brief scene the student needs to abstract the story's world. If there is a discussion of this at once, the student is then far better prepared to deal with the history of that world, including a series of costly wars, the decision to use legalized murder, and the commercialization of this custom. After finishing the story, the student can return to the exposition, confront the author's abstraction about the nature of man, and consider whether he thinks man is innately violent and competitive and thus whether legalized murder, as presented in the story, is plausible.

In addition to extracting such basic concepts from the exposition and dealing with them directly, the students frequently need help in recognizing mythological and historical parallels. For instance, few teenagers have enough historical perspective to follow Asimov's parallels to the breakup of the Roman Empire in his *Foundation Trilogy*. Early assignments need to be short and specific so that the teacher can provide support and explanation when needed to get the reader off to a secure start. As students read more and more science-fiction books and encounter variations in world models from book to book, they acquire a sense of what a world model is, and from that repetitive experience they may find it easier to understand some of the stuctures of today's world.

A standard principle in teaching is that one must begin where the student is (without allowing the initial weaknesses one finds to act as a self-fulfilling prophecy of how far he can be taken). We assume that most students have some kind of concept of the world and their relationship to its daily aspects. However, many seem unable to make abstractions about their experiences and cannot express what their reactions are or discuss what they perceive. The sensations are there, but they have not discovered the words to convey them. We believe that through conversations about the worlds in various science-fiction novels students will develop a vocabulary which will enable them to make some connections between themselves and the things they perceive in the world around them, thus releasing them from their prison of inarticulateness.

As the book progresses and the action develops, the sources of conflict may be the "evil" forces from another planet, or may come from within the world in the form of overpopulation, ecological catastrophe, and the like. But it is almost always something that affects large segments of the world's geography and population, and so gives the student some practice in dealing abstractly with ecological and sociological problems and approaches to their solution. This practice may also aid development of a social consciousness. At the very least the student has a series of vicarious experiences in which he identifies with the protagonist and assumes the character's awareness of relationships between countries, worlds, peoples, and so forth. The hero's ethic often requires responsible behavior based on recognition of the needs of the larger group, and identification with this familiar ethic provides the student with a base from which to venture into the exploration of new worlds and new ideas. It seems to us that students need an image for their developing egos which shows them their responsibility to the world of the future. Schools have always assumed that a student needs to know his heritage, but if the present-day student does not learn to take a responsible posture in relation to the future, there may not be a viable future. If, in education, the future comes to be seen as having as much importance as the past, then SF materials can be useful in communicating such concepts.

So far, we have been considering the ramifications of the literal meaning of SF stories. In addition, as we said earlier, an important use for SF is to help students learn to escape from the literal. The following illustration will help to explain what we mean. In *The Puppet Masters* we soon become familiar with the dreadful, slimy parasitic slugs and their effect on humans. We see Sam, the protagonist, controlled by a slug not once but twice. Sam's independent nature when he is himself is in sharp contrast with his behavior when he is hag-ridden by the slug; for example, he follows orders without question and neglects to eat, or wash, or change clothing. Cued by the details of Sam's physical condition after he has been ridden by a slug, students will often suggest that his situation is analogous to that of the person who uses drugs. That realization takes them one step away from the

CALKINS & McGHAN

literal, but not completely to the second step of the abstraction.

The implied parallel with the popular conception of the behavior of the Communist Party cell member requires explanation to the class born in 1958; what is comparatively recent to an adult reader is ancient history to a teenager. The students need to talk about why Sam hates the slug so much when he is free of it and why it is such a trial for him to submit voluntarily a second time. Otherwise, the leap to understanding that the slugs represent an idea which imprisons the mind—any *idée fixe,* ideology, prejudice, ignorance—may be an almost impossible feat: the student's literal mind seems to reject that extension of the words on the page.

The difficulties students have in grasping symbolic meanings is illustrated by a non-SF English class which had read Vonnegut's story "Harrison Bergeron." Their answers to questions asked before class discussion indicated that they knew the story was about equality, that people wore handicaps if they were intelligent, and that the story ridiculed inept radio announcers. No one in this better-than-average class made much progress toward seeing the point of the story. It begins with this paragraph:

The year was 2081, and everybody was finally equal. They weren't only equal before God and the law. They were equal every which way. Nobody was smarter than anybody else. Nobody was better looking than anybody else. Nobody was stronger or quicker than anybody else. All this equality was due to the 211th, 212th, and 213th Amendments to the Constitution, and to the unceasing vigilance of agents of the United States Handicapper General.

Here, we believe, Vonnegut is implying that there is a basic confusion between calling ourselves equal before God and the law, and insisting on sameness in every aspect of our life, so that we come to disallow individuality, prohibit excellence and reward only the lowest common denominator. After considerable discussion, when they re-read the opening paragraph of the story, still not one student could abstract the underlying idea that Vonnegut is criticizing sloppy thinking about equality. (One could argue that Vonnegut's thinking about equality is also sloppy, since he uses physical equality—the area where we are most genuinely different—to provide the ridicule and neglects to consider concepts of social, political, and economic equality, but that would lead us off the track.)

When asked directly about their difficulties in dealing with this story, the students at first said they "did not connect it with today's world," a typical response. One never knows quite how to interpret it: perhaps they saw it as some comment on the future which for some reason did not apply to them. Next, they said that they had difficulty because they found it hard to adjust to the world of the story. Apparently, when even fairly sophisticated high school readers find the world of the story to be radically different from their experiences, it takes most of their attention simply to adjust to the unfamiliar world: they need a chance to look at it carefully, to explore the degrees of difference, to identify the changes. Only then can they possibly make some connection between what is pictured and their daily life.

Frequently there is active resistance on the part of the class when discussion is directed to bringing out the various levels of meaning. Perhaps arriving at the surface information is so difficult that suggesting that the whole pattern of the story is only a pointer for a hidden meaning threatens their view of reality. Students seem to feel that anyone could make up anything he liked about the other levels of meaning, and that the whole process is some arcane exercise that does not really have to do with reading. The consistency of the relation between the surface meaning and the underlying meaning the author seems to be striking at is a correlation they refuse to acknowledge.

Students' problems with extended meanings are not just in seeing them, but in writing about them as well. While they seem to verbalize ideas well and their conversations often appear informed, it is not unusual to find that when they are called on to write analytical essays they do poorly, even after a good class discussion of the elements of the metaphor under consideration. Even when reasonably successful class discussions are fairly common, the problems of composition persist. There is little transfer from the group's verbal experience to the individual's writing effort.

The teacher's first reaction may be to blame himself for failing to properly present the material. But we believe that most students have simply not learned to consciously consider motivations for behavior, in literature or in life. Another explanation might be that students have not discovered how to have inner conversations with themselves. If they could consciously think through a talk in which they imagine themselves as two or three people, so that such an inner colloquy could mirror their group discussions, they might then be in a position to record their understanding as readily as they can record the events they "observed" in the book. With enough examples they can normally be led to connect a given term with some aspect of the vicarious experience they have had through reading and discussion. It takes repetition, and even then there may be hesitation, reluctance, refusal.

We conclude that students have few skills which take them below the surface meanings of their reading. They do not automatically apply the content of the story to the life patterns which bring them to school every day and take them to their jobs, out on dates, and home to argue with their parents. To extend such daily experiences to "society" is not their usual way of thinking.

CALKINS & McGHAN

One view of the situation that produces the difficulties we illustrated earlier is that the teacher is a representative of the language-community which educated him, and he in turn seeks to proselytize for it among his students. After all, when we want to communicate with others, the meaning of our words must be public, if not socially customary. A language-community, whatever group of individuals is involved, exists because it agrees on the usage of words. This matter of agreement on meaning is a difficult problem even with respect to the literal meaning (or denotation) of words in a pluralistic society such as ours. The problem of reaching agreement on the symbolic meaning (or connotation) of words and the subsurface level of meaning of whole works of literature is even more difficult.

Our sociological view of teaching and learning allows us to interpret the student's rejection of the symbolic meanings presented by the teacher as a form of xenophobia. Students fear and reject the strange and unusual ideas which come from the teacher's language-community. Similarly, the teacher's difficulty in reaching the students is in part due to the ethnocentric views of metaphor which he formed in his language-community. This ethnocentrism sometimes causes the teacher to insist on one extension of the literal as *the* right one. However, it seems clear to us that symbolic meanings are not absolute and eternal pan-cultural entities, but rather are the products of culture, and vary as cultures vary. The pedagogic issue is not whether "The True Meaning" has been discovered by the students, but rather that, whatever meaning has been accepted, it is accepted by mutual agreement based on common experience. Over a period of time the teacher has an opportunity to add enough of the "right" reading experiences to the students' lives so that more of them can grasp the underlying meanings which are implied or can be inferred. While those students whose prior experiences have been most similar to the teacher's find the symbolic ideas he presents easiest to grasp, all the members of the class can gain a greater understanding of figurative writing.

The ambience of the classroom is an important ingredient in developing the students' ability to escape from the literal. If a climate of goodwill and concern for completing the task at hand can be generated among the people in the room, then it almost seems that classroom discussions make it possible to catch ideas from the tone of the conversation. (How one produces the proper classroom climate that is the proper set of norms and expectations for behavior is a crucial question but one too complex to be addressed here.) With the body (at least occasionally) subdued to order in a given seat, discussion and examples and the social force of peer pressure can create a sequence of reactions which are somehow contagious, so that there is, as in the theater audience, a communication of understanding.

Although we can conceive of the existence of an educational package—or model—to help students escape from the literal, we cannot at this point be certain what the contents of the package should be. Perhaps all that is necessary is to provide a continuing series of experiences in which they proceed from the literal to the figurative and the allegorical time and time again, so that the journey becomes neither strange nor threatening. One could also have students begin systematically to approach subsurface meanings by developing lists of symbols and their meanings as part of their notes. We feel that such a routine will tend to make students sensitive to the possibility that a symbolic meaning may, from time to time, be intended.

One of the things we have not yet discussed is grading. Everyone hates grades, but we seem to be stuck with them. What is needed, we think, is a system which will tend to control their unfortunate influences. For this purpose we recommend a point system. Points awarded for each assignment can be open and public, that is, determined by the students and posted on the bulletin board if desired. A wide range of possible activities to earn points can be offered. For example, students can write summaries of sections of the books they read; answer questions about their reading; hold conferences with the teacher; participate in discussions; evaluate other students' papers; read unassigned books; give oral and/or written reports on movies and TV shows; listen to tapes and records; write stories and poetry; delve into the history of SF; create illustrations for books; write scripts from stories; publish fanzines; and write letters to fanzines or authors. Our system allows students the opportunity to redo papers or tests or to do "extra credit" work for more points, and thus enables the plodding hard worker to achieve the grade he wants so that his confidence builds up and his work improves. The more advanced student will benefit from the opportunity to put together work combinations which are better suited to her or his tastes. The final point count must of course be translated in terms of the local grading system, either at the beginning of the course so that the student will know what his goal is, or after all the results are in. It is important that each individual knows exactly how he got where he is, and that he had a perfectly good opportunity to be anywhere he chose on the scale.

Some classes must just be given the system. Others can participate in setting it up. In either case, most students quickly realize that it is something *they* can operate; they are not the helpless victims of the teacher's subjective judgment. Furthermore, because the point system allows for success without threatening irretrievable failure, the students' attention can focus more fully on the material of the course.

Once the amount and type of work is specified, it may be helpful to devise a flow chart which organizes the activities into a sequence so that the most important things will be taken care of first. Even with this initial organization some students will lag behind or jump ahead of the majority. The laggards should be coaxed along and given the extra assistance they need to make progress. The speedsters who finish

CALKINS & McGHAN

a book the first night need to be given another book right away. An in-class library of 100 to 200 SF novels provides "reading room" for the fast reader, and also provides the material for coming to know SF as a genre. In our experience, SF classes seem to be motivated to read more material than other English classes, and with an in-class library this tendency can be satisfied.

When the time comes to move from note-taking to essay writing, the students' task should be clearly identified for them. We find that a fairly standard and structured three-part form can be followed for essays. First, students give a general introduction to the book in which they answer "Who?", "What?", "Where?", and "When?" type questions. Second, they discuss in detail the events in the specific section of the story which they are going to analyze; third, they analyze an aspect of the novel which provides them an opportunity to express the figurative significance of the specific section. If the teacher feels it is necessary, he can even provide a model opening sentence or paragraph for any or all of these three parts, which the student would then be expected to enlarge upon.

A worthwhile technique is to tell the students to write their papers for someone who is not in the class and is therefore neither knowledgeable about the story nor privy to class discussions about it. This suggestion takes the paper out of the realm of a private conversation between the teacher and the student and makes it a public endeavor. This public nature can be further developed by removing names from papers and circulating them to other students, or even exchanging a set of papers with a nearby college English class, thereby enlightening both groups. With proper guidance, students can analyze each others' papers and benefit a great deal from participating in this process, as well as from reading what others have to say about their own papers.

Immediate feedback on the work should be provided to prevent the student's interest in his paper from cooling off, but this can be difficult in a class of thirty or more. One way may be to collect papers near the end of the hour and read a few aloud for comment. Or the essays could be done for homework which is collected at the beginning of the next period, and (if short enough) handed back with comments before students leave.

Most of our experience with SF has been in the regular high school program, about which we have spoken at some length above. However, we have also had experience teaching in two other kinds of programs: an "alternative" high school and an adult high school. Each type of student body imposes a somewhat different set of circumstances for teaching SF. The adults, for example, seem to start off at about the same level of skill and knowledge as the teenagers, but give more initial resistance to the teacher's effort to introduce second levels of meaning. However, once started they grasp the symbolism and reconstruct the *weltanschauung* of stories more rapidly, probably because they have more experience to draw on in identifying references and allusions. The alternative high school students (many of them potential dropouts) are the most difficult to work with using science fiction (or anything else, for that matter). They have at least as many reading difficulties as regular high school students, and other problems besides. The main characteristics of these students seem to be poor work habits and poor attendance—both brought on by the regular school's failure to provide them with opportunities to be successful. Their poor work habits make it difficult to cover very much material and their poor attendance makes it difficult to have the class discussions which help students to grasp the subsurface meanings and world concepts of SF stories. We recommend caution in using science fiction with this type of student. Minicourses may be better than semester courses; work contracts which spell out exactly what they must do should be negotiated at the outset of a course, no matter what its length. Considerably more individual discussion between teacher and students will be necessary to make up for the lack of class discussion due to high absenteeism and inconsistent work habits.

In the foregoing pages we have tried to give our view of the practical value of science fiction for high school students and have offered some plain opinions about who they are and what needs they have, as well as some homely advice about classroom materials and activities. We feel that our opinions of what can and should be done with SF in the high school certainly do not represent the maximum possible, and probably not the minimum either. Our opinions are relevant to general high school use of SF, and we hope that we have called sufficient attention to the nature and needs of students so that those teachers who will be using SF in high school will give careful consideration to the question of what can reasonably be expected to be successful in their situation.

SCIENCE FICTION IN THE ENGLISH DEPARTMENT

BY MARK R. HILLEGAS

Mark Hillegas, now a professor of English at Southern Illinois University, taught his pioneer course at Colgate in 1962. Thousands have followed him, in a score of different disciplines at every grade level. This thoughtful summary of his rich experience should be enlightening to all. As he says, SF often finds its warmest welcome outside the English department. One may see the course as a bridge between Snow's two cultures, but the traditional English professor is seldom much interested in the culture of science, too seldom willing even to admit that it exists. Mark's book, The Future as Nightmare *(Oxford, 1967) is an important study of the dystopian current in modern SF, flowing from Wells down to the present. His* Shadows of Imagination *was reissued in a new edition by Southern Illinois University Press in 1979.*

In 1967 in an article for *Extrapolation,* I looked back on having taught science fiction to college students for some five or six years. I was not altogether satisfied with the experience since I felt that a course in science fiction was received with something less than enthusiasm by professors of English, whose response often was, "You don't *really* think science fiction is literature?" So in 1967 I attempted my explanation of this seemingly common reaction. Professors of English were, by the very nature of their discipline, intellectually conservative (though not usually socially and politically so). They were, after all, concerned with preserving and understanding the literature of the past; and so it seemed understandable to me that they were not much interested in thinking about the future, an activity at the heart of a good deal of science fiction. Further, they were greatly concerned with style and taste; and science fiction was identified in their minds with pulp magazines. Finally, professors of English were usually hostile to science, largely because of the traditions to which they were heir. I thought it would be difficult to be interested in science fiction if one knew nothing about science and cared even less.

Then in 1974 I wrote again about teaching science fiction for Willis

E. McNelly's CEA Chapbook, *Science Fiction: The Academic Awakening*. With an apparent boom in science-fiction courses and with an apparent push by publishers to get in on a new market for texts, I tried to assess this phenomenon. As far as English departments were concerned, I pointed to the obvious—that their world had changed enormously (declining enrollments, changing patterns of interest among students) so that they were more willing to accommodate to courses called "science fiction." But at the same time I voiced my suspicion that the values and interests of many English professors had not changed greatly from what I saw them to be in 1967: science fiction was not literature for them; or, if they now had a glimmer that it might be, they were not knowledgeable about the subject. In addition, they and their students were even further down the road from reductionism to holism and despised science even more than in 1967. I went on to hypothesize that the courses in science fiction in English departments were usually—though not always—taught by younger men while the older men went on teaching what they knew and had always taught. Needless to say, they were teaching traditional courses to fewer and fewer students because "1066 and all that" had become increasingly remote to the young in America in the seventies.

I would now like to take a more positive approach to the possibilities for courses in science fiction, one based on my experience of teaching a variety of science-fiction courses over many years. To begin with, I should explain that I would tend to agree with Theodore Sturgeon who, just back from the Science Fiction Research Association meetings at Penn State, wrote in *The New York Times Book Review* for November 4, 1973, that science fiction was a "virtually undefinable literary area." Personally I still define science fiction as did Kingsley Amis in *New Maps of Hell* as a kind of literature that speculates on the consequences of real or imagined discoveries or knowledge in the sciences (physical, biological, and social), sometimes just for the fun of it but other times to make serious comment on the relationship to human life of these discoveries. But a glance at Jack Williamson's surveys of science fiction confirms that the usage of the term has broadened extraordinarily in recent years. The interesting thing is that, while "science fiction" is too general a term to be either prescriptive or descriptive, it nevertheless generates considerable excitement on the part of students. Still, the term has become so all-inclusive that, although one might reasonably title a course "science fiction," when one came to teach it he would inevitably have to narrow it down. It is to the possible courses under the heading "science fiction" that I will now turn.

One of the problems in teaching science fiction in English departments is, as I have already noted, that the professors have so little knowledge of and interest in science. If they turned to science fiction, they would tend, I think, to use techniques of analysis familiar to them. In my judgment, one of the most profitable of these literary

MARK R. HILLEGAS

approaches would be myth criticism; and so I can conceive of several of my colleagues who know the writings of, say, Joseph Campbell or Northrop Frye teaching with some success a novel such as Arthur Clarke's *Childhood's End*. I think a great deal of science fiction could profitably be taught this way. I myself have had luck with this approach in seminars for graduate students in English and suspect it would work well with reasonably able undergraduates. As for other kinds of literary approaches, such as stylistic, I have a feeling they would be less profitable; but this may be a bias on my part since I find boring these approaches to any kind of literature. I also think I see a new though still to be defined literary approach to science fiction which may be emerging at the moment in the work of several able young men at Canadian universities and in some of the articles in the lively new journal, *Science Fiction Studies*. From all this ferment I can foresee new courses developing which could be viable within the confines of an English department, both at undergraduate and graduate levels.

In connection with what I have just said, I should note that one of the courses from which I've had a great deal of pleasure is "Myths of Space and Time." It is not a traditional literary course but rather a multidisciplinary one in which we study in four different but related areas. The heart of it, of course, is fiction which deals with man's nature and place in the universe—for example, David Lindsay's *A Voyage to Arcturus,* Olaf Stapledon's *Last and First Men* and *Star Maker,* and C.S. Lewis's planetary trilogy. But parallel to such works and casting light on them, I also teach something of process philosophy and theology (Whitehead and Teilhard de Chardin) and cosmological speculation (the better popularizations), while using myth criticism (Joseph Campbell, for example) to attempt to reconcile man's mythic and religious attempts to explain his place in the universe with his scientific, objective vision. A related though different course which I have taught is one in the mythopoeic world of the "Oxford Christians" (Charles Moorman's phrase). It deals with the fiction of Lewis, Tolkien, Williams, and Sayers, and the poetry of T.S. Eliot. But except for Lewis's planetary trilogy, much of this material is pretty distant from science fiction. A perhaps more viable possibility, considering the tastes of English professors and the vagueness of the term "science fiction," would be a course in Lewis and Tolkien. For some young people, of course, science fiction is essentially no different from fantasy—the two modes seem interchangeable to them, and they read both in order to travel in their imagination to other worlds. The only difficulty here is that Lewis is a Christian apologist, which upsets many people, and Tolkien is enormously popular, which bothers those professors who tend to regard a widely read writer as not worth teaching.

Finally, before turning to the kinds of courses in science fiction which I find most exciting, I should mention two other possibilities for English departments. One is that there are a number of respected "mainstream" writers—Borges and Pynchon come immediately to mind—who have written what is very close to science fiction. English professors would rather enjoy teaching such authors. And second, an important part of a department's creative writing program could be the teaching of the writing of science fiction—something which would best be done by professional writers themselves. Having a science-fiction writer in residence would be good for English departments, helping them to shake their tendency to transfer bones from one cemetery to another. Several institutions, of course, have already had science-fiction writers in residence and also workshops in the subject.

But for me, as I have said, science fiction involves knowledge of science, not necessarily for extrapolation but certainly for speculation—which brings us back to the problem of the lack of interest in and knowledge of science on the part of professors of English. One remedy for this deficiency would be for professors to read regularly magazines of lay scientific and technical exposition—for example, *Scientific American* and *Popular Science*—and also the better books of similar popularization. I'm not sure, given their inclinations, that they ever will; but if they did, there are several possibilities for courses which I would like to propose. My essential point is that in order to teach science fiction as I would define it, one has to have some understanding and enthusiasm for science—not necessarily vast and extensive but at least *some*.

One idea for a course in science fiction of this sort would be one which plays skillfully with the consequences of a possibility—the ecology, say, of a planet with enormous gravitational attraction in Hal Clement's *Mission of Gravity* or a lunar vehicle sinking into moondust in Arthur Clarke's *A Fall of Moondust*. Skillfully done, a course of this sort could appeal to the imagination of undergraduates, providing topics for lively class discussions and for outside papers. But again I need to emphasize that it would require a reasonable amount of familiarity with the scientific and technical background of the fiction being taught.

I think the most important science fiction is that which has something significant to say about the relationship of scientific discovery and knowledge to human life. It ranges from diagnosis, satire, and warning to utopian projections of alternative futures. In this connection, I've had a good deal of success with a course I now title "Utopian Dreams and Nightmares," a course which I've taught over a number of years to graduate students and undergraduates. I start the course with Plato's *Republic*—the ancestor of all this kind of writing and a work so important it is still alive 2300 years later. The *Republic* isn't, of course, science fiction, but variations on its ideas reverberate in the later utopias and anti-utopias, which are in most cases a kind of science fiction. As part of the background, I also glance briefly at More's *Utopia*, Bacon's *New Atlantis*, Swift's *Gulliver's Travels*, Butler's *Erewhon*, and William Morris's *News from Nowhere*. But I give most attention to Bellamy's *Looking Backward*, Wells's *A Modern Utopia*, and then to the major anti-utopias of the twentieth century, particularly Zamyatin's *We*, Huxley's *Brave New World*, and Orwell's *Nineteen Eighty-Four*. Then I turn to the anti-utopias written by science-fiction writers beginning roughly in the fifties—say Vonnegut's *Player Piano*—and after that I return to utopias, notably Skinner's *Walden Two* and Huxley's *Island*. Toward the end of the term we discuss a fair amount of recent science fiction (say Brunner's book about overpopulation, *Stand on Zanzibar*) and also a few works of nonfiction that project possible futures (for example, W. Warren Wagar's *Building the City of Man* and John McHale's *The Future of the Future*). The course is extraordinary fun when I teach it to undergraduates in our university honors program—partly because they are able but also because they come from many other majors than English. It is less successful with graduate students in English.

And this brings me back full circle to the response of English departments to science fiction. I believe it is a very viable form, but it is, as I have already said, a form whose content escapes the grasp of a majority of professors of English. No matter how elaborate and sophisticated their techniques of literary analysis, without some sympathy and understanding for this content their attempts to teach it will remain relatively unsuccessful. I suspect that in general the best courses will end up being taught in other disciplines, where there are many professors at the same time both literate and knowledgeable in the sciences.

MISS FORSYTE IS DEAD— LONG LIVE THE SCI-FI LADY!

BY CAROLYN WENDELL

Unlike Mark Hillegas, who teaches SF to graduate students and honors seminars, Carolyn Wendell is fighting the battle of literacy, as she calls it, in a community college. Working with students "who may range from Albert Einstein and Virginia Woolf to Alfred E. Neuman and the Happy Hooker," she tries to get them to write complete sentences and to read almost anything. Her essay is a down-to-earth discussion of the ways she uses SF to reach the reluctant student. Her other fast-changing interests have recently ranged from sign language through the Erie Canal to dental crowns.

In the spring of my senior year in high school, *On the Beach* finally came to our one-theater town. The following Monday morning, my classmates and I trudged into Miss Forsyte's English class. Most of us had seen the movie that weekend and were still shaken. As those of you over thirty will recall, this was the cold war era: kids of my generation had air raid drills as often as fire drills, and our fathers built bomb shelters while our mothers worried how long canned goods could be stored for an emergency. Wakened by a siren at night, we would lie paralyzed, hoping it was fire or an accident, not the beginning of World War III.

That spring day, Miss Forsyte soon became aware that our thoughts were hardly on Bacon's prose style and that the daily buzz of conversation was a bit more frenzied than usual. Finally someone told her about the movie, and the room immediately became filled with fearful commentary on what it would be like to survive in a world doomed to death by radiation. Miss Forsyte looked aghast, then turned to me, as one of the more vocal of the young hysteriacs, and said, "My *dear* Carolyn, nothing like that ever has happened and, I assure you, nothing *ever* will!" That, she seemed to think, ended the matter. We returned to Bacon's search for truth and Pilate's refusal to stay for answer.

Miss Forsyte, I am sure, never read science fiction. Nor were any of its concerns even a part of her perceptions of reality and truth. She was firmly grounded in the comforting belief that things never change. As a result, she wasn't quite in touch with her students—nor was she in very close touch with the twentieth century. And so she missed a chance to reach, and teach, her students.

If there is one lesson that history—especially that history of the last seventy years—should have taught us, it is that things do not stay the same. Wise men have known this truth for centuries, but only in this century has it become so apparent to us who are not wise, only survivors in a world that seems different, if not every day or year, than at least every decade. On the first day of the science-fiction course I teach, I pass out a list of general questions asking about technological and social changes since the year of the students' birth—or, if they prefer, my birth year, 1942. Television, atomic energy, commercial jets, drugs, computers, open classrooms, liberated women and uncloseted gays, organ transplants, the pill—the list seems inexhaustible. And, my class and I gasp in chorus, all this in only a few decades. If, as Alvin Toffler has suggested, this rapid flux of reality does result in future shock, Miss Forsyte and those like her must be basket cases by now.

Maybe if they had read science fiction, they might have been better prepared. For one thing, they have missed a lot of fun—they've never ridden a sand worm with Paul Atreides, walked the streets of Winter with Genly Ai during a "mild spring blizzard," or met a Puppeteer or a Kzinti. But more important, it may be that this sort of imaginative literature is better preparation for the rapidly changing present than any other kind. Because science fiction predicts the future with a fair degree of probability? Hardly. None of us is ever going to walk the red deserts of Bradbury's Mars with its crystal towers. Nor is it likely that Clarke's Rama will float into our solar system and then speed away with its unsolved mystery. With only a few years to go, the chances for a Big Brother and Newspeak seem relatively remote—at least as detailed by Orwell (although there are frightening similarities). Isaac Asimov commented at the MLA Convention in December, 1974, after a heated debate on whether science fiction predicted the future, that all science fiction is correct—not because it accurately predicts the future but because it says, over and over, that tomorrow is not going to be like today, that things *will* be different. It is the possible world, not the probable world, that science fiction depicts. And in this, it is not so far removed from the traditional imaginative literature that people have been reading and writing for centuries and which has only rarely pretended to be the purveyor of hard fact and actual event: this has always been the realm of nonfiction rather than of fiction. Fiction writers have always dealt with possibility, not with actual facts transferred to paper. Science fiction simply concerns itself with a larger scope of possibility than does traditional fiction whose characters live next door and worry about the exact same things the reader worries about. The science-fiction character doesn't live next door—or even on the next planet—and his concerns may be similar to ours but they are not exactly ours because his society, his environment, even his very physical makeup may be greatly different.

Reading about this character is fun, but it can also provide a valid method for teaching our young about change: not what will be, but what might be. And in any case, the student might begin to realize that possibilities are infinite and that the future is not something that will happen to someone else some time, but that change is now and he is part of it, so that even current differences can be put into perspective. At the same time, since the writers of these science-fiction works are human, with human emotions and intellects, science fiction also suggests that some things do remain the same—primarily the basic physical and emotional needs of people, although the answers to these needs may differ greatly.

And it is these differences in the realm of science fiction that make it a valid subject for the classroom. Let me speak from my own experiences as a teacher. I teach at Monroe Community College in Rochester, New York. Our students come to us mainly from the local area, although every once in a while we pull in someone from farther away (the kid from Oklahoma who came for baseball and our police science program or the Filipino married to a doctor doing his surgical residency in Rochester). Many of our students are first- or second-generation Americans; they come from primarily blue-collar backgrounds. With our open admissions policy, Monroe attracts everyone and anyone, from all age groups, all ethnic groups, all levels of ability. Most of them are not readers; what spare time they have is devoted to part-time jobs (the majority work an average of twenty hours a week), television, and an occasional movie. I suspect most of their homes contain little reading matter, perhaps only the newspaper or *Reader's Digest;* thus, their reading habits are restricted to an infrequent popular novel (e.g., *The Godfather, The Exorcist*) or a vague "magazines and newspapers." The greatest percentage of our students want only a two-year degree which will qualify them for certain "career programs," i.e., they are here because they want to be policemen or women, nurses, department store managers, optical technicians, nursery school teachers, Kodak or Xerox employees, X-ray technicians, secretaries, etc. But this is, to those of us who teach them, a group every bit as important as those who enter Yale and Stanford. They are middle-class America, that majority called silent and passive and uninformed, who will live their lives of quiet desperation if we don't open a few doors and windows for them. And all of society will suffer if those windows and doors remain closed.

One of my favorite assignments in Basic College Writing a few years ago was a description of one day in the writer's life ten years thence. The results were so appalling that I stopped giving that assignment—my students were unable to see themselves doing anything significantly different from what they were doing in the present. For instance, one student in an evening class, a fireman, married, with children, said that the only thing he could foresee different in his future was a larger ride-around lawnmower. (I suggested to him that the unexamined life was not worth living; he, like Pilate and Miss Forsyte, did not stay for answer.)

These are the kids I want to, have to, reach. Classical literature will not do it. Eliot's "Waste Land" is incomprehensible to the fireman who wants a larger lawnmower. Shakespeare is incomprehensible to the kid whose greatest reading success was finishing *The Harrad Experiment* ("Shakespeare wrote in Old English, didn't he?"). Hawthorne doesn't make a dent ("Those Puritans sure were weird."); Hemingway is readable, but—bullfights? Faulkner's and Conrad's and Joyce's aesthetic innovations and convoluted points of view simply get in the way of the plot ("But I don't understand—what happened?").

I need a literature that will illustrate the strong possibilities of difference, that will be readable. Science fiction fulfills these requirements. The course has been offered several times at Monroe, and it has met with phenomenal success each time. It fills almost as soon as the registration line forms, and those who are closed out will put off their literary elective requirement until the next semester. Those semesters it has not been offered have been filled with howls of protest and pleas to, please, offer it the following semester. Kids who cannot pass an introduction-to-literature course because they have little patience with old ladies wearing motheaten fur stoles or young men who cannot make up their minds whether or not to kill their uncles will happily attend each meeting of a science-fiction class, stay past the hour to continue discussion, and write science-fiction stories whose freshness of approach and style would shock their writing teacher, who didn't think they knew what a sentence was. The difference? Simply the content and the style—the student likes it, it's different, he can read it and understand it, maybe because it retains somewhat the aroma of "non-school" stuff (i.e., the book you hid behind your *Silas Marner* during high school English class because Martians were infinitely more interesting than anyone named Eppie).

Although science fiction can be offered in any of numerous disciplines (and has, according to Jack Williamson's lengthy list, been offered in theology, history, physics, media, psychology: the variety is mind-boggling), it is most often the English department that offers it. This has caused many fans and writers to howl in agony; the genre has so long been segregated from "mainstream" literature that many of the science-fiction devotees now prefer a strict separation. Some have protested that English teachers could not possibly know enough about science to teach science fiction. Although I suspect similar complaints could be made about other groups (the writers who don't know enough about plotting and characterization to be able to write a novel, the readers who don't really understand the science they are reading about in a novel), I suppose the complaint about English teachers may be true in the context of some works. But there are solutions to this dilemma. One is to avoid those works that emphasize science over literary technique. If the teacher doesn't know the difference between a quasar and a laser, he should not teach stories about them. But if he just can't resist that fantastic story about a black hole, then he should do a little research (these things can be learned). Or—and this has been one of my most beneficial lessons from teaching science fiction—he might rely on his students. Let "Doctor Professor, Sir" step down from his podium and allow the kids to explain something to him. That glaring mass of hostility in the corner may be miraculously transformed into a dynamic lecturer on black holes (he hates English, but loves astronomy); for the first time in thirteen years of school, he may be able to contribute something to an English class. He may love the teacher forever; but, better than that, he may begin to suspect that there's more to this business of reading books than he had thought.

Also, more important, science fiction *is* literature. Because it utilizes the same techniques as mainstream literature, the student can learn in a science-fiction class the same literary methods he would be exposed to in a traditional introduction to literature course. The English teacher teaches a novel as literature, not as science. And, in many cases, science fiction is particularly usable for students who are inexperienced readers (as many of my students are) because it is literature without being self-consciously "literary." Irony and point of view can be taught as effectively (and possibly even more so) through Ellison's "I Have No Mouth, And I Must Scream" as through Joyce's "Araby." *Frankenstein* or *The Martian Chronicles* are excellent examples of atmosphere, setting, and theme. Allusion, imagery, symbolism, and characterization can be studied through Zelazny's "A Rose for Ecclesiastes." LeGuin's *The Left Hand of Darkness* illustrates the literary use of myth.

A good deal of science fiction is apt to sacrifice literary complexity for clarity of plot or extrapolation of idea; this does not mean that it's simple literature, only that it is frequently more approachable by the inexperienced reader. And one of the joys of teaching a science-fiction literature course is being able to compile a reading list that includes a range of reading difficulties, so as to appeal to as many reading levels as possible. Dick, who clutches a pen or a book as if it were a weapon about to be used against him, will be able to read and enjoy del Rey's "Helen O'Loy" and Bradbury's *The Martian Chronicles*. He will have some trouble with Sturgeon's *More Than Human* because of its disordered chronology and shifting points of view. *The Left Hand of Darkness* will undoubtedly lose him, but Susan (whose favorite author is Faulkner—the more complicated, the better), will probably be in my

CAROLYN WENDELL

office as soon as she's read it, demanding others like it.

Also, if Dick is "into" science or technology while Susan is dedicating her life to literature, the chances of their communicating may be slim. As our society has grown more and more specialized ("That's not my job"), academia has reflected this. For years, educators' attitudes have been: don't look at the forest, let me show you this tree. For most of us who have come through on the educational conveyor belt, this philosophy has resulted in an incredible narrowness of vision. The English major regards the scientist with grave suspicion (an amoral, fuzzy-haired automaton who eats electrons for breakfast and builds atomic bombs after lunch); the science major harbors similarly dark suspicions about artists and their audiences (illogical, ignorant souls who think that light switches work because of fairies in the walls).

In traditional academia, we fence off areas of human interest as if they were cattle and sheep ranges, rather than fertile fields for all people. Each of us becomes so involved in our own little bailiwick that we cannot see beyond the fences. And we wear these blinders when we offer our courses and when we talk to our students: a student could easily receive the impression that Einstein and Joyce lived on different planets when, in fact, each was obsessed with the idea of time and its perception by the human mind.

In recent years, there has been much talk of "interdisciplinary" courses, offerings which will help the student perceive the forest as a whole made up of individual but related trees. Science fiction is an obvious choice for a role in this development. It is literature, but it involves areas of human interest and endeavor that generally are not immediately involved in fiction. A story set in an overcrowded city (e.g., Ballard's "Billenium") may illustrate the horrors of overpopulation as well as a sociology lecture complete with statistics. *Dune* shows the complexity of an ecological system and its relation to culture and human behavior. *Childhood's End* depicts a logically and psychologically plausible encounter between human and alien when the latter lands on our planet. LeGuin's "Nine Lives" provides an opportunity to talk not only about cloning, but also about the nature of loneliness and friendship. Zoline's "The Heat Death of the Universe" uses the theory of entropy in the universe to parallel and comment upon the mental and physical exhaustion of a housewife. In each of these cases, the author has taken an abstract idea, concept, or theory from scientific or sociological research and used it for a story that puts the concept into individual, human terms. And because it is put into this identifiable form, with characters responding and behaving in specific ways, the story will make the concept understandable and relevant. This blending of disciplines, despite screaming from both sides about the impurities that result (watered-down science and sociology or watered-down characters and plots), will be attractive to those whose bent is toward the humanities or toward the sciences; they can learn from one another. A few years ago our school added to its catalog a "physics for poets" course; when I proposed my course, I suggested that we needed a "poetry for physicists."

Another of the appeals of science fiction to the current generation is that it is critical, often bitterly so, of the contemporary world. To a generation growing up with daily pollution counts, Watergate, "strategic" arms limitation, energy crises, and computers more interested in numbers than in names, the literature provides a stimulus to thought as well as an outlet for frustration and anger. I, as a teacher, want my kids to read, to respond, to think, and even to act. I at least want them to be aware of what is going on around them.

Frankenstein makes a good beginning point since it so well presents the case for human responsibility and the retribution for dereliction of that responsibility. From there, we read many stories that are social criticism (often satire) or, if not bitter enough to be satire, then social commentary. Many of these works may not lend themselves to lengthy discussion of literary technique, but will suggest implications and applications that extend far beyond the locale of the story itself. Ellison's " 'Repent, Harlequin!' Said the Ticktockman" portrays a rigidly conformist society where sameness is legally (and lethally) enforced. Spinrad suggests in his "The Big Flash" that the media and popular entertainers have a hypnotic and irresistible grip upon their audience, who could be persuaded by them to approve of even the worst horrors.

One of the most successful stories of this group, though, has been Reed's "Golden Acres," a story set in what seems to be a not-too-distant future: the elderly who are no longer wanted by their children are sent to Golden Acres where, when their funds run out, they are calmly and callously disposed of. The story regards the elderly with a mixture of wryness (two old ladies discussing their children agree that "43 is just about the cutest age") and bitter sympathy as the elderly hero and his wife move toward death which comes with the rumble of a "gigantic grocery cart." "Golden Acres" almost always foments discussion that runs well over the hour as the students realize and begin to explore and cope with the horrors of being old in a society where old is defined as "unnecessary and disposable."

And it is when discussion runs over the time allotted for the class that I feel especially happy about being the "sci-fi lady" (as I have been titled by some of my colleagues) because I know that my students are with me, that they're thinking, responding, and learning. They are learning about literature and they are learning about human responsibility to the life that exists on "this island earth." This is what should happen in a classroom. Unhappily, it too often does not happen in an English class; English Literature I, American Literature II, World Masterpieces, and others each semester go begging for students and frequently are cancelled by an administration that wants full classes in an era of "cost containment." Others that fill because they

CAROLYN WENDELL

are required are often only sparsely attended. Science fiction fills, and the students come and stay.

The obvious conclusion is that this is a literature that speaks to our students. It's the only class I have ever taught where students do not daily watch the clock, start piling up their books ten minutes before the end of the hour, and poise on their chairs' edges like racehorses at starting gates. It's the only class where not only will they read and be prepared to discuss the assignments, they will ask me to share their reading by bringing me their own copies of science-fiction books. It's the only class where a few will regularly follow me out of the room to my office, and deposit themselves in my chairs and on my floor to "talk some more." It's the only class where even the usually tedious task of paper-grading can be less than numbing because the papers may be enthusiastic and original. And it's certainly one of the few courses I have ever taught where I may learn as much from the students as they do from me because there is more excitement and more passion to communicate.

And former students do not forget the course: I recall one semester a few years ago when the course was not offered. I seemed to have an unusually large number of inquiries about when the course would be offered again, so I began to ask the inquirers where they had heard about it. My publicity agent has been a young man who received a D from me! Perhaps this has happened before in the history of academia, but the chances of praise coming from a student who did poorly are usually so slim as to be nonexistent. Also, I have on my desk at school a ceramic ashtray with a strange green blob reposing on its bottom; this was a gift from a student who, several months later, remembered a lengthy discussion of why SF monsters always seem to be green. And I have a film made by two students who decided a story we had read in class ought to be made into a screenplay. Again, these things happen occasionally in other classes, but they happen reliably in science-fiction classes.

Science fiction is worth teaching. Let's not be Miss Forsytes who ignore what is most exciting to our students. Let's teach it.

SCIENCE FICTION AND THE SCIENCE TEACHER

BY STANLEY SCHMIDT

Science fiction may be taught for itself—for technique and truth and literary beauty. It may be used to teach something else—reading or ecology or religion. In the physics department at Heidelberg College when he wrote this essay, Stanley Schmidt has done his bit of both. He also writes fine fiction. Speaking from this unusual background, he has significant things to say about both the science and the fiction in SF. Now editor of Analog Science Fiction Magazine, *he was recommended for the job by Ben Bova, who had observed and been impressed by his SF course.*

There are two fundamentals which should, I think, be borne constantly in mind by any teacher using science fiction in the classroom.

First, *science fiction is for fun.* It, like any other literature, may be much more besides, but its first purpose is (in a very broad sense) to entertain. Teaching methods should enhance, never detract from, the students' enjoyment of the subject.

Second, *science fiction is an* integrated *product of science and fiction.* It is not just science problems in fictional guise. It deals with at least as broad a spectrum of human problems as other forms of fiction. Nor is it merely mainstream fiction with pseudoscientific window dressing. The scientific elements, at least in science fiction at its best, cannot be removed without destroying the story.

Still, it is possible to use science fiction in a wide variety of instructional ways, with the emphasis ranging from the scientific to the integrated to the literary. This article will deal with approaches in that part of the spectrum where the scientific elements receive at least equal emphasis. Such approaches range from incidental use of science fiction in science courses to complete courses focussing on science fiction itself as a literary craft with scientific speculation as one of its tools.

Before considering possible ways to handle the science in science fiction, it seems desirable, if not downright necessary, to think a little about just how science and science fiction are related. Essentially,

STANLEY SCHMIDT

science fiction includes, in more or less integral and important ways, careful speculation about scientific matters. This does not mean "prediction," in the sense of trying to foretell what the future *will* be, but rather the examination of various things which *might* happen—and their consequences if they do. Such speculations can be roughly divided into two types: *extrapolation* and *innovation.*

By "extrapolation," I mean speculation which is based entirely on new applications and developments of well-established and understood scientific principles. For example, Poul Anderson and Hal Clement develop entire worlds, ecologies, and cultures, exotic but highly plausible, by meticulous application of what is already known about astronomy and physics and chemistry. Typical examples are Anderson's *The People of the Wind* and Clement's *Mission of Gravity.* Robert A. Heinlein develops very detailed future human societies which use completely new technologies based on old principles. See, for example, the catapults used for Moon-to-Earth shipping in *The Moon Is a Harsh Mistress*—and the explanations of both why they're used and how they work.

By "innovation," I mean speculation which depends on the assumption of new principles, such as faster-than-light travel, antigravity, or time travel. In my opinion, to be acceptable as good science fiction, such hypothetical principles must be introduced in such a way that they don't contradict any accepted principles *in any region of experience where the accepted principles have been directly tested.* That is, a science-fictional innovation should satisfy what I might call the "negative impossibility" criterion: nobody should be able to *prove* it's impossible at the time of writing. (Since we're learning new things all the time, it would be both unfair and impractical to require that it be demonstrably possible.) Whether or not this criterion is actually met by a particular speculation is not always an easy question. A serious attempt to answer it may force students (and teachers) to think as they have never thought before about what they mean by "know."

In well-done extrapolative fiction, much sound science is incorporated, made vivid, and explained lucidly. For example, one can learn a good deal about astrophysics and general planetology by reading an Anderson novel—and all while enjoying a new world that feels almost as real as the one he lives in. These are the kinds of stories most useful to a science teacher using science fiction to help teach science. But he must beware—stories with such solid extrapolation frequently also contain radically innovative, purely fictional concepts as well. And if such a story is well done, the purely fictional ideas will be explained in ways that sound quite as plausible as the well-established ones. Unless the reader already knows where the frontiers of present-day science are, he may learn a mixture of solid science and pure conjecture, with no way of telling which is which. For example, Isaac Asimov's short mystery "The Billiard Ball" contains a beautiful layman's explanation of general relativity's conception of the nature of gravity—which continues with no obvious break into an equally beautiful explanation of the purely fictitious "two-field theory" which leads (in the story) to antigravity and the production of energy from nothing. Moral: a teacher who is going to teach science through science fiction needs to know enough about the frontiers of science to know where the real ends and the fictitious begins.

Moreover, even if a story is purely extrapolative, it will seldom be designed to illustrate neatly a particular law of physics or chemistry or biology. More often, particularly if convincing and interesting worlds or life-forms are to be created for the story, the creation process requires consideration of (at least) astronomy, physics, chemistry, and biology in an inextricably interrelated way. (Which, by the way, I consider a very good thing for students to be exposed to. Too often conventional curriculum structures tacitly encourage them to think of the various named sciences as self-contained and tightly partitioned boxes—an illusion which I'm always delighted to shatter.)

For a student or teacher who wants to see the process of such thinking—either as an illustration of scientific principles and methods for their own interest, or as an important part of a science-fiction writer's homework—I highly recommend two of the essays in Reginald Bretnor's *Science Fiction, Today and Tomorrow:* Anderson's "The Creation of Imaginary Worlds" and Clement's "The Creation of Imaginary Beings." There are also several books which, though not specifically oriented toward science fiction, provide both good surveys of contemporary science and good examples of the kind of extrapolation which science-fiction writers do. Among these are I.S. Shklovskii and Carl Sagan's *Intelligent Life in the Universe,* Stephen H. Dole's *Habitable Planets for Man,* and Poul Anderson's *Is There Life On Other Worlds?* Of course, these cover only some of the fields of interest—and all the sciences are changing too fast to rely on books alone. It's a good idea to also keep an eye on periodicals, notably *Scientific American* and more specialized sources to which it makes reference, and the fact articles in the science-fiction magazines.

All that I have said so far pertains to science fiction's scientific content *per se.* Science fiction these days usually deals at least as much with the sociological consequences of scientific and technological developments as with the developments themselves. For example, Asimov's "The Dead Past" is superficially about a time machine and Harry Harrison's *The Daleth Effect* is superficially about a space drive—but even more important in both are the questions they raise about such issues as controlled research, secret science, and the social responsibility of scientists. The answers people find or invent to such questions will have far-reaching effects on the future of both science and society. The recognition of this fact has spawned—or at least contributed to—a proliferation of courses dealing specifically with the interactions of science and society. These courses are often taught at least partly by science teachers, and certainly science fiction provides a wealth of illustrative and speculative material on the subject—probably largely untapped by the teachers of such courses. And yet the widespread development of what might be termed a "science-fictional outlook"—the deep-down recognition that tomorrow is going to be different from today, and we'd better try to look far ahead in planning today's decisions—seems to be vital for developing sane policies for the future (which begins *now*). Where better to look for help in developing a science-fictional outlook than in science fiction itself, which has had more practice than anybody else? I would hope that at least some teachers of science-and-society courses might use selected stories to help make their points. A good source of guidance in this might be the group of essays (by Frank Herbert, Theodore Sturgeon, Alan E. Nourse, Thomas N. Scortia, and Reginald Bretnor) gathered under the heading "Science Fiction, Science, and Modern Man" in Bretnor's *Science Fiction, Today and Tomorrow*.

And I would certainly hope that the development of a science-fictional outlook would be at least a significant undercurrent in any *science-fiction* course.

This brings us to the subject of actual, specific ways in which science fiction can be taught or used in teaching. Broadly speaking, a teacher can either use it as a means to illustrate and illuminate other material, or make science fiction itself the main subject and develop other things (such as scientific principles and literary techniques and values) as tools of the science-fiction trade. I've done both myself.

Probably the simplest use is to introduce occasional science-fiction stories as supplementary reading (either required or recommended) to illustrate principles taught in otherwise relatively conventional science courses. Why bother? Because science fiction is fun. (So is science, but a lot of students are a long way from believing it.) To quote that great philosopher, Jack Point (in Gilbert and Sullivan's *Yeomen of the Guard*), "He who'd make his fellow creatures wise / Should always gild the philosophic pill." Not always, maybe, but I doubt whether it ever hurts anything—and if you have some reluctant students (as most science teachers do), you have to get their attention first. A good story can make concepts sufficiently vivid and intriguing to make students want to hear the explanation—sometimes even students who would find a textbook-and-lecture presentation alone hopelessly anesthetic. Of course, if the story is *required*, under penalties and on top of an already heavy load, it may become a chore which is resented rather than enjoyed—and that defeats the purpose. For this reason, I have never *assigned* stories to be used in this way, though I have made recommendations, such as Arthur C. Clarke's "A Meeting With Medusa" in connection with Jupiter in my introductory astronomy course.

(I'll mention another science course later in which stories *are* assigned, and apparently quite successfully. But in that one the stories aren't an *additional* load, but the core reading of the course.)

My own science-fiction course is exactly that—not a *science* course at all, but a *science-fiction* course, with equal emphasis on both words and the integral relationship between them. I teach it not as a physicist, but as a science-fiction writer. As such, I consider scientific speculation an important tool of my trade, but only one of them, and the others receive at least equal attention in my course. My major objectives are to introduce students to science fiction as a field of literature and to help them develop the "science-fictional outlook" I mentioned earlier. The most effective way I know to do that is to show them as much as I can about how science-fiction writers think and work—and then make them try to do likewise.

The actual conduct of this class is highly flexible, but does follow a rather well-defined general scheme. My methods were strongly influenced by my correspondence and conversations with John W. Campbell, who did so much to shape the development of modern science fiction, both as a writer and as editor of *Astounding/Analog*. Basically, they include three main activities: reading, discussion, and writing. I'll elaborate on this, and as I do so it will probably become apparent that my ability to use the approach I do is strongly dependent on the nature of the class: a small seminar, in an "experimental" program not attached to any standard department, and with an enrollment limited to approximately fifteen.

The reading and discussion aspects of the course are closely intertwined and run concurrently throughout the semester. The basic format is something like this. Each week I assign a group of readings chosen because of some broad thematic relationship among them. For example, an assignment might consist of a single novel or a group of short stories and novelettes dealing with, say, alien viewpoints. The following week I go to class armed with a number of provocative questions more or less related to that reading assignment (not necessarily to the common theme) as starting points for two-hour discussions. The content of these discussions is wide, variable, and somewhat unpredictable. They may deal with any literary, scientific, or philosophical aspects of the stories read; other directions similar speculations might take; or points about science-fiction writing and publishing in general.

With a few exceptions (some of them noted below), I don't feel obliged to cover any specific body of factual material or critical opinion. There are far more topics of interest than we could possibly cover, and I have relatively few absolute preferences about which ones we do cover. What is essential is that the discussions should be freewheeling and thought-provoking, goading students as much as possible to do the kinds of thinking about the universe and science fiction that good editors try to get writers to do. To this end, I'm quite willing to deviate radically from my "script" if student interest leads off in some other worthwhile direction, and I'm also quite willing to play a very vigorous devil's advocate for almost any viewpoint if it will force the students to think. I also find that the more informal the surroundings are, the better it works—sitting in a classroom with neat rows of desks facing an Authority on a pedestal tends to be fatal to the kind of thing I try to do. (Which, by the way, often happens quite spontaneously in bull sessions at conventions. Draw your own conclusions.) Even with all possible precautions, it often takes the better part of the first hour to get things really rolling—which is why I have 1 two-hour meeting rather than 2 one-hour meetings per week. (Usually we take a short break near the midpoint—but in a really good session, things may get so lively that nobody wants to stop.)

Lest you get the impression that there is no method in this madness, let me hasten to point out that there is a broad underlying "plot" in our sequence of reading and discussion topics—certain topics which I'm always careful not only to include, in a more or less definite order, but to stress strongly. We start with a group of diverse, impressive short stories and novelettes (e.g., Asimov's "Nightfall," Daniel Keyes's "Flowers for Algernon," Bob Shaw's "Light of Other Days" . . .) as an introduction to real science fiction. (Many students have very nebulous and/or erroneous ideas of what science fiction is. Some equate it with Japanese monster movies; many are surprised to hear that it includes "Flowers for Algernon.") In our opening discussions, both before and after this reading assignment, we worry the question of definition: what *is* science fiction? We never definitely resolve the question, of course, but we do manage to agree on some criteria for distinguishing clear science fiction from clear fantasy (of which I usually sneak a specimen into the opening assignment and ask the students to pick it out) and from clearly labeled but blatantly pseudoscientific "science fiction" (of which examples abound in movies and television). Central among these criteria is that of *plausibility;* as soon as the students' own efforts have gotten close enough to it, I introduce the "negative impossibility" test I spoke of some pages back, and the idea of extrapolative and innovative speculation.

To convey a real feel for these ideas, I find it very helpful to use detailed examples, showing the actual reasoning behind some speculation of both types, taken from actual stories. Here, as in most cases where I want to show "behind-the-scenes" aspects of science fiction, I draw my most detailed examples from my own work. (Not that I have any particularly high regard for my own work, but I am the only author whose backgrounding eccentricities I know well enough to talk about in a very detailed way.) We devote a sizable part of an early class to the question: how might man be able to travel to the stars? There are purely extrapolative ways which (in very recent years) are even talked about in polite scientific society—e.g., suspended animation, multi-generation crews on big self-sufficient starships, flight at relativistic speeds to take advantage of time dilation. All of these have been explored repeatedly in science fiction—to name just a few: A.E. van Vogt's "Far Centaurus," Heinlein's "Universe," Alexei Panshin's *Rite of Passage*, Poul Anderson's *Tau Zero*. The last of them, relativistic flight, provides an opportunity (and an obligation) to explain some of the main points of the special theory of relativity—and that in turn provides a bridge to a discussion of the classic innovative type of solution: faster-than-light travel (FTL).

It is commonly asserted (somewhat less commonly now, since Gerald Feinberg made it fashionable to talk about "tachyons") that the theory of relativity proves that FTL is impossible. I disagree, even as a physicist. Please note carefully: I *don't* claim to know that any form of FTL is possible. I do claim that we're not yet in a position to rule it out. This is an excellent opportunity to talk about the nature of knowledge, and model-building, and Occam's razor. In my class (and this is as close as I ever get to formal lecturing) I write the equations and draw the graphs that are commonly presented as proof that FTL is impossible, and I point out why a graph of energy versus speed does in fact rule out certain *kinds* of FTL. But then I point out that the "proof" that *all* FTL is categorically impossible is completely dependent on an extrapolation beyond tested experience—an extrapolation of exactly the kind that might have been used a hundred years ago to "prove" that there was actually nothing very special about the speed of light. I show an alternate way of extrapolating the graph—without contradicting anything that's been verified experimentally (a requirement of any new or expanded theory), but allowing for the possibility of FTL. This graph, in two slightly different versions (either of which would surprise me greatly if it turned out to be correct), has provided the basis for the FTL used in several of my own stories.

I don't stop there, of course—there's one more step which I must emphatically point out. Once I've made my innovation, by specifying the assumed shape of that graph, I must live with any logical consequences it forces on me. Some of those consequences, not surprisingly, would require substantial rethinking of theoretical physics (a process which has already happened at least twice in this century alone, with relativity and quantum mechanics). They also generate important parts of the resulting stories. (And some of them, incidentally, are strikingly similar to Feinberg's conjectures about tachyons, which I hadn't yet read when I worked this out.) Let me emphasize again, I do not claim that my sample graph is the way things are, or that I know FTL is possible. But I have taken considerable pains to satisfy my "negative impossibility" requirement, and I think it is quite instructive to show my science-fiction students what that entails.

A series of later discussions in the course are geared to developing

STANLEY SCHMIDT

that science-fictional outlook, and insight into what writers do, in a variety of ways. There is a session on "From idea to story," wherein I show the class the complete evolution of a story of mine ("Lost Newton") by showing them all the working notes and editorial correspondence that finally led to the published story. The original germ of this story was a technical idea ("quasi-materials" suggested by a whimsical analogy with some research being done at Bell Labs—a radically innovative idea, but with its conceptual roots in quantum mechanics, holography, and acoustics. Onto that was grafted a sociocultural "What if?" leading to thoughts about the history and philosophy of science—e.g., the roles of Galileo, Copernicus, and Newton, and how things might have developed differently if their circumstances had been slightly altered. Also on the subject of "idea to story," I show James Gunn's movie, "Lunch With John W. Campbell: An Editor at Work," which shows Campbell, Gordon R. Dickson, and Harry Harrison working out the beginnings of *Lifeboat*.

There are situation games. By now probably everyone has seen the one, used in many contexts, in which the participants are supposed to be stranded on the Moon, are forced to make an overland trek, and must decide what to take along. I've used that one, with a slightly different emphasis than it has received in some circles. I spice my list of available items with an unorthodox extra or two, divide the class into several stranded crews, and when they have all ranked their priorities (which they must do within a time limit) the various crews cross-examine each other about their reasoning. I insist that the reasoning be scientifically sound and make myself available as consultant to provide information not given about lunar conditions, laws of physics, etc. The students quickly discover that a very important part of problem-solving is the art of recognizing what's important and asking the right questions. Some version of this problem has become so familiar to so many people that I doubt that I'll use it again, but it has served me well enough in the past that I think the technique deserves more use. For example, one semester when I was unable to get Murray Leinster's "First Contact" for the class to read, I got the idea of having them write it instead. That is, I again broke the class into small groups, posed the central problem of the story to them, and gave them some time to try to come up with Leinster's solution or a better one. (I've done this a couple of times, now; it works best when they can read the story immediately after trying to solve the problem.)

And finally, after the students have all read and discussed a variety of stories and seen something of the evolution of stories from ideas, we have an "idea session." On this occasion, everyone is to come to class with at least one idea (anywhere from barely conceived to half-baked to highly developed) which might form a basis for a story. The class and I then kick several of these around, examining them for the story potential and partially thinking out one or more ways that they might be developed.

None of these possibilities, of course, are pursued to the point of complete development in the full-group idea session. The importance of that session is to get the whole class thinking and exposed to a variety of ideas and solutions, as a bridge to the final phase of the course, writing: the production of an original science-fiction story. I have no delusions of producing science-fiction writers this way (though it could be one small step in the process for a sufficiently talented and self-motivated student). The important thing is that everybody, at least this once in his life, should go through the kind of thinking that lies behind a good science-fiction story, taking an idea and pursuing it through to some sort of conclusion. The whole-group idea forum provides a range of ideas but pursues none of them far enough to write; for his story, each individual must take one idea and think it out in enough depth to produce a tangible and hopefully worthwhile result. The conduct of this project is patterned as closely as possible on professional publishing practice, which by that time the student is somewhat familiar with. I am an editor; the student is an author. All he must do is sell me a story. (One flaw in the analogy with professional publishing: when I accept a student's story, all I can offer him is a passing grade, which no known bank has been willing to cash.)

Early in the game—shortly before midsemester—each student has an individual conference in which he and I discuss the story he intends to write. During this, I try to point out (mainly by asking questions) any holes or additional potentialities I see in his ideas, and work them down to a concrete situation and characters. By the time he leaves, we are agreed on a more or less definite direction the story's going to take. He still has lots of work to do, but at least he knows roughly how he's going to direct his efforts. By another deadline (still well before the end of the semester) he submits the story—*not* a rough draft, I keep insisting, but the best effort he can produce. If I think it's good enough—meaning I think it might have a chance on the professional market—I'll accept it and recommend that the student submit it to somebody who pays real money. On rare occasions I have even done this, thereby completing the student's writing requirement on the first try (though for some reason such students have tended to be reluctant to try to sell their wares). Usually, however, I return the story with a rejection letter posing questions and/or suggestions about how it might be made acceptable, and pose a deadline for a rewrite. The rewrites are rarely of professional quality either, of course, and I don't seriously expect them to be. But I do insist on seeing a real effort in that direction. How much *science* is involved in this depends very much on the type of story, but very often there is some. To give a rather crude example, a story containing a planet with a "dense atmosphere of hydrogen and oxygen" will not be accepted no matter how beautifully written it is.

STANLEY SCHMIDT

The course just described is pretty obviously slanted to show science fiction from a writer's point of view. I think there are definite values in this, and it's a slant that students don't often get to see. In general, both they and I enjoy it and get something out of it. However, the problems of writing are such that I wouldn't recommend that quite the same approach be attempted by anyone without some science-fiction writing experience—preferably professional—behind him. I don't think I could have done it creditably ten years ago, and I don't think I do it as well now as I should ten years hence. I have spent so much time on it here simply because it's the approach I am personally most familiar with, and others may find some elements of it helpful.

What other options are available to a science teacher who's not a fiction writer? Gerald P. Calame has done an enthusiastically received seminar for senior physics majors at the U.S. Naval Academy, based on "The Science in Science Fiction." Briefly, his approach consists of reading an assigned story each week, related to one or more definite scientific themes, following which designated students are responsible for leading a discussion of the scientific theme on which the week's story was based. He has described his course in considerable detail in an article in the *American Journal of Physics* (February, 1973), which I recommend to anyone contemplating this type of course. Among other things, this article includes an extensive listing of stories used, their background themes, and lists of references dealing with those themes. Not surprisingly, the authors and stories chosen fall heavily into the "hard-core" extrapolative category, with such writers as Poul Anderson, Hal Clement, and Larry Niven prominently represented. For example, Niven's "Neutron Star" is listed, with five references in *Scientific American* and *Science* dealing with the background themes of tidal forces, neutron stars, and gravitational red shift. I can recommend one recent anthology as a valuable addition to Calame's listing of sources for such a course: Isaac Asimov's *Where Do We Go From Here?* This is a collection edited with just this sort of use in mind—stories high in both entertainment value and scientific interest, accompanied by Asimov's commentary and discussion questions and a list of background references.

Both Calame's course and mine are small seminars, his for senior physics majors, mine for a heterogeneous mix of students of all undergraduate years and majors. Both have found the demand at least equal to the supply. What advice can I offer to a teacher at a large university or high school who might have to face a hundred or more students at once? I find myself on somewhat shaky ground here; I have no personal experience with trying to teach science fiction to such a crowd. I'm afraid I would find the prospect somewhat intimidating; I'm sure I would have to part with the most characteristic features of my own present course to accommodate such a class. And yet there will be places where the job must be done—and good teachers will find ways to do it well. Hopefully they are already doing so; I just haven't been there to watch.

One obvious possibility is to use the same kind of subject-story relationship that Calame does, but with the format adapted to the lecture hall rather than the seminar room. That is, let the stories speak for themselves, and then lecture on the science behind them—hopefully with some opportunity for audience participation, if only questions from the floor. This method would seem, in fact, to be rather widely adaptable. Many of the same stories could be read and enjoyed by students at many levels, from high school all the way through college, and the level of the lectures adjusted to that of the audience.

But there are pitfalls. I think it would be especially important in such a class that the lecturing be done with concern not only for accuracy and clarity but for "showmanship." Lectures (including my own, I fear) can be deadly dull. Using stories helps liven things up and infuse interest in the material—but then, in a sense, the lectures are competing for interest with the stories. If they don't compete well, the students may quit listening; if your lectures are bad enough, they may even quit reading. If you try to compensate by *forcing* them to do the work—by such devices as some of the kinds of tests that are easily given to large groups—you alienate them even more. All of which just drives you further and further from the original good idea of using their *interest* in science fiction to get them to learn.

Such things can happen, I think, no matter how good the readings and the teacher's intentions. That possibility would be one of my major concerns if I found myself giving such a course. The decreased personal contact with such numbers makes it even harder than with a small group to tell when such things are happening—so I would make a special effort to get feedback and to be sensitive and responsive to any danger signs.

But as long as I did these things, I see no reason why I should not be able to make such a course work. And my chances would be significantly enhanced, I think, if I consciously reminded myself now and then that science fiction is for fun.

And courses about it—however educational—should be fun, too.

STANLEY SCHMIDT

SCIENCE FICTION IN A COMPUTERS & SOCIETY COURSE

BY PATRICIA S. WARRICK

This essay is illuminating. Reaching far beyond the limits of any course in computers and society, it is a broad philosophic exploration of a major SF theme. Though there have been stories enough about computers—generally evil computers—we've hardly begun to sense the social impact of our fast-evolving thinking machines, even in SF. Patricia S. Warrick is a professor of English at the University of Wisconsin-Fox Valley, Menasha, Wisconsin, with an undergraduate degree in biochemistry. She has co-edited SF anthologies for classroom use and written essays for Critique *and* Extrapolation *as well as a book,* The Cybernetic Imagination in Science Fiction, *published by MIT Press in 1980. She is currently working on a study of Philip K. Dick.*

At the risk of sounding negative, let me begin by stating there are many things science fiction cannot do in implementing the objectives of a course in Computers and Society. The solid foundation of the course must be a rigorous text in Computers and Society, and lectures that augment and illuminate the textual material. But there are a few things science fiction can do, and these things it does very well. Consequently, the possibilities of using science fiction as supplementary reading are worth exploring.

Courses in Computers and Society characteristically attract both students in the hard sciences, such as biology, chemistry, physics, etc., and in the social sciences and the humanities. The students must familiarize themselves, in general terms, with the *functions* of the computer and also its *applications*. The objectives of the course, once all students are acquainted with the functions and uses of the computer, are to help them become sensitive to the present and possible *social effects*—both short term and long term—of current computer applications. Alternative applications to present uses are also explored. Next, a dialogue hopefully will occur between the students in the sciences, social sciences, and humanities—aimed at defining *value systems*. The *actual value system* underlying current computer usage is examined. Further, an *ideal value system,* that ought to determine the uses man makes of technology, is formulated.

Of what use is science fiction in accomplishing the objectives of the course? First, admittedly, it is a gimmick—a device to make the course more attractive to the prospective student. Science fiction is popular literature; it is fun. I feel this use of science fiction to attract the student to the course is defensible. The course is a relatively new one, and usually does not have the sort of established clientele who take the course because it fulfills a requirement. The humanities or social sciences student, who often shies from courses in mathematics and the hard sciences, may find the course less threatening if part of the reading is science fiction. On the other hand, science students very often are already enthusiastic readers of science fiction. It is a good vehicle to attract their interest, and from it they can move to nonfictional consideration of social problems and value systems. Such considerations lie within the boundaries of the social sciences and the humanities, areas a science major often feels are outside his field and do not interest him. Science fiction may therefore function as a bridge between the two fields.

Beyond being a marketing device for the course, what can science fiction do? It can permit the use of a more rigorous and demanding text without frightening the student away. Some texts now available for the course are, unfortunately, bland and simplistic in their approach. They are presumably pitched at this level on the assumption that otherwise they will be over the heads of, and consequently threatening to, the non-science major who considers taking the course. It would seem desirable to avoid this superficiality. Choose instead a rigorous text in which the subject and the issues are explored in depth, and then lighten the reading with a few carefully selected science-fiction novels.

The use of science fiction also allows a team-teaching approach in the course. A literature instructor, for instance, familiar with the use of fiction for social criticism, can handle this aspect of the lectures and discussions.

Beyond these points, the greatest value of science fiction to the course is its effectiveness in presenting the issues and dramatizing the conflicts that arise as computer technology expands in society. Science fiction explores the individual's loss of privacy and freedom, and his dehumanization in a mass technological culture. It examines the impact of automation and increased leisure. It considers the significance of bureaucratic power augmented by computer technology. All of these issues should be treated in a course in Computers and Society.

Novels can serve as a starting point for the vigorous debate that, one hopes, will occur between student and students, and student and

PATRICIA S. WARRICK

instructor. Ideally, science fiction can stimulate that discussion—increasing its breadth, depth, and originality. Science-fiction stories start with the question "What if?", proposing a condition or setting other than the presently existing one. They present a spectrum of answers to the question or problem. Any alternative the imagination creates can be worth examining. Reading science fiction often stimulates the student to think more imaginatively in problem solving. He begins to consider the alternatives other than those he has been conditioned to expect may be possible and desirable.

Science fiction can present the social issues and problems with much more power than can statistics or abstract discussions in a text. The student faced with generalized statements often offers little response. But the story presents a concrete example—particular people in a particular situation—and the student finds it easier to respond to a particular example than to a generalization. Further, the characters in the story hold certain values. The plot explores what happens when those values are either frustrated or fulfilled. Thus, the story works as a model of a value system.

Using formal models or analogies to help visualize something that cannot be directly observed is common in science—for example, the model of the atom. Literature also uses models—symbols or interacting sets of images—although they are usually created by intuitive rather than logical thought processes. These images model mental and emotional states, relations between individuals, social systems, etc. The literary model of a system, granted it is less formal and precise than a mathematical model, is a functional one for the purposes of the course. It is a dynamic model that can picture changing states.

The literary model works particularly well in modeling value systems. The student studying the model can grasp more readily the effect that a value system has on the individual's reaction to social change. As he examines the values of the protagonist of the story and either accepts or rejects them, he defines his own values. He explores the values of a culture set on another planet, for example, and notes that because of an environment different from that on Earth, people have had to develop a different value system to survive. He begins to understand that many values are relative, not absolute. Valuation is a dynamic process; value systems are not eternal. As technological change occurs, the value system may need to respond with change.

The instructor discussing values in general terms finds himself in a difficult position. On the one hand, if he tries to present objectively and nonjudgmentally the positions of conflicting value systems, he seems guilty of being neutral about the uses of technology. His objectivity implies that one need not take a stance. On the other hand, if he argues in favor of the value system he espouses, he seems to be imposing his view on the students and violating their right to make independent choices. The use of science fiction to model values solves this difficulty. The instructor can lead a discussion about the implications of the value system the protagonist endorses, and still maintain an objective stance himself. Thus he can withhold expression of his own value system until the class has explored through discussion the alternative value systems.

Limitations of Available Material

Before we look in detail at fictional material that can be used in the course, let us spell out what science fiction *cannot do*. It is generally of little aid to the student in learning how computers *function*. As the narrator says in Robert Heinlein's *The Moon Is a Harsh Mistress,* "Explaining how a computer works to a layman is as difficult as explaining sex to a virgin." Science fiction has not surmounted that difficulty. Many novels take the function of the computer as a given and proceed from there. This is probably a virtue because too much of the fiction that portrays in detail the function of the computer is inaccurate in its descriptions. The knowledgeable computer science student can have fun noting the inaccuracies, but the student without this background is only confused. In my reading suggestions, I have tried to avoid novels with gross inaccuracies in descriptions of functions.

Moving beyond computer functions to computer *applications,* we find all varieties of present and possible applications of computers portrayed in science fiction. But to use science fiction to acquaint the student with the wide range of computer applications would require an anthology of short stories collected specifically with this objective in mind. None is available. When the student's science-fiction reading in the course is limited to three or four novels, he cannot be exposed to a comprehensive view of computer applications.

Given that science fiction can only serve as supplementary reading, two factors limit even further its potential as a teaching tool in the course. First, much of the good fiction portraying the computer and automation is not available. There are well over 100 novels and probably four times as many short stories in which the computer plays a crucial role in the plot development, or in which the setting—critical to the story—results from automation. But the bulk of the short stories originally appeared in science-fiction magazines and so are not generally available today. Groff Conklin has edited an excellent anthology, *Science Fiction Thinking Machines* (1954), reprinting stories about computers and electronically operated robots; but it is out of print in paperback. *Inside Information: Computers in Fiction,* (1977) edited by Abbe Moshowitz, a recent anthology of fiction about computers, is currently available. Moshowitz, an associate professor of computer science at the University of British Columbia, designed *Inside Information* so that it can be used in a Computers and Society course. However, its effectiveness in the classroom is limited by the large number of selections and the use of excerpts from novels. Students would find the thirty pieces of fiction difficult to recall, and additionally the excerpts would make dull reading because the dramatic tension is vitiated when a piece is sliced from a novel and read out of context. *Inside Information* is more useful for the instructor, providing brief essays by the editor on various topics, a good overview of fiction about computers, and a comprehensive bibliography. I will limit my suggestions for student reading to novels and only those currently available in paperback, since hardcover prices seem too high to ask the student to pay for supplementary reading material.

The second factor limiting the potential fiction as a teaching tool is the negative view of the computer presented in much of the novel-length fiction. Two dark visions keep appearing. In one, the computer replaces man as a worker. Resentfully, he rises up in a modern Luddite rebellion and smashes the computer as the weaving looms were smashed by the workers in nineteenth century England. In the other view, the computer, godlike in its power, tries to enslave man, reducing him to a robot servant. Such negative views do not aid the student in exploring positive alternatives in future computer usage.

The prevailing negative image of the computer in science fiction undoubtedly reflects the growing distrust of science and technology that has occurred since World War II. First the atomic bomb, then pollution, overpopulation, and other ecological disasters have led to a loss of optimism. Faith in science and technology, marking the nineteenth and early twentieth century, has begun to erode. This change is reflected in fiction, where dystopian literature has replaced the earlier utopian writings. Much of the negative response toward technology generally has been directed against the computer—probably unfairly, since it is not the only technology altering man's social and physical environment. But the computer as a discrete entity is more visible. It is also, perhaps, more threatening because it replaces mental rather than physical labor, as earlier machines have done; and man has always regarded his mental capacity as his unique gift.

Science fiction portraying computers and computerized robots is much more recent than science fiction generally, which dates back to the nineteenth century. The first story to portray a computer was John W. Campbell's "When the Atoms Failed" (1930), but more stories about computers did not appear until just prior to World War II, and they were not abundant until the fifties. By that time, dystopian literature began to predominate. This may explain somewhat why so many novels display a negative attitude toward the computer. Another reason is that twentieth century literature generally portrays the individual struggling to come to terms with and survive in mass society. Since computers until very recently have been owned by organizations and bureaucracies, not individuals, the economics of the situation puts computers on the side of the forces that oppose the individual. Very recent buying trends, as a result of minicomputers, are beginning to change this pattern, but generally the change has not yet been reflected in the fiction.

The first work of fiction to be published describing a robot that is clearly computer controlled is Harl Vincent's "Rex," written in 1934. It was followed by two short stories both benign in their view toward machine intelligence. The robot is beneficent and subservient to man. Lester del Rey's "Helen O'Loy" (1938) is a story of a robot female household servant. She is so kind, helpful, and faithful that her owner falls in love with her. They live a long and happy life together. Asimov's first robot story, "Robbie" (1940) describes a robot who is a baby-sitter for an eight-year-old girl. The robot is gentle and dependable, and as the story climaxes, he saves her life. "Robbie" was the first of three dozen stories Asimov has written about robots and computers, and in all of them he gives a very positive picture of the potential of computers. His work is a refreshing exception to the generally bad press computers have been given by science-fiction writers.

Let us look now at the available science fiction and how it can be used in the course. Reading suggestions in five different categories follow, with a summary of the content of each novel, and also a brief indication of the social issues dramatized.

The Negative View of a Computerized Society

I think the negative view of most science-fiction novels about the computer is significant, and should not be ignored in selecting fiction for the course. The most productive approach would be to identify this negativity by beginning with a dystopian novel. Such a novel can work effectively in defining the emotional response the layman tends to have toward the computer. It is new, strange, powerful. He typically reacts with fear. He has had unpleasant encounters with the computer through errors in billings, magazine subscriptions that could not be terminated, etc. He has turned from a name into a number because that is the form in which the computer can most easily process his records. Automation of work may cause the loss of his employment. His irritation is understandable, as are his fears. Further, some of his fears are justified. The development of data banks does threaten his privacy; the modeling of social structures on machine images does result in dehumanization.

Three dystopian novels embody powerfully the fears and apprehensions that people have about computers. Any one works well in class. They are Yevgeny Zamyatin's *We*, Kurt Vonnegut's *Player Piano*, and Ira Levin's *This Perfect Day*. Each novel presents a future society where the masses are controlled by technocrats who enforce conformity. Depersonalization, alienation, and uniformity reign. Privacy has been lost. Man has been rendered obsolete by an intelligent, infallible machine.

PATRICIA S. WARRICK

We, the earliest of the three novels, has become a literary classic. It was written in Russia in 1921, but has never been published there. While the computer as such does not appear in the novel, the society protrayed is a totally programmed one, entirely based on numbers and the logic of mathematical reasoning. Homage is paid to The Machine. People have numbers, not names. *We* is good, and *I* (the individual and his imagination) is evil. The perfect state has been achieved, where there is stability, peace, order, perfection, reason, and—presumably—happiness. But the narrator, D-503, is unhappy because he comes to recognize the violation of human nature when the individual is programmed to function on a clockwork schedule. He cannot function merely as a standardized part in a giant machine. Nor can he function only as a reasoning creature, for man is also a creature of feeling and intuition and creativity. A revolution finally occurs as a little group of dissidents, headquartered in the green natural world beyond the wall that encloses the perfect city, attempts to assert its right to poetry, intuition, and the creative imagination. These have been banned in the "perfect" state built according to reason. They cannot be permitted, for imagination creates new forms, and changes result. The revolution is speedily put down by the authorities, who perform lobotomies on all numbers to excise their imagination. The novel is very powerful and very well written. It is particularly interesting for a Computers and Society course because Zamyatin was educated as an engineer and he makes extensive use of mathematical imagery in the novel. The complexity of meaning, the irony, and the symbolism in *We* demand a rigorous reader. Bright students become enthusiastic about the novel as they discover its rich meanings, but less able students may dislike it.

Another dystopian novel, similar to *We* in many respects, is Ira Levin's *This Perfect Day* (1970). Levin's dystopian future society is entirely run by computers. Each person is assigned to a specific rôle—as determined and programmed by the computer—so that everyone will be happy and society will be serene. Each individual voluntarily goes for a drug treatment whenever he realizes he is deviating from his assigned norm and beginning to be "different." Chip, the protagonist, decides to avoid the treatment, and his individuality develops to the point that he plans a revolution against the system. He gathers a small group of followers who succeed in blowing up the computers and over-throwing the technocrats who use them.

Both *This Perfect Day* and *We* explore the tension between freedom and happiness. If man is free to choose what he will, wrong decisions—producing unhappiness—will occur on occasion. The exercise of free will thus produces unhappiness, but paradoxically, man is not happy if he does not have freedom. Both novels also explore the individual's struggle to maintain his uniqueness in a totalitarian bureaucracy.

In *Player Piano* (1952) Kurt Vonnegut, who once worked in the public relations department of General Electric at Schenectady, New York, uses irony to make his social criticism. He portrays an electronic utopia set in the near future. The novel achieves its power because Vonnegut creates his future society with great restraint. He has done only a small amount of extrapolation from the present, and so it is easy to believe that something like he describes could happen. Through automation and the resultant increase in productivity, poverty has disappeared and wars have ceased. The good life seems to have been achieved, but we soon find this is true only for those with high IQ's; they are the elite who run the bureaucracy. For those with an IQ of under 140, there is nothing to do, and they can find no meaning in their lives. Although unemployed, they do not suffer physical deprivation because they are provided with the necessities of life, and even a few luxuries. But they feel useless and bored, and dream about the good old days when they worked on the production line.

The unemployed, along with a few sympathetic engineers, lead a machine-smashing rebellion, but it is halfhearted and ends in defeat. As the story ends, people are sorting around through the wrecked machines looking for workable parts so they can begin to rebuild them. Vonnegut pessimistically seems to suggest that despite the resentment of the unemployed citizens toward the machines, they have been enmeshed in a machine world for so long that they can conceive of no other way of life.

Any one of these three novels dramatizes effectively the fears of machines and automation that currently haunt many people. Creating a mental model or image as they do, the novels can be a good starting point for a student discussion about the causes of these fears and whether they are justified. Each novel defines the humanistic values of individuality, freedom, creativity, and work; and shows the resultant anxiety of the individual when these values are violated.

Each novel, intentionally or otherwise, makes the point that machine smashing is no answer. Given the problems of our overpopulated, polluted planet, with most nations already industrialized or moving in that direction, a return to a pastoral culture is not possible. The answer is not to destroy technology but to humanize it. These dystopian novels model only the problems, not possible answers, but those problems are presented vividly and memorably.

The Positive View of Computers
Having started with dystopian fiction and used it as the springboard to a discussion of the causes underlying the current antimachine sentiments, we can move on to literature that has a more positive view of the computer. One of the best books is Isaac Asimov's *I, Robot*. This is a collection of nine short stories originally published in the magazines between 1940 and 1950. Asimov, who has a doctorate in bio-

PATRICIA S. WARRICK

chemistry, is optimistic about the positive potential of science and technology; and this attitude is displayed in all the stories in *I, Robot.* Two of the stories, "Escape" and "The Evitable Conflict," are about computers; the others are about robots, which Asimov regards as mobile computers. The stories trace the development of computers and robots. In the first story, "Robbie," a rather crude robot is portrayed. In subsequent stories the robots become more sophisticated. In the final story, a very complex computer capable of worldwide economic planning has been developed, and is presented as the hope of mankind. The first story is set on Earth, the middle stories are set on other planets because anticomputer sentiment on Earth has banned further development here, and the final stories return to an Earth setting, where with the passage of time the anticomputer sentiment has dissipated.

The stories are interesting for three reasons. First, they are all grounded in sound science and logic. Second, the stories follow a problem-solving approach: a problem is first defined; then as much data as possible is collected and evaluated; next, a hypothesis is erected, providing a basis for a set of predictions about the solution of the problem; finally the predictions are tested. If they are incorrect, the process must be re-examined until the difficulty is discovered. This, of course, is the scientific method. Third, the stories are interesting because they contain the famous Three Laws of Robotics formulated by Asimov. First, a robot may not injure a human being, or through inaction allow a human being to come to harm. Second, a robot must obey the orders given it by human beings except where such orders would conflict with the First Law. Third, a robot must protect its own existence as long as such protection does not conflict with the First or Second Law. As Dr. Susan Calvin, the protagonist of the stories, points out, these Three Laws—with which all the computers are programmed—are only a restatement of principles that many of the world's ethical and religious systems are built on. The laws provide an interesting starting point for a class discussion of morality in the use of computers.

Some of the stories in *I, Robot* are better than others, although all are entertaining. Two are particularly interesting in the computer applications they picture. "Evidence" is the story of a political campaign and election in which one of the candidates is accused of being a robot. This raises the interesting question of how artificial intelligence is to be differentiated from human intelligence. Also raised is the question of whether a computer, programmed with all the available data, might be able to make better political decisions than a human. "The Evitable Conflict" gives a very positive image of a future world stabilized economically and politically with the aid of a computer. There is no unemployment, overproduction, or shortages; and so war and famine are unknown. The Machine is in control of mankind. But according to Asimov's view, its control is more benign than the runaway economic and social forces that had dominated mankind during earlier periods.

Asimov's recent anthology *The Bicentennial Man* (1976) contains six stories about computers and robots, including the award-winning title story, "The Bicentennial Man," one of his finest pieces of writing. Several of the stories in this anthology pair with stories in *I, Robot*, but the later stories picture artificial intelligence as having evolved far beyond its level in the earlier fiction. Now robots possess intuition, emotion, and the ability to make judgments, and the possibility of machine intelligence being both superior to and likely to dominate human intelligence is introduced.

Specific Computer Applications and Their Social Effects

The third group of novels is less broad in scope than the dystopian novels we examined in the first category. They do not draw a picture of an entire society, but instead explore a specific computer application and the possible social risks of that use. The group is rather extensive, and the choice of a novel or two depends on the instructor's particular interests.

One application portrayed is the use of the computer in the military. The first electronic computers were developed during WW II to caculate artillery trajectory tables. After the war the Air Force developed a defense system with its nerve center inside Cheyenne Mountain near Colorado Springs. The military attempted to keep these developments secret, but science-fiction tales began to appear picturing this computerized warfare preparation and what its consequences for society might be. Mordecai Roshwald's *Level 7* (1959) is the diary of Officer X-127, assigned to the lowest level of a military bomb shelter built underground to house military personnel and equipment. His duty is to stand guard at the Pushbuttons, a machine devised to rocket instant atomic destruction toward the enemy. The pushbuttons are numbered 1, 2, 3, and 4; each subsequent button allows a larger rocket charge to be deployed. Button 4 releases enough weapons to assure final and complete devastation of the enemy. Because of an equipment error, the mechanism is triggered, and the enemy is wiped out. But before this happens, the enemy defense system is activated, and it obliterates all above ground in the United States. Radioactive fallout after the bombings makes life on Earth impossible. Eventually all those underground perish when their power system fails.

Eugene Burdick and Harvey Wheeler's *Fail-Safe*, published three years later, is a novel very similar to *Level 7*. It portrays two automated military machines—Russian and American—poised and ready to launch a pushbutton war. Due to a mechanical error, the United States system is activated. Even though the error is detected almost immediately, the automatic attack system has been set in motion and cannot be stopped. American planes fly to bomb Moscow. The President phones the Russian Premier to advise him of the tragic mechanical error. He hopes to avert a counterattack by the Russians. But the Premier is skeptical of the explanation. Only by ordering the bombing of New York City can the President offset the bombing of Moscow and avoid a Russian reprisal that would mean total war.

Both *Level 7* and *Fail-Safe* explore an automated warfare system that causes a devastating catastrophe when the system malfunctions. Two other novels also deal with mechanized systems, but they move beyond the military to explore civilian systems and their failure. The first novel is very short and a very old one, but it is one of the greats. E.M. Forster's *The Machine Stops* (1909) does not contain a computer *per se,* but does portray a fully automated society. Passivity and alienation affect all the citizens. Having become fully dependent on the machine, they are unable to cope when the machine fails and the system collapses.

Christopher Hodder-Williams's *Fistful of Digits* (1968) is a recent and realistic presentation of the same theme—the mechanical failure of the system. It is a story of the development of a gigantic network of electronic equipment which operates to control dams and most other mechanized functions of society. The system becomes so complex that no one really understand it. When it begins to malfunction, people are powerless to correct it. They have developed so much faith in electronic technology that they have lost belief in their own capacity to cope.

Another use of computers is by political candidates campaigning for election to office. Marketing expertise combined with computer analysis of voter reactions seems likely to revolutionize the electoral process in the United States. A novel providing an excellent picture of this radical change being effected by the computer is Eugene Burdick's *The 480* (1964). Burdick describes a presidential election campaign in which the campaign manager designs strategies on the basis of simulations made with a computer. Using 480 categories of voter types, the simulations can predict the positive or negative reactions of these "uncommon" or uncommitted voters on a variety of issues. Party-line Republicans and Democrats are ignored since their votes are already committed. The campaign strategies are aimed at the uncommitted votes, and are planned to raise only the issues where, according to the simulations, a positive response is certain. Often these issues are minor. The public debate of major issues crucial to the current national and international situations is ignored. Burdick's novel is in fictional form, but based on strategies already being used on a small scale when he wrote the book. Burdick, who is a political scientist, sees a violation of the democratic election process in this technique. The novel is a powerful example of two things: the radical change in social processes that can occur as a result of computer applications, and the manipulation of the unsuspecting general public, uneducated in the possibilities of electronic technology.

The Steel Crocodile (1970), written by D.G. Compton, also portrays the massive control and manipulation that becomes possible with the aid of the computer. The steel crocodile is the metaphor for science, biting away at the unknown and continually producing more knowledge, regardless of what the results of that knowledge may be when utilized by technology. The novel is set in England, where the Colindale Institute—with the aid of a supercomputer—secretly files and correlates all the research findings of the European community. A key group of scientists then privately decides whether or not certain research should be discontinued because its consequences seem to be at odds with what the group defines as the good of society. Their recommendation to a government that it withdraw its financial support from a project can effectively terminate further research. The conflict in the novel develops when a sociologist joins the group of scientists and then develops moral qualms about whether the advance of science should be controlled. This novel provides a good starting place for a discussion of the moral responsibility of the scientist for the fruits of his research.

The 480 and *The Steel Crocodile* both examine the control and manipulation of groups of people made practical with the use of the computer. Michael Crichton's *The Terminal Man* (1972) pictures one individual and the way the computer is used to control him. Harry Benson is a computer scientist. Following a head injury, he experiences periodic epileptic seizures during which he becomes violent. A team of neurosurgeons connects his brain to a computer that, theoretically, will control his behavior and prevent the seizures. But rather than being cured, Benson turns into a violent killer as a result of the surgery, and finally meets a tragic death. The point the story makes particularly well is that mere good intentions are not enough in developing new technology. The motivation of the neurosurgeons is above reproach: they want to help Benson. But the outcome of their experimentation is quite opposite from what they had intended.

Another area covered in a Computers and Society course is the philosophical and social implications of the development of artificial intelligence. Machine intelligence is explored in a number of science-fiction works. The novel that provides the best vehicle for a class discussion is Frank Herbert's *Destination: Void* (1965). (A revised edition of the novel was published recently.) Herbert creates a drama on a spaceship that is clearly analogous to the situation of man on Earth. Herbert is very positive in his attitude toward the development of artificial intelligence. In the novel, a spaceship, carrying 3,000 dormant passengers in hibernation tanks and manned by a crew of four scientists and engineers, is sent out on a space colonizing venture. A major mechanical failure creates a crisis that can only be survived if high-level artificial intelligence is developed. The questions raised by the crew are two: Can it be done? If possible, should it be done? One crew member is trained in computer science, another in biology, the third in chemistry, and the fourth in psychology. The psychologist is also the chaplain of the ship, and he presents the arguments that oppose the development of artificial intelligence. There are limits beyond which man should not go in pursuing knowledge. Development of intelligence superior to man's is one of them. Further, the intelligence may turn out to be an uncontrollable Frankenstein's monster that might as well use its power against man as for him. But despite the chaplain's arguments, the position of the computer scientist finally prevails: high-level machine intelligence is necessary for the survival of the spaceship *Earthling,* and so its development—granted it involves risk taking—must proceed.

Arthur C. Clarke's *2001: A Space Odyssey* (1968) is also a good portrayal of artificial intelligence. HAL, a very complex computer with six independent power systems, becomes schizoid because he has been programmed with a secret that must not be revealed to the crew members of the spaceship: he is to kill them when the space flight has proceeded to a certain point. Midway through the novel, most of HAL's systems are destroyed by a crew member, and thereafter the computer plays no significant part in the story. Hence, the role of artificial intelligence is not as major in this novel as in Herbert's *Destination: Void.* Both novels follow a pattern that is almost a convention in science fiction drawing a picture of high-level artificial intelligence: the computers are presented as possessing consciousness and self-awareness.

A very recent and very impressive study of the development of artificial intelligence is James Hogan's *The Two Faces of Tomorrow* (1979). Currently employed by Digital Equipment Corporation as a Senior Sales Training Consultant, Hogan is thoroughly knowledgeable in the field of computers. The substance and accuracy of the material he provides is impressive; however, the length of the novel (392 pages) would seem excessive to many students. A more workable novel for use in the course is Hogan's *The Genesis Machine,* to be discussed in the next section.

The development of high-level machine intelligence is not likely to cause an immediate social problem since it lies well in the future. Two problems are much more immediate and pressing: 1) the threatened loss of privacy through the development of data banks, and 2) the possible loss of human vitality and creativity as more and more of man's work is taken over by machines. Unfortunately, the science fiction most effective in presenting these problems is not easily accessible. On the first, data banks, Kendell Foster Crossen's *Year of Consent* (1954) and Poul Anderson's classic short story "Sam Hall" (1953) both give powerful portrayals of societies where the government, with the aid of electronic files, totally controls the lives of its citizens. Crossen's novel is out of print. "Sam Hall" is reprinted in Conklin's *SF*

Thinking Machines, currently available only in hard covers. On the second issue, loss of vitality and creativity, two lighthearted satires deserve mention even though they are not currently in print. Shepherd Mead's *The Big Ball of Wax* (1954) creates a computerized future society where the only role that remains for the passive masses of people is to consume pleasure. Finally, the ultimate technology for pleasure consumption is produced. A technique is perfected for recording on tape the pleasure sensations in the brain of a consuming individual. When this tape is played for another individual—hooked up to sensitive equipment—he has the same pleasure sensations without actually consuming. *The Silver Eggheads* (1961) by Fritz Leiber is equally humorous and as entertaining as *The Big Ball of Wax.* In its future society giant computers write bland novels, robots perform most functions, and humans have little to do. The novel writers in the society merely tend the "word machine," to give a colorful human image of authors to the general public. When the writers rise up and smash the computers, planning to write their own books, they find they have lost the ability to be creative. Both of these novels are so effective in their social criticism that one hopes they will be reprinted.

The Potential of Computer Technology

As we look back over the fictional works I have cited, we see that most of it is better at pointing out negative social effects of computer applications than in portraying positive uses. The fiction extrapolates from present possibilities of undesirable effects rather than creating new and positive possibilities. One of the most effective uses of science fiction in the course may well be to point very powerfully to our present predicament: we are better at defining problems than at finding solutions to them. We seem to be experiencing a failure of the imagination and the spirit. Criticism is certainly the precondition of a change for the better, but in itself it is not creative.

Problem definition is, finally, self-defeating if it is not countered with creative solutions. If we are to have an improved future, we must begin to have positive visions of what it will be like. Frightening as technology may seem, our culture is so inextricably bound up with it that we cannot return to a pastoral society. Smashing computers, the resolution of the plot in too much science fiction, is not a solution. Using computers creatively to solve problems is. Given our present situation—the growing world population, finite resources, and the interrelatedness of all aspects of our technological social system—the long-range planning necessary to world survival cannot be accomplished without the computer.

One of the few novels presenting this positive and comprehensive view of computer usage is Robert Heinlein's *The Moon Is a Harsh Mistress* (1966). The story is set on the Moon where an underground colony—whose environment is regulated by computers—has been established by Earth. The leaders of the colony recognize that recycling of all resources and careful ecological balance are necessary for long-term survival. But their resources are being exploited by Earth, and this exploitation will eventually make life on the Moon impossible. The narrator of the story, Manuel Davis, is a highly skilled computer technician. He joins with two other persons, a political scientist called the Professor and a woman named Wyoming. They organize a revolution and lead a war of independence against the Earth. Manuel turns to the computer (or more precisely, a computer program), nicknamed Mike, for assistance, and Mike becomes the real leader and decision maker in the war. He computes ballistics data and controls rocket flights in the struggle against Earth. He aids in planning; he computes the probabilities of success as various alternatives are considered; he registers votes when an election is held on the Moon. The eventual success of the Moon colony's struggle for survival results from the creative use the leaders make of the computer.

The novel is not primarily about a computer. It is political in its theme: a study of the organization and implementation of a revolution. But its setting is a technological future world where computers are a vital part of the political process, both national and international. It is comprehensive and accurate in its portrayal of the computer, and very positive in its view of the potential of computer technology.

James Hogan's *The Genesis Machine* (1978) is unquestionably the most powerful novel available to use in discussing the potential of the computer in man's future. The narrative portrays the struggles of a young physicist and computer scientist to maintain his integrity against the pressures of the military, who demand that he utilize his knowledge and expertise to create more deadly weapons. The setting in a large research center is drawn with detail and accuracy, and the discussion of contemporary astronomy and physics is substantial and interesting. Critical opinion rightly hails Hogan as a powerful new writer in the tradition of Isaac Asimov and Arthur Clarke. In the innovative resolution of the complex but well-handled plot, the computer is used not to make but to end war. The student, given a bit of help with the astronomy and physics if he is not a science major, will read the novel with great interest and in the process will get a good picture of the current use of computers in research. He will also be interested in debating the question of the responsibility the scientist has for the use or misuse of the knowledge and technology produced by his research. If only one novel were to be used in the course, *The Genesis Machine* would certainly be that novel.

Philosophical Issues

Do we live in a probabilistic or a deterministic universe? If the latter, computers can effectively be used to simulate and predict the future. If the former, is man's intuition more effective? Robert Silverberg's well-written novel, *The Stochastic Man* (1975), explores these questions and provides a good springboard for discussion of logical versus intuitive modes of thought.

Is man's brain nothing more than a "meat machine" as some computer scientists claim, or does a "ghost" in the human machine make man forever different from a robot? As man increasingly utilizes computers in his society, does he risk turning himself into a mechanical creature? Philip K. Dick dramatizes these questions with a brilliance no other writer achieves, a brilliance that has earned him the reputation of being probably the finest science-fiction writer alive today. He explores these questions in several of his novels, but the best one to use as a teaching device is his *Do Androids Dream of Electric Sheep?* (1968). In this post-holocaust world, man has destroyed most life forms in his environment and built electronic animals as replacements. Robots in human form (Dick refers to them as androids) are used for a variety of tasks. Because their level of intelligence is so high, they become resentful of being used as slaves and turn against man. The novel thus pits man and robot—indistinguishable in appearance and action—against each other. This structure allows Dick to explore the question of whether a real difference exists between man and high-level machine intelligence. Avoiding tedious philosophical discussion, Dick dramatizes the issues in a powerful story full of suspense. In the resolution of the conflict, he defines an ethical position guiding man to preserve humanistic values and to avoid becoming a machine even though he lives in a totally mechanized world.

In conclusion, let us summarize the strongest merit of science fiction in the course. If we agree that a healthy debate on information technology and all its present and possible applications in society is desirable, then how do we get that debate? How do we counter the student's tendency toward passivity and no response? Or his tendency toward a programmed, conventional response? How do we sharpen his awareness of the radical nature of technological change? One way is through the use of science fiction.

Science fiction can provide a vehicle for genuine dialogue in the class. Because it is inherently interesting, it stimulates the interest of the student. It can model with economy a whole social system, and—more important—the individual struggling to maintain his selfhood in that system. It dramatizes the conflict between the humanistic values of freedom, individuality, creativity, and the pragmatic values of material abundance, growth, progress, love of power and efficiency. The model each science-fiction author presents is imaginative, innovative, unconventional, and future-oriented. Each asks the student to respond with these same qualities when he considers what we want to do with computers, and whether our purposes are socially desirable.

SOCIAL
SCIENCE FICTION

BY LEON STOVER

With his essay in the first section of this book, Leon Stover has illuminated the origins and meaning of SF. Moving now from historical theory to the college classroom, he presents revealing explications of four fine novels he uses at Illinois Institute of Technology in his course in social science fiction. Besides the novels, he also uses Above the Human Landscape, *a textbook anthology of short fiction edited by Willis McNelly and himself, which emphasizes SF as a literature of ideas and social criticism.*

In the beginning, commercial science fiction was devoted to glamorizing laboratory research and new product design, as I have indicated in an earlier chapter, "Science Fiction and the Research Revolution." The progress of industrial science and programmed innovation was the theme, and still is, in what is called "hard-core" science fiction. Inevitably a counter-theme developed, protesting the social costs of modern technology. The two themes, however, are both ideological responses to the research revolution, the original one finding it uplifting and the other dehumanizing. Beyond that is a residual category of techno-neutral themes, which might just as well be grouped under the rubric of "social" science fiction. It is as if the genre began with carpenters praising their tools, rejoicing in the moral superiority their new hardware gave them, only to turn against it, the carpenters blaming their tools for bad results. And then came stories about the carpenters themselves, the issue of good or bad tools put aside for those of man and society. Heinlein said it in "The Roads Must Roll." Ostensibly a story about the fascinating new technology of a futuristic transportation system, it is really about the problem of duty among the engineers who maintain it. "No, it's not the machines, it's the men."

This large category, which at its best has brought science fiction to maturity, I cannot hope to survey. What I can do is report on the four novels that have worked well of late in my course, "Social Science Fiction," taught at the Illinois Institute of Technology since 1965. They are, in order of treatment (with time frame):

1) Arthur C. Clarke, *2001: A Space Odyssey* (past and future).
2) Frank Herbert, *The Santaroga Barrier* (present).

3) George R. Stewart, *Earth Abides* (a future that is a return to the past).
4) Harry Harrison and Leon Stover, *Stonehenge* (past).

Science fiction evidently can be about the future, the present or the past. But when it is not futuristic, or if it does not touch on issues of science and technology, what makes it science fiction? With an answer to that question I will conclude.

2001: A Space Odyssey

Filmgoers mystified by the meaning of *2001*, the movie written for MGM by Stanley Kramer and Arthur Clarke, will find the latter's novel based on it has restored to clarity much of its intended idea, not fully visualized on the screen. Yet the film offers the most important clue of all, its opening and closing bars of music, the World Riddle theme (C-G-C) from "Thus Spoke Zarathustra" by Richard Strauss, who said of this tone-poem that it was his homage to the philosophical genius of Nietzsche:

> I meant to convey by means of music an idea of the human race from its origins, through the various phases of its development, religious and scientific, up to Nietzsche's idea of the Superman.

Nietzsche himself compacted the idea in one of his most famous aphorisms, from a book of the same title as the tone-poem, "Man is a rope, fastened between animal and the Superman."

Accordingly, the novel breaks into three parts. The first deals with man's apelike ancestors, the next with his phase of scientific development, and the last with his ultimate destiny. The progression is Apeman, Spaceman, Superman, the middle term bridging the other two. Man as we know him is only a transitional form to be overcome, a "dangerous going-across," Nietzsche says, as on a tightrope over the abyss between past and future.

For a picture of human origins, Clarke draws on the controversial "killer ape" thesis of Robert Ardrey in *African Genesis*. Our primate ancestors, the apemen of genus *Australopithecus,* were peaceful vegetarians when during Pleistocene times a change of climate desiccated their habitat, the African savannah, and they were faced with extinction unless they took advantage of the animal food walking all about them. It was learn to kill, eat meat, or die. They learned, following a mutational change in behavior caused, as many mutations are caused for the benefit of natural selection working toward new adaptations, by the impingement of cosmic rays on the gene structure. The apemen evolved to become men, endowed with the bigger brains to master the ever-changing complex of human culture and technology, starting with weapons of the hunt. Humanity got its creative intelligence from those killer apes who learned how to kill food animals, predators—and each other. Thanks to that accidental ray upon the crucial gene, that "gift from the stars," as Ardrey puts it, man became man. But the gift of mind is tainted with the heritage of the flesh, and the killer apes became murdering men, who even now have brought themselves to the verge of nuclear war.

Clarke translates that "gift from the stars" into a literal gift from alien beings of pure energy. Because in all the galaxy they have "found nothing more precious than Mind, they encouraged its dawning everywhere." On the planet Earth they saw hope for a line of evolution like their own, leading out of mortal bodies into a condition of incorporeal intelligence. Their first step was to place a teaching machine in the midst of the apemen, a crystalline monolith that projects how-to images of killing warthogs with a club.

In the film the teaching machine is a mysterious black monolith that attracts the attention of one of the more curious of a band of apemen, who is somehow inspired by it to invent the principle of the lever, an extension of the power of the arm. He picks a long bone out of a crumbled warthog skeleton, which he bashes to pieces in a slow-motion sequence, his great hairy arm lifting up and crashing down, the flying debris intercut with images of a live warthog falling under his blows. This first triumph of technology, the hunting club that will make for killing and meat eating, is underlined by the C-G-C World Riddle theme, climaxing in full orchestra and organ. The weapon is tossed into the air in a fit of exaltation and, in a wipe that disposes of several million years of evolutionary history, the bone in its toss becomes an H-bomb in orbit.

As the apemen once were faced with extinction, so now are their descendants, only this time the threat is from themselves. The space age is that dangerous time of going-across. Then explorers on the moon trigger a signal device, emitting a beam toward the planet Jupiter and advising the aliens of human progress thus far. A ship is built to follow in its wake, equipped with an intelligent computer, HAL, in addition to the human crew. HAL kills all the crew members but one, who has the wit to escape. Machines being functional extensions of the men who made them, the thinking machine HAL carries forward the original sin of the killer apes. The survivor is Mission Commander Bowman, who is taken by the aliens to a mocked-up hotel suite somewhere beyond Jupiter. There he dies a natural death, and is reborn at the next stage of existence, a Star Child.

The film cuts at this point to a view of Earth seen from outer space. The camera moves aside to include another luminious disc nearby. It is a transparent globe that contains an alert, watchful embryo of cosmic proportions, looking down on Earth with the eyes of Bowman, as he prepares to liberate all humanity from the disabilities of material existence and promote it to the superman status he has attained. This embryonic figure is a symbolic show, for the sake of visualizing something on the screen, of Bowman's attainment to a state of disembodied intellect.

But the Star Child is no superman of Nietzschean philosophy. It is a creature of modern physics, to which Clarke gives plausibility from the transformation of matter into energy. It is also a creature of metaphysics and Christian Platonism, which looks to the release of the eternal soul from its vile garment of flesh. The dualism of mind and body provides a ready explanation of evil. Mind is imprisoned in the body and, if it were free, the problem of evil would be overcome.

The Santaroga Barrier

Santaroga is a small California town that appears utopian but is not. People there take a drug named Jaspers, infused in their locally made beer and cheese, and the result is a sense of community so strong they refuse to buy anything from the outside "money-industrial world." A psychologist named Dr. Gilbert Dasein is sent by an investment corporation to discover what is the "barrier" that keeps branches of its chain stores closed in Santaroga. He is not the first, nor the last, to investigate. Several of his predecessors were killed by Santarogans, as he himself kills his successor after taking their drug Jaspers and going native.

The clue to the meaning of this drama is the name of the hero, *Dasein,* a word basic to the vocabulary of the existentialist philosopher Karl Jaspers. That the Santarogans take a drug named after Jaspers is blasphemous, for the community they make under its influence is the opposite of the authentic one he would have people make by way of intellectual effort—all the more so because their critique of mass society is exactly his. They end in creating the same inauthentic anonymity of the outside world from which they claim to have escaped.

Dasein in German means "just being there" (*da-sein,* there-being), and refers to the crude empirical existence of the individual before he achieves a human personality, if he ever does. Dr. Dasein does not. He fails the test of existence, and falls away from the process of becoming. He has not the courage to meet the challenge of human freedom, the action and work of exercising choice, preference, descision.

> He had no group, no place in a hive of fellow-activity, nothing to shield him from personal decisions that might overwhelm him.

The dread freedom to live or not live up to the future possibilities of self, distinguishable from others, is too much for him. The drug Jaspers easily takes him, self hiding from self and disappearing into the Santaroga hive-average, where action and purpose is no more than a "dance of bees."

LEON STOVER

Personal autonomy, however, does not mean man who is a man for himself alone, a mere individual. Selfhood can be disclosed only in being with others, in a cooperative struggle to make spiritual progress from just being there in the world to concern about our existence. Communication makes the man and community. But consciousness of the life situation is difficult, writes Karl Jaspers in *Man in the Modern Age,* because its radical dehumanization by a mass-production, mass-consumption society has transformed personal relations into commodity values. It is a world of crude empirical existence, from manipulators to manipulated, the former denied transcendence in their very intolerance of the same in the latter. Everything goes against self-clarification, from the conformist tendencies of excessive organization in the work place, where the standard of achievement is the average functional capacity, to the mobilization of a debauched popular taste in the marketplace. Given the consensus needs of a classless multitude of average people, few can find the opportunity to learn even the desire to be themselves. The individual is atomized and reduced to an object of utility with "no more genuine individuality than one pin in a row."

The Santarogans have made the same diagnosis of mass society and mean to escape it. But their counter-culture replicates the very feature of the outside world they deplore, "everybody . . . everywhere alike." If people outside are like pins in a row, those living in Santaroga form an equally mindless mass of identical parts, like bees or drops of water. Santaroga is like the waters of a placid lake, "serene, contained, every droplet knowing its neighbors." The drug Jaspers has created for them the illusion of community based on deprived selfhood. They claim Jaspers is their "Consciousness Fuel," but it fuels a sense of other awareness at the total expense of individual awareness. They have not even the awareness individually of their collective hostility to outsiders, and the deaths of the investigators they murdered they believe resulted from unfortunate accidents. Self is so little realized they have no understanding whatever of the depth of their resentment, which at bottom is a fear and loathing of selfhood.

For Karl Jaspers, a community must be *a* whole but never *the* whole, the collective will a unification of strong wills. But the Santarogans are not strong in themselves, for they lack inner promptings. They think the drug creates vital sympathies, but it does not. They mistake empathetic awareness for consciousness of self-in-society. Like minds have no more to communicate than a placid lake has water to flow. In the still waters of personal oblivion do they appease the struggle for personal autonomy. In the saving security of a social whole unimbued with individuality do they evade the trouble and effort that freedom demands, and not face up to the hidden poison of their dissatisfaction. Sooner or later this resentment, now turned outward, will turn inward and they will confront their own true natures. And since they lack self-reliance, they will not survive the confrontation. Perhaps those whose reaction to the drug is adverse, the moron-rejects of the community, have already done so, only to lapse into nullity and become one with nothingness.

Earth Abides

George R. Stewart received the first of the International Fantasy Awards for this, his only novel to fall into the SF genre. A retired professor of English from the University of California, Berkeley, he is also the author of nonfiction works which, like his novels, all touch on some aspect of American history or culture.

Earth Abides is no exception. It inverts the famous story of Ishi, the last wild Indian in North America, a story recently retold by Theodora Kroeber in *Ishi In Two Worlds* (1962). Ishi, the last member of the Yahi, a tribe of California Indians long thought to have been extinct, emerged from his Stone Age world to live in the early twentieth century world of trolley cars and electric lights. He was rescued by an anthropologist at the University of California, and taken to live in its Museum of Anthropology, then located in San Francisco, where he passed his remaining years. He showed the anthropologists the native Yahi way of making and hunting with a bow and arrow, and of making fire. With these lessons Ishi paid his way and enjoyed the fruits of civilization, which for him were mainly glue (for the easier feathering of arrows) and matches. His name in Yahi means "man."

The hero of *Earth Abides* is named Ish, which in Hebrew also means "man." Ish is one of a very few to survive a pandemic disease to see civilization collapse and his descendants return to the life of Stone Age hunters like that of Ishi. Ish is the last of the civilized Americans as Ishi is the last of the aboriginal Americans.

Naked, hungry, and weakened by snakebite, Ishi stumbled into industrial America on August 29, 1911. The last of the Yahi, he wandered down from his native hills into the corral of a slaughterhouse near Oroville, California. There he fell exhausted, was jailed as a "wild man," was finally recognized for what he was, and was taken to the museum.

Weakened by snakebite, Ish in *Earth Abides* stumbles out of the same hills into a dead civilization, its populace wiped out almost without exception by some deadly virus. He had been studying the ecology of the Sacramento Valley, Ishi's tribal home, for a master's degree at the University of California. Throughout the novel, Ish watches with ecological detachment the transformation of a world emptied of men.

He returns to his home in a suburb of San Francisco, overlooking the Bay and the Golden Gate bridge. The few survivors he gathers around him facetiously call themselves the "the tribe." Everybody forages in stores for food and other goods, trying to maintain the old way of life under new conditions. One couple brings home a bridge lamp and a fancy radio set, even though no electricity is available. Even Ish,

LEON STOVER

the only one to think about the future, holds school and teaches spelling and arithmetic, although the world is so depopulated it cannot sustain occupational specialties based on literacy.

At last Ish realizes the futility of his classroom lessons and school is dismissed. He then teaches the children a game, which he knows will have to become a way of life once there are no more store goods to scavenge; otherwise, the tribe would degenerate into a bestial existence, devoid of human dignity. What he teaches them is how to make and use the bow and arrow, and how to·make fire without matches, the same technology he knew from his study of anthropology to have been the basis for successful living by our pre-civilized ancestors.

In time, the tribe departs the crumbling ruins of San Francisco. By then Ish is an old man and the tribe, now composed of skilled hunters, sets out to cross the Bay Bridge to new lands.

Crossing the bridge, Ish slows to a stop. Before he dies, he reflects on the course of human history and the fate of his grandchildren and others of their generation, who squat in a half circle around him.

> They were very young in age, at least by comparison with him, and in the cycle of mankind they were many thousands of years younger than he. He was the last of the old; they were the first of the new. But whether the new would follow the course which the old had followed, that he did not know.

We are left to wonder if it will or not.

But the moral of the novel is certain. Inverting the story of Ishi, Stewart dramatizes the humanistic fact that man is man, be he civilized or tribal; that a Stone Age culture is just as valid a setting for being human as is an industrial culture.

Stonehenge

All fiction may be analyzed in terms of plot, character, and setting. From this rhetorical perspective, science fiction may be judged apart from its content in terms of an emphasis on setting, just as detective fiction is given to plot and mainstream fiction to the development of character, plotted for that purpose in a familiar or unobstrusive background. But in science fiction, background is foreground, setting is hero. In Robert Heinlein's *Beyond This Horizon,* for example, the content is about the future of genetic engineering. Its characters and their plot entanglements, however, are mere vehicles to give play to the setting, an imaginary society in which that new technology has important consequences. The same rhetorical method can be applied to the present *(The Santaroga Barrier)* or to the past *(Stonehenge).*

When Harry Harrison and I wrote *Stonehenge,* we were conscious of the fact that, rhetorically speaking, we were writing a science-fiction novel. We were not writing a historical novel, but a novel *about* history, whose purpose was to authenticate the past. Historical novels rarely attempt this trick; they usually take culturally modern people and their problems and project them against a painted backdrop of researched historical detail. But in *Stonehenge,* the proto-Celtic culture of the ancient Britons is not used as ornamental detail but as a key element in the reconstruction of a warrior society in the condition described later by Homer and the sagas of the Irish Celts. It was a serious effort to dramatize a solution to the Stonehenge mystery in light of archaeology, classical accounts of the Gaulish Celts, and Indo-European epic literature.

When the novel was first published, the dagger carving on the inner face of stone No. 53 was believed to have represented a Mycenaean dagger and therefore a Mediterranean connection dating back to about 1500 B.C. That connection is dramatized in the person of the novel's hero, Ason. But since then, a revision of the chronology has pushed the date of the final phase of Stonehenge back to 2000 B.C., which is about 500 years before the rise of Mycenae. Therefore the dagger is a native one and the monument itself a strictly local accomplishment.

All the same, my political interpretation of the monument still holds, that it functioned as a tribal assembly place, the father of the mother of parliaments. In *Stonehenge: The Indo-European Heritage* (Chicago, 1978), of which I am senior author with a historian, the idea is argued in scholarly fashion. Thus has a new theory of Stonehenge come to light after having been tested playfully in a science-fiction novel.

LEON STOVER

TEACHING POLITICAL SCIENCE FICTION

BY MARTIN H. GREENBERG AND JOSEPH D. OLANDER

*In shifting combinations, Pat Warrick, Marty Green-
berg, Joe Olander, and others have been turning out
a whole galaxy of deftly selected anthologies designed
to use science fiction to brighten introductory courses
in anthropology, psychology, sociology, political science, and even American government. Professor
Greenberg is Associate Professor of Regional Analysis
and Political Science, University of Wisconsin—Green
Bay, and Joseph Olander is Vice President for Academic Affairs at the University of Texas—El Paso.
Here, they discuss the classroom uses to SF to explore
the political dimensions of the world we live in. The
essay concludes with a well planned syllabus, citing
specific SF titles.*

Although the term science fiction belongs properly to the twentieth century, the device of creating a fictional world by which to
explain or criticize the existing world and to propose social and political
alternatives is a very old technique. Plato, in *The Republic*, developed
a fictional world which illustrated his conception of a perfect and just
society. Later, in the sixteenth century, Sir Thomas More speculated
about ideal political and social conditions when he created his fictional
world of *Utopia.*

These classics of speculative fiction may serve as prototypes for contemporary science fiction which also aims at social and political criticism and alternatives. Certainly, the history of modern science fiction
is filled with examples of works, both short stories and novels, which
deal with distinctly political themes and subjects of interest to the
political scientist. Two classics of modern literature—George Orwell's
Nineteen Eighty-four and Aldous Huxley's *Brave New World*—employ
the device of speculative fiction to offer political criticism. Orwell, by
extrapolating the tendency of government to control the freedom of
the individual, especially the freedom to think and express dissenting
points of view, created a world of totalitarian horror. In 1932, Huxley,
with brilliant predictive insight, drew a utopian world in a highly
technological society in which an individual is happy as a result of
having been conditioned to desire only what the state would allow.
But, Huxley asks, what price happiness if an individual receives utopia
in exchange for the freedom to choose? A "wrong" choice may result

in unhappiness, but it may also be a small price to pay for the prerogative of maintaining integrity of self and of expressing it in individual choices.

Both Orwell and Huxley were essentially writers of so-called mainstream literature who happened to use science-fictional devices infrequently. It really remained for the science-fiction specialty magazines—the pulps—to develop what later became known as "social science fiction," a body of literature within science fiction which contains short stories and novels related to social and political themes and subjects.

From the late nineteen-thirties on, the most significant magazine was *Astounding Science Fiction* (now *Analog Science Fiction / Science Fact*) under the editorship of John W. Campbell, Jr. Campbell was the most influential force in science fiction for almost two decades. His attitudes regarding political and social issues were very controversial. In his later years, he became a supporter of the views of George Wallace and was frequently associated with a variety of "conservative" positions.

But Campbell's basic outlook on politics also reflected the dominant characteristic of science fiction during the forties and fifties. He stood for an intense distaste for the power and role of government, especially "big government." Perhaps because of this original impetus, science fiction was, and continues to be, one of the last refuges of "rugged individualism" in American letters. Time and again, science fiction projected the individual against "the system," whether the system was ecological or bureaucratic in nature. In most stories, particularly during the period 1926 to 1962, the individual emerged victorious in this struggle. Many science-fiction writers seemed to adhere to the "great man" theory of history with its emphasis on the talented individual struggling to overcome the problems of the present and to determine the shape of the future.

Yet the rugged hero did not merely rely upon strength and cunning; he also relied on his intellectual prowess. For it was talent *and* scientific training that enabled these heroes to prevail. Not unnaturally, political power often belonged to those who possessed a great deal of expertise. In fact, future societies were frequently portrayed as technocracies, in which those who have mastered the secrets of science rule over the uneducated "barbarians."

But the great bulk of science fiction written before the end of World War II was not concerned with social and political themes. More sophisticated—and more frequent—treatment of political issues began to appear in the pages of *Galaxy Science Fiction,* a magazine founded after World War II and edited by H.L. Gold. Galaxy featured stories and serialized novels on social and political themes with an emphasis on the logical (and often satirical) extrapolation of present trends and ideas. Its pages featured the work of such authors as C.M. Kornbluth,

Robert Sheckley, and Frederik Pohl.

Pohl is a particularly important figure in the development and popularity of social science fiction with political relevance. As the successor to Gold at *Galaxy* and as editor of *Galaxy's* companion magazine, *Worlds of If*, he continued to place emphasis on social and political SF and also wrote a number of important works on these themes. Today examples of politically relevant science fiction are produced regularly, although government and the political process in general are usually depicted in unfavorable terms, perhaps reflecting the general disillusionment with politics and politicians which seems widespread.

Finally, the history of modern science fiction includes the development of science-fiction films, which should not be overlooked by the teacher of political science. Unfortunately, many of the classic science-fiction novels with political significance have not been reproduced on the screen, but this may be a temporary situation. Nevertheless, a number of good productions are available on a rental basis for classroom use, including major films derived from that very special category of science fiction sometimes referred to as "near-future science fiction." Examples include the outstanding *Dr. Strangelove*, adapted from the novel *Red Alert* by Peter George; *Fail-Safe; The Manchurian Candidate;* and a good adaptation of *Seven Days in May*.

It should be noted that these films are sometimes only marginally science fiction and that all of them are from books written by writers outside of the science fiction community proper. An exception to this general condition is *Fahrenheit 451*, an excellent and reasonably faithful treatment of Ray Bradbury's classic of the same title. These films can best be used in the classroom in conjunction with the novels on which they are based, a technique which is popular with students and effective in teaching. Moreover, *The Twenty-First Century*, narrated by Walter Cronkite, is worth using in class and is available at reasonable rates through the Film Series produced by James Gunn at the University of Kansas.

Many of the short stories and novels mentioned in relation to political themes and subjects cut across political categories and thus can be used diversely in teaching. Most of the short stories contained in this essay can be found in Martin H. Greenberg and Patricia Warrick, eds., *Political Science Fiction: An Introductory Reader* (Englewood Cliffs, N. J.: Prentice-Hall, 1974), and Joseph D. Olander, Martin H. Greenberg and Patricia Warrick, eds., *American Government Through Science Fiction* (Chicago: Rand McNally, 1974), both now out of print.

One of the most important and frequently appearing themes in social science fiction is political authority and its implications for the individual. Political authority is most frequently presented as extremely centralized in modern science fiction, the exceptions being those works which examine the theme of anarchy. Control by central authorities is usually rigid, brutal, and uncompromising. A subcategory within this theme may be referred to as the "resistance story." In this form, the United States appears as having been conquered and occupied, frequently by the Soviet Union, China, or some unidentified Asian power, and a resistance movement has developed in order to fight the occupation and to restore individual liberties.

These resistance movements form the plot of numerous science-fiction novels like *Beyond This Horizon* by Robert A. Heinlein. Perhaps the finest novel of this type is *The Man in the High Castle* by Philip K. Dick, in which the United States has lost the Second World War and is divided at the Mississippi River between German and Japanese Occupation Forces. Another device in this category is the creation of a setting in which a dictatorship has come to power in a vacuum following a natural disaster or a nuclear war, such as the excellent and underrated *Doomsday Morning* by C.L. Moore.

Other novels with significance for the theme of political authority include: *Doppelgangers* by H.F. Heard, a work that is also useful for discussing the concept of competing elites; *The Status Civilization* by Robert Sheckley, one of the best discussions concerning the stratification of authority and power to be found in any form of literature; *Alien Island* by T.L. Sherred; *The Stars Like Dust* by Isaac Asimov, which is especially insightful for the way it develops the concept of tyranny; and *The World Inside* by Robert Silverberg, a subtle and powerful book which may require the teacher to provide fairly extensive guidance for the student.

With respect to the theme of political authority, Eastern European science fiction presents a good opportunity for the American political scientist. This science fiction is finally becoming available in English translation, principally through the efforts of MacMillan (New York), which has undertaken a series of translation projects. European science fiction, like most American science fiction, is basically anti-system and pro-individual. Its themes and plots give salience to attacking the inefficiency, tyranny, and impersonalization of large bureaucratic structures. *Memoirs Found in A Bathtub* by Stanislaw Lem is perhaps the finest novel in this category by a European author. *Hard to Be A God* by Arkadi and Boris Strugatski presents a good Eastern European view of the issues of authority and control.

Other useful and insightful novels by American and British authors on political authority and control include: *Sundog* by B.N. Ball, an excellent portrayal of totalitarianism; *The Last Starship from Earth* by John Boyd; *Orbit Unlimited* by Poul Anderson; *The Sirens of Titan*, perhaps Kurt Vonnegut, Jr.'s best science-fiction novel; *Colossus* by D.F. Jones, one of the best treatments of political decision-making available; *The Weapon Makers* by A.E. Van Vogt in which the slogan "The right to buy weapons is the right to be free" allows for a discussion of issues ranging from the meaning of freedom to gun-control legislation; the famous and perhaps too familiar *Dune* by Frank Herbert;

The Day of the Star Cities by John Brunner, which is preferable to his more famous *Stand on Zanzibar* and *The Sheep Look Up* for political content; *The Lincoln Hunters* by Wilson Tucker; *Revolt in 2100* by Robert A. Heinlein; and *Camp Concentration,* a difficult but worthwhile novel by Thomas Disch.

Another major political topic which has received much attention in science fiction is ideology. It is generally assumed that science fiction is "conservative" in its political values. While this statement may be true of many books which contain overt political references, it is clearly not true when one examines the literature in broad perspective. Science fiction is largely disposed to favoring various forms of social and political change. It implies that the future holds possibilities which may be radically different from the present. Whatever else it may be, science fiction does not hold much promise for those interested in maintaining the status quo.

But this statement is not equal to asserting that science fiction treats human motivations as constantly changing; indeed, men and women are portrayed in much science fiction as being driven by desires for power and material gain. Similarly, governmental forms and structures are typically dictatorial, totalitarian, or representative, although recently more radical forms of communal political arrangements have been featured. Nevertheless, the inevitability of change, brought about largely through technological and scientific developments, is a hallmark of science fiction and can be interpreted as subversive of the present. It is interesting to note that several Soviet science-fiction writers have served prison terms for their works, and the Spanish science-fiction magazine *New Dimensions* was periodically harrassed by Spanish authorities.

Further evidence of the ideologically critical nature of modern science fiction is contained in the work of writers like Robert Sheckley, Frederik Pohl, C.M. Kornbluth, and Mack Reynolds, who have consistently attacked many of the most cherished American political, social, and economic institutions in their fiction. The writing team of Pohl and Kornbluth was especially noteworthy for this type of story, and their novels *The Space Merchants, Gladiator-at-Law,* and *Search the Sky* are considered classic political satires. Reynolds is perhaps the single most persistent political critic in contemporary science fiction, although his work is very uneven in quality. At his best—as in the short story "Radical Center"—he is an acutely perceptive observer of the American political scene.

Currently there is a major debate taking place in critical studies of contemporary science fiction with significant implications for the political scientist interested in science fiction. The debate centers around the alleged absence of a Marxist perspective in American science fiction. Although the personal political preferences of science-fiction writers may be only tangential, it is interesting that one of the major early fan groups—the Futurian Society of New York—had a more or less "official ideology" well to the left of center. Many of these fans, who were in their teens during this period, became leading science-fiction writers, editors, and critics, although, like everyone else, their political beliefs are subject to profound changes over time.

One noteworthy novel which examines a communal society in detail is *Rogue Queen* by L. Sprague de Camp, a work which exhibits a fascinating social and political structure as well as artistic quality. But perhaps the most important work which examines the Marxist world view (probably unwittingly) is the *Foundation Trilogy* by Isaac Asimov, consisting of *Foundation, Foundation and Empire,* and *Second Foundation.* It can be interpreted as pseudo-Marxist because its frame of reference postulates a science of "psychohistory," which allows for the prediction of the broad outlines of the economic, political, and social future for thousands of years.

Clearly, the *Foundation Trilogy* should be used in any political science-fiction course.

On the other side of the political continuum, fascist and "right-wing" ideology has also received attention in science fiction. *Fahrenheit 451* by Ray Bradbury is, among other things, an attack on the anti-intellectualism of fascism. *The Iron Dream* by Norman Spinrad is also a fascinating treatment of the fascist perspective. Robert A. Heinlein's *Starship Troopers* is one of these relatively rare works which has succeeded in dividing the science-fiction community. Its controversial nature derives from its extolment of military values. Its political views—for example, that only combat veterans should have the right to vote—form the basis of a society which may approximate an amplification of the Japanese code of *bushido.*

Other important novels rich with insight for discussing political ideology include: *Cat's Cradle* by Kurt Vonnegut, Jr.; *Anthem* by Ayn Rand, a controversial book which makes a powerful statement on behalf of "rugged individualism"; *A Case of Conscience* by James Blish, which attempts to tie the religious dimension of the human condition to politics; *The Star King* by Jack Vance, an interesting study of political power, and *Ring Around the Sun* by Clifford D. Simak. Finally, another Heinlein novel—*Stranger in a Strange Land*—can be useful because of the ideological implications of the communal society presented in it.

The acquisition and use of political power is a subject which has also received attention in science fiction. Competing elites are well presented in H.F. Heard's *Doppelgangers* and Isidore Haiblum's *Transfer to Yesterday.* Political leadership is dealt with in such novels as *Double Star* by Robert A. Heinlein, which is additionally useful for its emphasis on political strategy, and *Past Master* by R. A. Lafferty. Shorter fiction on this subject includes the Nebula Award-winning "Call Him Lord" by Gordon R. Dickson, which deals with the elusiveness of requisite leadership qualities; "The Short Ones" by Raymond E. Banks, which underscores the idea of elite recruitment by a plot which manipulates the lives of miniaturized beings; "Eternity Lost" by Clifford D. Simak and "Death and the Senator" by Arthur C. Clarke, both of which treat the perennial question of honesty and ethics in politics. Finally, two other works on the uses and abuses of political power are important: *The Genocides* by Thomas M. Disch and *The Unteleported Man* by Philip K. Dick.

Another subject treated in science fiction is political change, or the means by which political power is transferred. In democratic systems this occurs through elections, but in most political systems throughout history political change has occurred largely through violence. Science fiction is especially rich with works which feature extralegal and violent political change. This conflict element is pronounced in science fiction, perhaps largely because stories of conflict are popular. Social systems which work perfectly and are conflict-free are likely to be very dull reading.

Although most of the novels and short stories mentioned earlier in connection with the subject of political authority can be used beneficially to examine the concept of political change, there are several novels and shorter works which are distinctive. They include *Beyond This Horizon* by Robert A. Heinlein, *The Stars Like Dust* by Isaac Asimov; *Agent of Chaos* by Norman Spinrad, a vastly underrated and neglected novel which presents a good opportunity to discuss the nature of change and the meaning of order; " 'Repent, Harlequin,' Said the Ticktockman" by Harlan Ellison, a favorite of students, which considers the concept of nonviolent resistance; "Burning Question" by Brian W. Aldiss, similar in theme to the Ellison story but set in a poorly disguised Vietnamese situation; ". . . Not a Prison Make" by Joseph P. Martino, which develops the principles of guerrilla warfare and then shows how they can be countered; Keith Laumer's excellent "The Right To Resist" and "The Right To Revolt," which are best taught together; and the very powerful short story by J.G. Ballard, "The Assassination of John Fitzgerald Kennedy Considered as a Downhill Motor Race."

Science fiction dealing with nonviolent forms of political change—political campaigns, elections and electoral behavior in general—appears much less frequently than do stories about other forms of political change. But the relatively few examples which do exist are among the most imaginative stories to be found in social science fiction. The three most important novels in this category are *The Eclipse of Dawn* by Gordon Eklund; *The Joy Wagon,* a much lighter work, by Arthur T. Hadley; and *Bug Jack Barron* by Norman Spinrad, in which a television interview host uses the media to propel himself into political prominence.

The short stories in this category are even better than the novels.

Among them are two stories by Isaac Asimov—"Evidence," one of his famous Robot stories in which a political candidate has to prove that he is not a machine, and "Franchise," in which one chosen "representative" citizen determines the direction of political life; "Beyond Doubt" by Lyle Monroe and Elma Wentz, which is concerned with underhanded electoral practices; "2066: Election Day" by Michael Shaara, in which a computer scans the entire population to find the best-qualified person to be president—and finds none; "May the Best Man Win" by Stanley Schmidt, which focusses on the technical rules governing candidate eligibility; "The Delegate from Guapanga" by Wyman Guin, which looks at an alien election conducted through mental processes possessed by a group with special powers; and "The Children of Night" by Frederik Pohl, which stresses the role of public relations in elections.

The international dimension of politics has not been neglected in science fiction, although the teacher should be aware that many books on this theme are nothing more than naively romantic cold-war-in-outer-space stories. Nevertheless, one of the classic themes in science fiction is the "first contact" situation between Earth people and aliens, a theme which parallels the problems encountered when representatives from different cultures and political ideologies attempt to deal with one another. Structurally, future international systems in science fiction are characterized by a federal or unified nature. They typically presuppose the disappearance of the nation-state. Since confrontations between aliens and Earth people, invader and defender, and explorer and native life form are basic to science fiction, concepts and techniques such as gaming, diplomacy, deterrent strategy, and bargaining can be employed in imaginative settings.

Some of the better science fiction in this category includes *Who?* by Algis Budrys; *The World of Null-A* by A.E. Van Vogt; *Colossus* by D.F. Jones; *Level 7* by Mordecai Roshwald; and *The Syndic* by C.M. Kornbluth, which presents an international system controlled by professional gangsters. Shorter fiction includes "Crab-Apple Crisis" by George MacBeth, a funny but equally chilling tale based upon Herman Kahn's escalation ladder; "The Day They Got Boston" by Herbert Gold, which discusses the idea of selective retaliation; "Triggerman" by J.F. Bone, a strong story about the rôle that instinct plays in diplomatic and military decision-making; "The Helping Hand" by Poul Anderson; and "Superiority" by Arthur C. Clarke, which can be used for presenting some of the military dilemmas the United States faced in Southeast Asia.

In addition, there is a large group of stories which focus on conflict-resolution techniques. Typically, they involve dispute-resolution through combat by individuals or small groups representing whole cultures or nations, such as "The Survivor" by the late Walter Moudy, in which international dominance is determined every four years, Olympic

Games style, by teams from the United States and the Soviet Union; and "Arena" by Fredric Brown, in which planetwide survival is determined by individual combat between Earthman and alien. Alternative conflict-resolution methods are explored in "The Link" by Cleve Cartmill; "The Pacifist" by Mack Reynolds; and "Thunder and Roses" by Theodore Sturgeon, all of which employ a uniting-against-adversity theme. Finally, most of Keith Laumer's "Retief" stories, which feature an intergalactic diplomat as the hero, are valuable for insight into international politics.

An area which has been neglected by science fiction is "Third World" politics. Although a partial treatment is available through extrapolations of science fiction which deals with international themes, good science fiction on this subject is not available, with one exception. Mack Reynolds's double-novel *Blackman's Burden* and *Border, Breed, Nor Birth* is insightful.

A field which is becoming increasingly important to political science is political anthropology, a study of the ways by which political institutions and practices are created and ritualized. In science fiction, this topic provides interesting opportunities for speculation. For example, an entire subgenre in science fiction, known as the "post-holocaust story," focusses on how social, political, and economic institutions are reconstituted after civilization collapses because of a natural or manmade disaster. In these situations, themes related to political anthropology abound. Examples include the long-neglected but recently rediscovered *The Long Tomorrow* by Leigh Brackett; *Farnham's Freehold* by Robert A. Heinlein; *Earth Abides* by George Stewart; *Polymath* by John Brunner; *Greybeard* by Brian W. Aldiss; and *Gather, Darkness!* by Fritz Leiber.

Moreover, insight into political anthropology can be gained from an assessment of the relationship between language and politics. Several works are available, the most important of which are *The Languages of Pao* by Jack Vance; *Babel-17* by Samuel R. Delany; and "Brave New Word" by J. Francis McComas.

The purpose of this discussion has been to delineate categories of modern science fiction which contain political themes and subjects of interest to the political scientist. By portraying the potential development of political trends today and by presenting alternatives to those trends, science fiction offers a potentially rich literature by which humans and their political relationships—actual and possible—can be studied. Society is complex, and attempts to describe and explain how political systems function are necessarily difficult because a great number of variables are operating. The process of abstraction and conceptualization omits the richness and discreteness of human relationships.

Simplification, regarded by some critics as a weakness of science fiction, actually becomes one of its strengths, in much the same way that more formal models of political systems allow for an assessment of the more complicated—and more interesting—world for which they stand. The fictional world and people depicted in most science fiction are created with enough detail to embody and animate adequately ideas but with enough restraint to avoid submerging them.

In addition to illustrating concepts, the reading of science fiction may sharpen our awareness of the political implications of technological systems and science. Science fiction portrays a variety of societies, both utopian and dystopian, which are creatures of technological and scientific developments. These portrayals dramatize one of the contemporary world's major political dilemmas: Who is to be the political and literal master—humans or their technology?

Finally, science fiction provides a good opportunity for the formulating of political futures. Scenarios which involve developing alternative political futures are becoming increasingly common in high schools and universities. The formulation of alternative futures not only exercises the imagination but also—and perhaps this is more important—allows for a critical examination of present social, economic, and political reality.

A Political Science Fiction Module: Introduction to Political Science

Week One: Ideology and Political Philosophy
"Freedom" by Mack Reynolds
The Foundation Trilogy by Isaac Asimov
"The Last of the Deliverers" by Poul Anderson

Week Two: Political Leadership
"The Short Ones" by Raymond E. Banks
Doppelgangers by H.F. Heard
"Call Him Lord" by Gordon R. Dickson

Week Three: Elections and Electoral Behavior
"Evidence" by Isaac Asimov
The Joy Wagon by Arthur T. Hadley
"2066: Election Day" by Michael Shaara

Week Four: Political Violence and Revolution
"Burning Question" by Brian W. Aldiss
Revolt in 2100 by Robert A. Heinlein
" 'Repent, Harlequin,' Said the Ticktockman" by Harlan Ellison

Week Five: Diplomacy and International Relations
"Crab-Apple Crisis" by George MacBeth

Level 7 by Mordecai Roshwald
"The Day They Got Boston" by Herbert Gold

A Political Science Fiction Module: American Government

Week One: Politics and Political Culture
"Radical Center" by Mack Reynolds
The Space Merchants by Frederik Pohl and C.M. Kornbluth
"The Oogenesis of Bird City" by Philip José Farmer

Week Two: Politics and Policy-Making
"Hail to the Chief" by Sam Sackett
"Polity and Custom of the Camiroi" by R. A. Lafferty
"Request for Proposal" by Anthony R. Lewis

Week Three: American Political Processes
"The Children of Night" by Frederik Pohl
Bug Jack Barron by Norman Spinrad
"Franchise" by Isaac Asimov

Week Four: Political Change in the United States
"The Right to Revolt" by Keith Laumer
"The Right to Resist" by Keith Laumer
Seven Days in May by Fletcher Knebel

Week Five: American Foreign Policy
"Triggerman" by J.F. Bone
Who? by Algis Budrys
"The Survivor" by Walter F. Moudy

A Political Science Fiction Module: International Politics

Week One: The Nation-State
"Remember the Alamo!" by R.R. Fehrenbach
The Syndic by C.M. Kornbluth

Week Two: Foreign Policy
"Isolationist" by Mack Reynolds
"Fighting Division" by Randall Garrett
Red Alert by Peter George

Week Three: International Conflict
"Superiority" by Arthur C. Clarke
Starship Troopers by Robert A. Heinlein
"Red Moon Rising" by Robert Bloch

Week Four: Conflict Resolution
    "The Cave of Night" by James Gunn
    "Peacebringer" by Ward Moore
    "Thunder and Roses" by Theodore Sturgeon
    "Pacifist" by Mack Reynolds

Week Five: Diplomacy
    "Truce or Consequences" by Keith Laumer
    "Good Indian" by Mack Reynolds
    "First Contact" by Murray Leinster

GREENBERG & OLANDER

SCIENCE FICTION
AND PSYCHOLOGY

BY ROBERT PLANK

Robert Plank teaches the psychology of literature at Case Western Reserve University. The author of The Emotional Significance of Imaginary Beings, *he has contributed to books on Alfred Adler, Arthur C. Clarke, Robert A. Heinlein, C.S. Lewis, and J.R.R. Tolkien, and to professional journals. His essay here begins with a thoughtful look at SF and literary criticism. He reports in detail the use he makes in the classroom of one selected SF work, then returns to the theory of SF and psychological criticism.*

SF is literature. Literature deals with people's inner and outer lives imaginatively. Psychology deals with the same subject scientifically. Studying the one leads to studying the other.

It should be as simple as that. Well, it isn't. "Mainstream" literature creates models of individuals. SF builds "alternative worlds." Twain's Huckleberry Finn, Steinbeck's Joad family are people. We know their likes. Psychology can scrutinize them. It cannot scrutinize life forms on planet X in galaxy Y. Planet X may be magnificent, living there may be glorious beyond anything on Earth. Merely to think of it may satisfy our finest longing; but it would not arouse our scientific curiosity.

That may explain why psychologists eschew SF (at a guess, of a thousand scientific papers published by psychologists, one deals with SF), but it does not explain why the practitioners and critics of SF are reserved about psychology. In a guest editorial in *Analog,* James Gunn notes that "teachers of science fiction are not just in English but in history, sociology, engineering, political science, religion, philosophy, chemistry, physics, and many more disciplines, no doubt." To me, being in one of the many more disciplines, it comes natural to ask, why doesn't he list us? Working as a psychoanalytically oriented psychologist to boot, I can't help wondering: could there be some reason why people would shy away from the idea that SF might be studied from the angle of psychology? Why they would ignore the fact that some queer researchers who do just that actually exist?

It is the contention of this chapter that the field of our exotic research, now largely fallow, can be fertile. The psychological study of SF has a great potential; to make use of it in teaching has great utility.

Fair warning is in order here, though, that we'll have to range rather wide to make our point.

The area of our inquiry is of course but one part of that much broader entity, the psychology of literature. Let us see how this little creature (stepfather: Department of Psychology; stepmother: Department of English; age: tender) is trying to grow into its life task of bringing together those two step-parents who sometimes give the impression of never having been properly introduced to each other.

When asked by an English scholar what we can hope that psychology of literature will achieve, I am tempted to paraphrase Kennedy: Do not ask what psychology can do for you, ask what you can do for psychology—and obversely to a psychologist. It should be able to do both, of course, but this may be far from obvious.

The skein is best unravelled from the reader's end, for it is as readers that we approach the subject. The normal and natural class procedure is that the students read a certain piece of literature or hear it recited, or watch a play, a film, a TV program; it comes essentially to the same thing. Then it can be discussed.

We may be snowed under with questions. How does fiction affect the reader? (Or does it?) Which one affects which reader? How does it do it? We can ask about a specific work, or a category of works. This has been done long before SF existed or was recognized. Aristotle for instance explored the psychology of the effect of Attic tragedy. His theory of catharsis through terror and compassion is still a cornerstone of the edifice of theories on what is usually called audience response. SF can very well serve as one such category to be studied; but there is no particular reason to think that its study would be either more or less fruitful than that of other forms, modes, genres.

Students do not usually particularly like to analyze their own reaction to a work, which would be the almost indispensable prelude to the study of the reactions of others; neither do they do it particularly well. Do we here have the sensitive spot where people do not want the psychologist to look in too closely? Perhaps so, perhaps not. Let us turn to where the student's interest turns: to the work itself.

The psychological study of a work of literature is not literary criticism. The psychologist does not try to explain what the author may have wanted to convey. He has no business, *qua* psychologist, to say whether the work is good or bad (though he will often be sorely tempted to step out of his role). He is not particularly interested in the author's sources, he is only tangentially concerned with structure, form, and style (though the more he understands of all that, the better the job he will do). Literary craftsmanship is for him irrelevant. As the ornithologist gives as much attention to the blackbird as to the nightingale, so he deals impartially with the highest literature and the lowest. The grist for his mill comes from the work's content. What is content?

To grow up and to grow into their role in society, individuals need

ROBERT PLANK

to know "life"—i.e., human beings and their interaction. Basically that comes from the individual's personal experience. But this is not enough. It never was, and the more complex our world grows, the wider our radius of possible interaction becomes, the less does it suffice. An immense amount of understanding and knowledge of the human world is not absorbed from mother's knee but is brought to the individual by literature (fiction, in the widest sense: anything from a novel down to a TV commercial). This role of literature is often underrated, but there it is.

Now fiction can discharge this function only to the extent to which it gives a true picture of human beings, of what they do and what is done to them, and why, and how they think and feel about it. Most works worth the price of a paperback do. Most works of literature are realistic. "Mimetic" would perhaps be the better word, but let us not get into subtle distinctions. Some circular reasoning lurks here, but may it suffice to note the problem how we can be sure that the writings we consider *are* true to life.

The manner of presentation is in this context unimportant. Shakespeare has been called nonrealistic because people in real life do not speak in iambic pentameters (which is what so many of his characters speak in), nor do they hold soliloquies (which some of his characters do). But obviously this does not matter. What matters is whether what the author shows is true to life, not how he shows it. In terms of the dichotomy performed by C.S. Lewis in Chapter VII of *An Experiment in Criticism* (Cambridge University Press, 1961), we are interested in the "realism of content," not in the "realism of presentation."

Realistic works can be read in many ways. One is to read them like case histories—Tolstoi's *Anna Karenina* as though it were the story of a woman taken in adultery, Hesse's *Siddhartha* as the story of a man who spends his life seeking its meaning, etc. We can go so far as to claim that psychologists have learned more about human nature from characters in literature than from real case histories. Freud, for one, was generous in giving creative writers the credit due them. It may be said, of course, that this is just where Freud's weakness lay; but that is a different chapter, one not for this book.

Let us face facts: SF cannot share in all the credit earned by mainstream literature. It is not the forte of SF to draw characters and to describe their inner life and external fate "true to life." Innumerable critics have taken note of this weakness; many of them have derided SF for it, have given it bad marks as it were. That is a bit silly. SF writers have not *failed* trying to create lifelike, "three-dimensional" characters and life histories; they have not tried. Their aim—we all know it, but some critics don't—is something entirely different: to depict conditions, societies, worlds different from ours due to fictitious innovations, specifically scientific or technological novelties.

This is the unique hunting preserve that SF has all to itself, and here psychological exploration is promising. Let the main body of the psychology of literature consist of the study of characters, where SF can not significantly contribute. To the study of how human societies work under different conditions SF is relevant, while mainstream literature hardly is.

It's a two-way street. In the classical scientific experiment we change one element in a process and see how it affects the result. Our possibilities of treating entire societies thus are quite limited. We cannot, for instance, create a galactic empire in order experimentally to see how it works. We can, however, make mental experiments of that sort—which is exactly what SF does. Psychology can help SF by putting its findings at its disposal. Predictions can be extrapolated from these as to what would make such a fictitious society tick (or not tick, as the case may be). Psychology in turn can learn from the mental experiments of SF.

If audience response and characters in a work are two main areas of the psychology of literature, the study of the author's mind is a third equally important domain. In reading and analyzing literature we often come to the point where we ask no longer, why does a character act in a certain way, but, why did the author choose to make him act thus? Why does Quixote fight windmills—why does Cervantes let him? Why does Hamlet hesitate to avenge his father—what made Shakespeare think he would? Why do the brothers Karamasov wish their father dead—why did Dostoievsky write his greatest novel on this subject?

With some works of SF or fantasy, where the customary laws of causality and motivation are simply not applicable, *only* the latter type of question makes sense. To ask why Gregor Samsa is changed into a beetle (if it is a beetle) is meaningless; to ask why Kafka made this metamorphosis the cornerstone of his tale is very meaningful indeed. On a lower level of literary merit and a correspondingly higher level of popularity, there is no asking why Mike in Heinlein's *Stranger in a Strange Land* uses his strange powers the way he does. Since there are no people with such powers, psychology cannot tell. It is important to ask, though, what fantasy may have led the author to invent a being who can make a person "be not" by simply so wishing (in this case, the infantile fantasy of omnipotence).

Here the psychology of literature can most fruitfully interact with SF—or rather, with nonmimetic literature, including, in addition to SF, much of fantasy, utopias, etc. (often given the overall name of "speculative fiction;" I personally prefer the term "heterotopia"). The reason can be easily demonstrated by an example.

In our real world adults live more often than not in the state of marriage. Many of them have children; and if they do, the probability that the child will be male or female is about even. The realistic writer is compelled by his commitment to "tell it like it is" to present to us

ROBERT PLANK

characters who are likely to be married and whose children are in about equal numbers sons and daughters. Not so in speculative fiction. The type known as "mad scientist" in particular is almost always a bachelor or a widower, and he almost invariably is either childless or has one daughter. I hope this observation will become known as Plank's Law. (Why "almost" invariably? That is a different story and would lead us too far afield.)

The speculative writer, not forced to form his characters and situations in deference to their probability in real life, forms them by projecting into them, with less restraint, something out of his own inner life. He is closer to Shakespeare's model:

. . . as imagination bodies forth
The forms of things unknown, the poet's pen
Turns them to shapes, and gives to airy nothing
A local habitation and a name
    (*Midsummer Night's Dream*, V, 1)

He has a *greater degree of freedom*. The realistic writer obeys the demands of his craft. SF expresses more openly the writer's inner urges, and this makes it so especially valuable as material for psychological study.

And now, before we feel the lack of breathable air at these heights of abstraction, an example from a seminar on the psychology of imaginative literature I recently taught. There were twenty-three students in the class, a number found too large to allow enough of them to participate in a relaxed and yet productive discussion. On a student's suggestion we therefore devised the following format: A book is assigned for reading. At a predetermined date (the class met for seventy-five minutes twice a week) the students cluster in informal separate groups and spend the first half of the class time discussing the book. Each group elects a reporter. The class as a whole gets together for the second half of the time, and the reporters sum up their group's discussion. My role in this is limited to going from group to group "visiting," and to chairing the second half of the session. No instruction or guidance is given to the groups as to which problems they should focus on or how they should handle them, although some traditions develop naturally in the course of the semester.

The reporters then write up their speeches, I consolidate them, and my writeup is photocopied and distributed at the beginning of the following session. This session, and sometimes a third, is devoted to discussion by the entire class, in which I may take an active part.

Orwell's *Nineteen Eighty-four* was assigned. On the date set for it, twenty-one students were present. They formed (spontaneously, not by design) three groups of seven each. The three reports follow. As it happened, I did in this instance but a minimum of editing, chiefly some tightening up. E.g., in 3–a the original text said, ". . . in addition to the external restraint, Winston did not possess . . ." I left out the "to the external restraint," it having already been mentioned a couple of lines higher up.

Orwell, *Nineteen Eighty-four:* Questions and statements for discussion, as reported on behalf of the three small discussion groups.

Group 1:
a) What are the top people of 1984 really after? O'Brien says for power only—or is it for the wealth? The top personnel have servants, excellent food, etc., while the mass of the people are poorly fed, poorly clothed.

b) Why does O'Brien prolong the arrest of Winston and Julia, give them the book, and hold off for a while?

c) Changing the vocabulary does not change a person's emotions. Julia is an example. With a limited vocabulary and after growing up in an environment in which sex was dirty and love did not exist—except love for the Party—she still loved and found sex beautiful. There must be others like her then (who probably don't rebel, out of fear).

d) We would like the entire class to discuss the significance of "Under the spreading chestnut tree . . ." The song is used on pp. 66 and 241. Rutherford and Winston both react in the same manner when they hear the song—or do they? Are they both experiencing the same thoughts or emotions?

e) Could this happen today? Everyone in the group except me said yes, citing Watergate, farming controls, police laws, etc., as events that could lead to a 1984. Consider here the development and extent of doublethink; also the control (success and failures) of Hitler and Castro.

f) Is the society of 1984 efficient? The majority said no—people are poor; the only job we know of is "changing history and the past."

g) Discuss the passage on p. 197: "They got me a long time ago . . . You know this, Winston . . ." Did Winston really know this?

Group 2:
a) They were able to find out what he feared most—was or wasn't the torture by use of rats classical conditioning?

b) They may have used (arrested) Parsons to frighten Winston.

c) When Winston said he was "better than the Party," they played the tape of him saying he would throw acid in kids' faces—it shows, if you believe in a cause the end justifies the means.

d) Winston was a victim of doublethink because he liked his job, rationalized his work by saying he was not forging but "substituting one piece of nonsense for another"—ironic because what he did was

ROBERT PLANK

exactly what he was against.

e) Proles are better off than Party members—"Ignorance is bliss."

f) What effect did mother and sister have on Winston's behavior?

g) The Freudian principle: avoid pain, strive for pleasure (food drive).

Group 3:

a) The concept of freedom: Winston did not ·have any "freedom." There were the pressures of external restraint, as when he was taken to the Ministry of Love for punishment; the basic purpose here, of course, was to condition him to accept and honor Big Brother. In addition, Winston did not have the freedom of choice. This was the result, presumably, of the reduction of words so that people's thoughts would be constricted and narrow.

b) The group also looked for parallels between 1984 and present-day society. There was resemblance between "doublethink" in the book and the language invented by the past administration, particularly around "Watergate." Also, *Nineteen Eighty-four* not only represents a form of governmental repression and subversion, but also a mood of despair and alienation—a warning to people of today despite a corrupt government not to allow their emotions to be suppressed to the point of despair.

c) Is it possible for a government to have more direct control over children than do the parents? What made this possible in 1984?

d) What is the purpose of the "hate period"? Is it to reduce the aggressive drive of man, or is it a means in which sexual passions are expressed? Or, is there an interaction between these drives?

A critical review of the three discussions reported here will have to keep in mind that these were students (in this case, college undergraduates, chiefly juniors and seniors): to apply the standards of professional scholarly work would be inappropriate. Likewise, if you taught the same subject in a similar manner in high school, expectations would have to be materially scaled down. Personally I think the discussions were very good, considering all factors, and the reporters did an excellent job. (I want to take this opportunity to thank the students who took part in the discussions, and particularly the three reporters, Cathy O'Donnell, Merle Owen, and Laura Steckler, who did the work embodied here and who have kindly permitted me to use it.) They, of course, could only summarize what had been said.

Bewilderment seems to have been the foremost response that *Nineteen Eighty-four* evoked in these readers, as well it might. One does not get the impression that they were awed, that the book gripped them and shook them, as it equally well might. When I recommend SF on totalitarianism—the genuine article, such as *Nineteen Eighty-four* or Ernst Jünger's *On the Marble Cliffs;* no special precaution is needed for stories like Ira Levin's *This Perfect Day*—I am used to warning my students not to read the book in the evening, unless they want to spend a sleepless night. My concern has turned out to be unwarranted: they all sleep well. Perhaps this generation that prides itself so much on being unsentimental and "on top of things" is not easily gripped or shaken, or willing to admit it. Yet, some of the questions in our reports are downright naive. But then, these enviable young people haven't had the experience of totalitarianism. Americans generally haven't, but many soldiers in World War II have seen the concentration camps.

Nobody who grasps the scope of Orwell's imagination would think that the present is similar. Watergate may point in the same direction, but the difference between the common cold and viral pneumonia is obvious, though perhaps those who have had both would more easily see how obvious. Orwell's point is missed when the "efficiency" and "productivity" of his terrifying structure are discussed as though we were dealing with a society having values comparable to ours.

The answer to some questions is too pat (1–c, 3–a) while in other instances probing did not go beyond formulating a question, where an attempt at least at answering would have been within reach (1–b, 2–f, 3–c). Item 1–d is especially interesting: the discussants failed to see the total pattern of Orwell's allusions to childhood; on the other hand, it is remarkable that they meaningfully connected two widely separated passages where the same song is evoked. Occasionally, psychological clichés ("conditioning," "brainwashing," "Freudian principle") raise their ugly heads. Ambulating from group to group, I could catch some of the process of the discussion which had to remain unreflected in the final product. I noticed for instance that item 2–e was urged by the two minority students in the class, an instance of empathy with the underdog that seems to me significant, seeing that most of the critical literature on *Nineteen Eighty-four* pays as little attention to the proles as they were given by that mechanism of tyranny.

All this, of course, was food for the subsequent full class discussion, and I was able to enrich it by supplementing the book with references to Orwell's life and to some of his earlier works. I tried to steer into two main problem areas: the pertinent traits of Orwell's personality—the pattern of offered trust and perceived betrayal, his insistence on unpolluted language, his ready suspicion; and the machinery of the structure he had conjured up, with emphasis on the interplay of dominance and submission, the substitution of aggression for sex, the distorted father images, and of course again the significance of trust and betrayal.

Could we have done the same for any other novel, any other author? Certainly. The result would not have been inferior, but different. There are mainly three reasons why I think *Nineteen Eighty-four* an apt choice. Two are interconnected: the special quality that the work shares with other SF (in the wider sense, including utopias–in this case, "negative utopias," "dystopias," call them what you may) and that sets it apart from the "mainstream," and second the literary quality.

My observation that the greater degree of freedom in SF makes it especially suited for psychological study does not claim extreme originality. "Mainstream" scholars may not be aware of it, but among specialists in SF it has reached even those who cannot be said to be markedly perceptive. Arthur Asa Berger, discussing Italian "erotic horror comics" such as *Satanic,* remarks (*The Comic-Stripped American,* Penguin Books, 1973, p. 213) that "the very crudeness and childishness of these stories suggest that they must be particularly meaningful, since the artists and writers lack the ability to give their works any sophistication and *are unable to hide or repress their dreams and fears"* (my italics).

Lack of ability is an allegation new to this argument. We must give it at least passing attention. If we remember that we are not engaged in evaluative criticism, it might appear at first blush that a bad book can be just as good stuff for psychological analysis as a good book. If we think, however, of the "degree of freedom," we may go on to the thought that a bad book would be even better for our purpose. What distinguishes the good writer from the bad writer is not merely that the good writer is more eager to satisfy the demands of his inner mental processes than the public's demands, or that he is more concerned with considerations of taste, probability, intellectual level, psychological depth—all inhibiting factors. More important, he needs and applies more inhibition because, though he may be more sincere, he knows so much more about himself, there is so much more to be sincere about, while the bad writer may spill his most objectionable fantasies without even knowing it. As it is true that the nonmimetic writer is freer than the mimetic writer, so it can also be said that the bad writer has, and uses, a greater degree of freedom. He presents his fantasies more in the raw, and so his works may be even better material for psychological study than the better works are.

Let us not stop to ask where SF comes in here (Berger, remember, talks about comic books, a somewhat related but happily different line of literature), but let us rather hasten to add that the question is somewhat moot: the teacher of SF, as the teacher of any literature, must consider that the students' time should not be wasted on bad literature when it can be devoted to good literature, and that it is part of his obligation to help develop his students' taste and ability to discriminate and to appreciate the best. The Lord knows this can be an uphill road, so this may become the overriding consideration, and bad literature may be firmly banned from class, even if better literature were from the point of psychology only the second best.

Orwell clearly meets any reasonable standard. He may not have been the peer of Shakespeare or Goethe; but most certainly *Nineteen Eighty-four* is not, the Lord be praised, on a level with *The Exorcist*. Of course, many other works could be chosen as well as Orwell's; e.g., the novel that is so often mentioned in tandem with *Nineteen Eighty-four* because of its external similarities, though the ideological thrust goes in quite different a direction, Huxley's *Brave New World*.

The third reason applies to all SF or speculative fiction worthy of its name because of what sets it apart from all other fiction. Mainstream literature, facing the future, asks, what shall we individually become? SF asks, what shall become of us collectively? We are learning in the university of hard knocks how topical this is. Empires have crumbled all through history. This time history has a new lesson: the empire you save may be your own.

The ascendancy of SF is one fruit of our learning our lesson, but we are reluctant learners, and the value of SF may be thought to lie elsewhere. George Steiner, a critics' critic and a scholars' scholar, reviewing a book on *The Adventurer* by Paul Zweig in *The New Yorker* (Jan. 20, 1975, pp. 94-97) says:

> It is the adventure story, the telling of the tale, which has kept the heart awake from the time of the Greek bards . . . But from the seventeenth century onward, the Western concept of "action" and of what constitutes true adventure alters radically. . . . In the modern sense, adventure has become internal; it lies in the play of consciousness. . . . It is in science fiction, which he all but ignores . . . that Zweig would have discovered those great currents of action and adventure he finds lacking in the modern novel.

We may rejoice in such an accolade from a man not suspected of yielding to popular taste, but we may disagree. I for one believe that what really distinguishes SF is something different.

A great exhibition of archaeological treasures dug up under the jurisdiction of the People's Republic of China during the first quarter century of its rule was shown in three great North American cities (Toronto, Washington, Kansas City) in 1974–75. A splendid and melancholy sight. Almost all the exhibits came from tombs. There they were, the corpses encased in jade and gold, the crocks and bowls to keep their food, and their horses and servants and utensils, all fashioned in enduring bronze to assure them imperishable honor among the other corpses.

So the Chinese were not better off than we. The dream is everywhere, rooted in a ubiquitous defect (ineradicable, perhaps; as the poet says, "High heaven and earth ail from the prime foundation"), a defect of human comprehension, from distant China to pre-Columbian America, and to the lands from which Western civilization arose, the fantasy of

ROBERT PLANK

individual physical survival. And where does the universal fantasy lead? To the grave; and to the grave robber.

Yet there has been another fantasy, as venerable and as durable, a dream that seeks its fulfillment not in our own survival but in the survival and the lasting glory of something greater than ourselves: a land, an idea, mankind, the world. Imagination has looked for the embodiment of that "airy nothing" in history and in distant places. Thomas Mann's speculation about Atlantis is a late example. Now SF looks for it in "alternative worlds," thus claiming the inheritance of an old and noble tradition.

This leads us back to our starting point, but also beyond most of current SF. Still, to explore the yearning for a country "closer to the heart's desire" would be another worthy subject for the psychology of SF.

SCIENCE FICTION
AND RELIGION

BY ANDREW J. BURGESS

Those who find conflicts between science and religion may be surprised at this use of SF to teach religion, but Andrew J. Burgess outlines his approach with convincing logic and clarity. Now Chairperson for the Religious Studies Program at the University of New Mexico, he has taught Religious Studies at Case Western Reserve University and Cleveland State University. His writings include Passion, "Knowing How," *and* Understanding: An Essay on the Concept of Faith *(Scholars Press, 1975). What he says here will interest many others in addition to teachers of religion. There is a point, it seems evident, where SF and religion tend to converge.*

I must confess at the start: I am not a teacher of science fiction. Not, at any rate, if teaching science fiction means presenting the breadth and literary power of the works. My concern is less to teach the genre, or even the religious subspecies, than to *use* the writings in the discussion of religious issues. Thus what I have to say will be directed not so much to literary critics as to religion professors and to others from various fields who dip into science-fiction materials with similar ulterior motives.

Courses have indeed been devised to teach religious science fiction, often with fair success. Whatever the difficulties of such courses, they can guarantee enjoyable reading, lively discussion, and some mind-bending reinterpretations of ethical and religious views. The book list might be a formidable one, including such staples as the C.S. Lewis space trilogy, James Blish's *A Case of Conscience,* Walter Miller, Jr.'s *A Canticle for Leibowitz,* Philip José Farmer's *Night of Light,* David Lindsay's *A Voyage to Arcturus,* and Michael Moorcock's *Behold the Man.* With books like these, how can one go wrong?

Academic authorities, however, are apt to take a dim view of courses of this sort, and for good reason. Measured against Augustine, Aquinas, Maimonides, Luther, and the rest, the science-fiction writer looks unimpressive as a teacher of religion, and it is easy to see why the project of replacing the standard texts with speculative novels meets with little support. The novelist's first obligation is to tell the story; keeping the theology straight is far down his list of priorities. An old tradition in science fiction forbids transgressing the known limits of science, but no such restriction inhibits the author from blending together doctrines from different religions without giving notice, or from creating sensational new religious doctrines to fit the plot. The stories are primarily "science" fiction, not religious fiction. Very often the religious angle comes in late and seems designed chiefly to fog over with pseudo-mysticism a shaky plot structure. The reader who is well versed in different religions can enjoy himself sorting out the various traditions and distinguishing what is creative from what is banal. The college student, whose grasp even of his own heritage is often extremely feeble, only becomes confused.

Nonetheless, science fiction can be used to teach religion. I refuse to believe that an area of study that has found a place in the curriculum for poetry, film, drama, and virtually every other splendor of the human spirit cannot find a use for this style of fiction, which is among the most idea- and issue-oriented media we know. If precedent from ancient tradition were required, I would call upon the Biblical apocalyptic writers (for example, in the books of Daniel and Ezekiel), whose works are filled with strange visions of the creation and destruction of worlds. Apocalyptic is not science fiction (although the relation between the two is an intriguing one, well worth investigating), but the kind of daring needed to portray one's faith apocalyptically is surely no less than that which would be required to put theology into a science-fiction framework.

Despite the limitations of space novels as classroom religion texts, they could serve some functions which no other kinds of literature perform.

For one thing, science fiction creates an emotional backdrop against which certain sensitive issues can be discussed. A person's faith is such an intimate matter, closely tied together with his attitudes toward his family and his tradition, that it is difficult to display in a public forum. Genuine doubts and convictions are easier to speak of in terms of a story set on Arcturus than closer to home, say, in Akron. Of course, as a person matures he learns to speak of his faith in psychological and sociological abstractions, but something is lost in the process. A story setting, by keeping the concreteness of the problems, prevents them from losing their point.

The kinship between religion and science fiction goes deeper than a mere tactical teaching device. The two are natural allies. Most major religions make cosmic claims; and, where the awareness of the cosmos expands, the religious consciousness ought to expand with it. Imaginative literature helps to free a person from childhood fixations and envision God in ways appropriate to the space age. Unfortunately, much of science fiction portrays a kind of Conan the Conqueror rather than the Creator of Heaven and Earth, but some of the best of the literature breaks through such limits and shows a picture of God which would be hard to match anywhere.

There are, besides, some issues in religion which simply cannot be illustrated except in the far-out reaches of space and time. The notion of a state of innocence, for example, which plays so large a part in Western religion's understanding of sin and responsibility, has always asked for the imagining of a perfect society somewhere. To be valid the notion does not have to be actualized—indeed, perhaps actualization would undermine the concept—but it is natural to want to see the possibility of such a perfect state in concrete terms. Thus, when the Edens of the Near East turned out to be dried-up deserts, people looked elsewhere for the ideal. At one time the New World was supposed to provide a perfect "state of nature," but it would be a bold soul today who argued that America was free from guilt. C.S. Lewis, when he described the state of innocence, placed it as close as Venus (Perelandra); and it is a measure of the speed with which spaceships are hurtling back the frontiers of space that Venus now seems to be in our backyard, and hence an implausible site (even if living conditions permitted) for an ideal society.

For some purposes, and for some issues, we simply cannot do very well without science-fiction materials. The trick is to learn to limit what is hoped for from the course to what can reasonably be expected in the available time. Background, structure, timing, are as important in such a class as in any other.

Certain limitations must be placed on the scope if a class using science fiction is to work. What these limits will be may be disagreed on, but some limits there must be. Here are those within which I work:

1) The readings should be limited to the Jewish and Christian traditions. The main reason for this is the probable background of the students. In order to profit from so ambitious a project the student will need all the background he has, and more besides. A secondary reason for this restriction in scope comes from the materials themselves. Writers who draw on themes from Eastern religions find it very easy to trade upon the ignorance of their readers and to blur basic distinctions among the religions.

2) The bulk of the reading should be standard non-science-fiction material of an historical or methodological sort, built around a specific problem or theme. Although many courses using religious science fiction do not follow this practice, it is a central requirement for a sound course. Students can be imagined for whom solid background material is not necessary, but they are unlikely to show up in large enough numbers to make a class.

3) The science-fiction readings should be short, straightforward (insofar as this is consonant with the nature of speculative fiction), and as close to identifiable traditional conceptions as possible. The readings are there to illustrate issues and suggest new solutions, not, at least

not primarily, to send the student off on a trip all his own. Lewis and Blish are among the finest of the authors in the accurate presentation of religious views which are close enough to historical traditions to be illuminating about those traditions. For simplicity, however, it would be difficult to better the way Vercors's *You Shall Know Them* takes up the question, "What is man?" In the story a "missing link" is killed, and the reader is then caught up in the fascinating argument and counterargument of the trial which is to decide whether such a killing is murder. Best of all, the ending is sufficiently ambiguous so that one cannot rest with it and must go on to find a more adequate solution.

Short stories which fit a given theme are not always easy to come by. Because religious themes stand frequently on the fantasy end of the science-fiction spectrum, *Fantasy and Science Fiction* is a likely magazine source. Three anthologies of religious science fiction from which the teacher can pick and choose are: *Other Worlds, Other Gods* (various religious views), *Flame Tree Planet* (Christian), and *Wandering Stars* (Jewish).

4) Several conflicting stories should be selected on the same issue. Better yet, there should be only one main issue for the course. The reason for the conflicting stories is that selecting only one story is liable to allow the student to rest with that story as the definitive solution to the problem. It takes two contrary stories to make a debate, and three or more, plus vigorous reading in the religious traditions and some hard thinking, before a student will be able to create a position of his own.

What, after all, does it mean to teach religion? If rote learning is all that is desired, the use of science fiction can only be an intrusion. But understanding a creed or a theology involves more than learning to repeat it. A person has to search out how and why the doctrines were made. For this purpose there is no substitute for the effort of following through the development that lies behind the doctrines, step by step, until they reach their present form. The student needs to get inside the doctrines sufficiently so that he can build them anew for himself and see how they were put together. A good exercise to check the depth of one's understanding is to try to develop the theology in new ways, in terms of a later situation or in answer to objections which it never had to meet, and yet to stay true to the distinctiveness of the original. What would Augustine have had to say to a particular view of modern psychology? The question can only be speculative, but the quality of the speculation given in reply says something about one's grasp of the man.

The beauty of the science-fiction approach is that it cuts off the possibility of simply reciting old phrases. Because today's world is gone, the situation in which speaking takes place differs in a bewildering variety of ways. Of course the teacher has to pick the fictional world carefully, both for its intrinsic coherence and for its appropriateness in illuminating a particular doctrine. But that is hardly a limit—only a condition; and whatever Martian or Venusian theologizing may result can have all the playfulness and exuberant freedom of the original story.

In the beginning is the idea. In my own case, the inspiration for the first course came from reading a short story by Ray Bradbury entitled "The Fire Balloons" (The Illustrated Man). The plot has a group of Episcopal priests sent as missionaries to Mars. Finding that the Martians have glowing, spherical bodies which move freely through space, the leader of the priests makes a model of a sphere, puts a candle within it, and places it upon the altar of his chapel, as a symbol of what the incarnation of Christ will be to those with Martian bodies. For, as he explains to his shocked followers, since Christ needs to be portrayed as Italian to the Italians, and Chinese to the Chinese, the Martian Christ ought to have a Martian body. Reading this, I was reminded of a different solution to the priest's problem which comes in the speeches of the "eldila" (angels) at the end of C.S. Lewis's Perelandra. Handling this question in a class, however, turned out to require calling on the resources of linguistics, anthropology, and psychology, as well as Christology. In fact, to make the problem real, I had to create a special kind of course. But on that topic, more later.

Other ideas produce other kinds of courses. Because students are frequently repelled by the bizarre style of the apocalyptic writers who wrote in the period between the Old and the New Testaments, two professors at Luther Seminary, St. Paul, decided to lead off the readings with a modern analogue—science fiction. The actual proportion of the readings devoted to science fiction (H.G. Wells and Ray Bradbury) was small, but the point was made, and the apocalyptic images took on a startlingly contemporary cast. Moreover, the appropriateness of the comparison between the old and the new speculative writing did not depend only upon the similarities between them. Not until the student could clearly state how apocalyptic is *not* science fiction would he truly understand what apocalyptic is.

Once the basic issue has been isolated in several science-fiction stories, the possibilities are limited only by the perseverance and cunning of the instructor. The question "What is a Jew?" for example, has attracted a number of outstanding writers, among them William Tenn in his delightful "On Venus, Have We Got a Rabbi" (Wandering Stars). In this story the First Interstellar Neozionist Conference, on Venus, is in an uproar because the Bulbas from the fourth planet of the star Rigel have applied for accreditation as Jews. And why not? They can produce Jewish birth records going back for centuries. When they recite the sacred prayers the whole assembly is moved. What is more, they tell how they have suffered pogrom after pogrom for their Jewishness. The problem is this: the Bulbas look like lumpy brown pillows

ANDREW J. BURGESS

with short gray tentacles. And what does the Talmud say to that? But on Venus, have they got a Rabbi! Any professor who cannot take Tenn's story, and Rabbi Smallman's solution, and start off a discussion of Judaism, is probably teaching in the wrong field.

The whole secret of effectively using religious science fiction to teach religion is to construct the course plan with a balance of stories and text materials, so that the student can apply the stories to deepen his understanding of religious issues. More often than not, science fiction will merely provide the spark which ignites otherwise inert traditional material. Back in my rocket-launching days at college I used to gather with some chemist friends each Saturday night on top of the science building to watch the latest creations. There was a flash, a soul-satisfying explosion, and then the rocket shot off a few feet in one direction or another. A course which simply puts together science-fiction writings could be like those rockets—good on flash, but poor on distance and direction. A plan that uses science fiction as a starter or to focus issues is no less exciting than one made up only of stories, and often a good deal more productive.

Some of the same principles which have been discussed apply also when one is dealing not with a reading course but with a writing course. The reading of science-fiction works is in any case also basic to a class in writing, since the stories and novels provide models for the students' work. Moreover, regular reading assignments and reports are a good way to provide structure to a writing curriculum, which tends to have no work producible for discussion until near the end of the term.

The critical juncture in such a writing course comes at the time when the student presents the outline and sketch of his story for private criticism. In any writing course this point would be important; in a course teaching religion it is decisive. In order to develop a story which brings to bear a solid body of religious knowledge, the student is going to need help in locating the relevant source materials. If there is a theme or issue in common among the science-fiction readings and student stories, a reading list can be provided that will give general aid, but some specific suggestions will still be needed for each story.

The test of the grasp which the student attains over the material will come not only in the story he writes, but also in how well he can explain to his classmates why he wrote as he did. To this end I have required that each story be accompanied by a defense, in the usual term paper format, which explains the story in terms of the sources used.

What may easily be overlooked is the way in which the Bible itself offers countless possibilities for variations on its narratives. Of course, the prospects for slam-bang gadgetry are there too, as in all science-fiction writing. There is a temptation either to provide a mechanical account of every remarkable event in the scriptures, or else to multiply miracles. But if someone carefully studies the Biblical stories to find what they say, it is surprising what diverse and creative results can follow. Even so slight a story as that of Balaam's ass, for example, provided Anthony Boucher with a source for two completely different tales—"Balaam" and "The Quest for Saint Aquin" *(Other Worlds, Other Gods)*.

Good story writing of this sort need not take one away from the essential idea of the original. Sometimes, indeed, it is only after writing such a story that one appreciates what was said. There may be very little left of the Biblical narrative from which one began and that mostly in insignificant details or bits of conversation, but if the writer has in fact understood the original, the new story may pick up some of the point of the old and state it afresh, somewhat as a modern composer may pick up a classical musical theme or idea and make us hear it as we have never heard it before.

In addition to courses using the reading or writing of science fiction, there are many worthwhile hybrids. The first course I designed of this sort, on the topic of incarnation and communication, began as a standard reading class, but soon developed into a corporate project in which the students had to work themselves out of a science-fiction situation. The idea for the method came from a course entitled Creative Engineering taught at M.I.T. by the late John Arnold. In order to steer his students away from the usual cookbook approach to solving engineering problems, Professor Arnold assigned the class to create products for the inhabitants of an imaginary planet, who are hatched from eggs and have an altogether different physical and social environment from ours. One ingenious student designed an egg-shaped car, arguing that the car would be structurally strong—and besides, such a people would feel psychologically more secure in a car of that shape! In my own course, the function of the imaginary planet was different; it provided the setting in which communication of religious concepts might be attempted between human beings and creatures with a different kind of body (insect-shaped, with a humanoid slave race). By asking the question, "How does the type of body (and the related social structures) affect the ability to transmit religious concepts?" the class was led to analyze concretely some conceptual connections between conviction and emotion and between religious language and form of life. Moreover, instead of having individual projects, the class was divided into teams (physical environment and story line; biology-sociology; linguistics and communication) that produced materials which were edited into a composite class report.

Part of the excitement of dealing with science fiction comes from the desire not just to read about highly speculative situations but to participate in them, and when a class can preserve some of that initial excitement, learning is easy. In a course recently developed at a congregation in Evanston, an approach along these lines presented fu-

ANDREW J. BURGESS

turology and the future of Christianity. The future-directedness of both Christianity and Judaism fits here perfectly. On the other hand, one can also set the time machines backward for a course project; there is abundant material in the literature, for example, that could help a group test out in detail what a "quest for the historical Jesus" would really involve.

In the end, there is no universal format into which courses using science fiction to teach religion can be programmed. More than with most other curricula, each course of this sort has to be custom-designed to fit the issue handled. The results are apt to be a bit rough and unpredictable, open-ended, full of spectacular victories and spectacular defeats. But the course will have two great advantages over a more conventional approach. The one is the joy and the power of the stories themselves. The other is the kind of student who loves science fiction and is attracted to the class, and who is puzzling over religious issues. Such a student will neither accept the stock answers to religious questions, nor will he rest content with vague abstractions; he will insist on envisioning the future in concrete terms. Unpredictability and open-endedness, moreover, are just what he demands. Having such allies in the class does not assure success, but it does mean that however the class goes, all will succeed or fail together.

Bibliographical Note

The anthologies referred to are: Jack Dann, ed., *Wandering Stars* (New York: Pocket Books, 1975); Roger Elwood, ed., *Flame Tree Planet* (St. Louis: Concordia, 1973); and Mayo Mohs, ed., *Other Worlds, Other Gods* (New York: Avon, 1974). Other recent anthologies are: *Chronicles of a Comer and Other Religious Science Fiction Stories* (Atlanta: John Knox, 1974) and *Signs and Wonders* (Old Tappan, N.J.: Fleming H. Revell, 1972), both edited by Roger Elwood; and *The New Awareness: Religion Through Science Fiction* (New York: Delacorte, 1975), edited by Patricia Warrick and Martin Harry Greenberg. There are also a pair of novella collections arranged around the themes: Terry Carr, ed., *An Exaltation of Stars* (New York: Pocket Books, 1974; three stories centered on the nature of transcendental experience) and Poul Anderson, *et al.*, *The Day the Sun Stood Still* (Nashville: Thomas Nelson, 1972; three stories in answer to the question "What kind of world might exist where the basis of faith is replaced by certain knowledge?").

Secondary sources on religious science fiction include: Erminie Huntree Lantero, "What is Man?" and "What is Time?" *Religion in Life*, 38 (Summer 1969), 242-55; and 40 (Autumn, 1971), 423-35; Lois and Stephen Rose, *The Shattered Ring: Science Fiction and the Quest for Meaning* (Richmond: John Knox, 1970); Gerald Heard, "Science Fiction, Morals, and Religion," in *Science Fiction: The Future*, ed. Dick

Allen (New York: Harcourt, Brace, Jovanovich, 1971), 291-306; and Andrew J. Burgess, "Teaching Religion Through Science Fiction," *Extrapolation*, 13 (May, 1972), 112-15.

In addition to the standard sources, the following works may be useful for background on special topics, particularly those dealing with extra-terrestrial life: Sylvia Louise Engdahl, *The Planet-Girded Suns* (New York: Atheneum, 1974) and Stanley L. Jaki, *Planets and Planetarians* (New York: Halsted Press, 1977), both dealing with the history of the belief in extra-terrestrial life; E. L. Mascall, *Christian Theology and Natural Science* (London: Longmans, Green, 1956), 36-46; Pierre Teilhard de Chardin, *The Future of Man* (New York: Harpers, 1969), 101-44, and *Christianity and Evolution* (New York: Harcourt, Brace, Jovanovich, 1969), 229-36; Andrew J. Burgess, "Earth Chauvinism," *Christian Century*, 93 (December 8, 1976), 1098-1102; and Norman Lamm, "The Religious Implications of Extra-Terrestrial Life," in *Faith and Doubt: Studies in Traditional Jewish* Thought) New York: KTAV, 1971), 107-60. An extensive bibliography on such topics is included in Cyril Ponnamperuma and A. G. W. Cameron, *Interstellar Communication* (Boston: Houghton Mifflin, 1974), 215-19.

The most helpful non-fiction works of C.S. Lewis here are: "Religion and Rocketry," in *The World's Last Night* (New York: Harcourt, Brace, Jovanovich, 1960), 83-92, and several essays in *Of Other Worlds* (New York: Harcourt, Brace, and World, 1966). A basic resource is the monthly *Bulletin of the New York C. S. Lewis Society* (466 Orange Street, New Haven, Connecticut 06511).

I wish to thank Charles J. Brady (University of Dayton), Wendell Frerichs and Roy Harrisville (Luther Theological Seminary), Rose Gruenler and Marvyn Mahle (Hiram College), Rev. Dow Kirkpatrick (Evanston, Illinois), Robert Reilly (Rider College), and Charles G. Waugh (University of Maine at Augusta), for sharing with me their experience teaching religion with science fiction materials. I am also indebted to Sylvia Louise Engdahl and Robert Plank for many helpful suggestions.

ANDREW J. BURGESS

PHILOSOPHIC INSIGHT THROUGH SCIENCE FICTION: FOCUSING ON HUMAN PROBLEMS

BY ROBERT E. MYERS

We like to define science fiction as the literature of ideas. Here, Robert E. Myers offers strong support for that sometimes-challenged claim. He's a professor of philosophy at Bethany College in West Virginia. His works include one volume of some special interest to the editor of this book: Jack Williamson: A Primary and Secondary Bibliography *(G. K. Hall, 1980). He has been using SF for several years in his philosophy courses. In this essay, he not only highlights the parallels between SF and philosophy, but outlines the subdivisions of philosophy and makes useful comments on the specific SF titles he uses in the classroom to introduce such topics as epistemology, metaphysics, logic, and ethics.*

Philosophic insight through science fiction? This claim may sound more than a little strange at first and it may alienate both many science-fiction authors and many professional philosophers. However, in spite of these possibilities, I affirm that philosophic insight is possible through some science fiction. This is more than an accident, for philosophy and science fiction stand in a special relation; it is true that this special relation and its constructive potential have not been fully developed *overtly*. Most good science fiction and an evolving (or perhaps rediscovered) concept of philosophy have, if not instances of technical "sameness," at least "family resemblances" of concerns and questions and central focus.

I. Both Fields Emerging from Periods of Trauma

Traditionally both science fiction and philosophy have been viewed as "abstract" and as "worthless." In a culture that is basically pragmatic, the terms "abstract" and "abstractions" often carry strongly negative connotations and it is quite easy to argue that if something is abstract, it is therefore worthless. In one of those delightful contradictions which a culture can embrace, we have cried for specialization but decried abstraction. Only with the greatest of difficulty are we beginning to realize that the generalist may be needed more today than more specialists; we are still trying to shake off this trauma. Both science fiction and philosophy seem to be emerging from periods of traumatic struggle.

Reflecting somewhat the attraction of specialization and the security of working with "closed definitions," science fiction and its scenarios tended to be assigned to a pulp status in a double sense by "knowledgeable literary critics": value-laden judgments consigned "Sci-Fi" (SF) to the pulps to indicate not only economically cheap publication but insignificant subject matter as well. In a striking sleight-of-hand (or of logic), it was decided that since SF did not fit the closed definition of literature at hand, it was without redeeming qualities and could be safely ignored. (This is what Jack Williamson refers to as the time SF was seen as "a kind of subliterate nonsense.") More recently we seem to be recognizing: the need for a more general definition (the philosopher might suggest the open-textured nature of literature); the advance of SF to a subgenre (perhaps becoming a genre) of literature; the literary competence of many SF writers; and the creative potential in their works.

Reflecting a somewhat different aspect of specialization and a kind of "guilt" because philosophy didn't seem to have the precision (and "successes") of the sciences, philosophy tended to develop into a closed "professional" activity, on the one hand, and an antiscientific but pro-Angst semi-literary activity, on the other hand. The tools of critical analysis were held for and by those who qualified as full initiates; those tools and the resulting "analysis" from the proper manipulation of these tools were in a real sense "abstractions." Although training and qualification for initiation were long and arduous, once initiated and qualified, the philosopher could discourse with other professional philosophers of similar training. (Please note that philosophy was far from the only discipline caught in this tendency.) But too often those who were on the verge of asking philosophical questions of importance either could not pass the test of technical linguistic and conceptual tool-wielding or could not understand the significance of the "abstract" models presented by professional philosophers. More recently we seem to be recognizing: the inadequacy of being divided into two camps which decry the merits of one another and hold counsel only with their own members, Analytic specialists on one side, Existential writers on the other; the discovery—some of us would insist: the rediscovery—that the task of philosophy is more than analysis alone and more than an existential shock alone; and the need for and the creative potential of a philosophy that deals with human problems in at least generally understandable human terms.

In this period of emerging from traumatic experiences in their his-

ROBERT E. MYERS

tory, perhaps more of those involved in these particular fields of science fiction and philosophy are better able to recognize their common concerns than most practitioners in either field were able to do previously. Perhaps both can come to terms with the phenomenon of becoming "respectable" or at least more respectable. Perhaps those in science fiction can admit openly that their stock in trade is ideas and especially philosophic ideas. Perhaps those in philosophy can admit openly that some science-fiction stories present more detailed accounts of particular solutions or philosophic stances than they have done recently (e.g., Plato did rather well). Perhaps we can come to recognize that the best of both fields is complementary and focuses on and has central impact on the human being and his/her concept of him/herself.

II. Similar Concerns, Complementary Treatment: Ideas and Human Problems

Both science fiction and philosophy tend to attract people who are "reflective," persons who are fascinated by ideas and who have an interest more in "possibilities" than in "just the facts." Even the most extreme SF story of other worlds, other times, and other life-forms involves the imagination and emotional processes of the human reader; most SF stories with fewer extreme variables may be more completely integrated into the reader's thought process and ideas.

Both science fiction and philosophy trace out the consequences of actions, beliefs and decisions and evaluate them. Both, certainly the best of both, probe the sanctum of assumptions which we usually either ignore or try to protect from examination and change. "What if . . .?", that favorite of science fiction, is just as much a favorite of philosophy—as are "If this goes on . . ." and "If only . . .", also. That "What if . . .?" question, if taken seriously, opens us up in such a way that it can probe our concept of human nature, of what it is to be human and ask ourselves how we, as such human beings, would respond to changed conditions.

For example, practitioners in both fields may ask: *What if:* —this present tendency goes on unchanged? What consequences will follow? —one commitment of our belief-set is indefensible and is changed? —one part of our sociopolitical framework were to change and/or become dominant? —one of our creations were to win control over its creators? —God were far different from what the main religious traditions have led us to believe? —our thinking process were somehow altered and the accepted criteria for distinguishing truth/falsity were thus changed? —technology were more value-laden (good-evil) than we believe it to be? —human beings were readily expendable and replaceable and thus of little value? Although obviously not all thinking people write or read science fiction and philosophy, still both science fiction and philosophy tend to attract "thinkers," probers of the status quo, of unexamined assumptions, people who are interested in ideas and in concepts and in speculating about them in a disciplined way.

At this point it might well be asked: We all know that Socrates, the philosopher's philosopher, was supposed to have said "The unexamined life is not worth living," but did anybody significant in science fiction really say this kind of thing about ideas, thought, and reflection? Some quick examples: John W. Campbell enumerated the professions represented among the readers of his magazine and summarized their special resemblance by saying, "Generally speaking, these people are philosophically inclined. They enjoy thinking. They enjoy speculating and figuring out problems." Isaac Asimov suggests that "the better science fiction" "is not primarily concerned with new inventions but with human beings. [This kind of SF] has a little thought to it." This kind of science fiction he describes as "that field of literature which deals with human response to advances in science or technology." Anthony Boucher, commenting on critic Bruce Franklin's claim that science fiction is *realistic* fiction, noted: "Almost always the writer of good science fiction is writing about his own time but, by casting the story in the future, he can say things he couldn't get by with if it were set in his own time." Theodore Sturgeon believes that good science fiction is "telling a story of humanly understandable problems with humanly understandable solutions, all of which could not occur without a scientific aspect." Ray Bradbury asserts that "we are so enamoured with gimmicks in our society" that we ignore "human reactions to inventions"; what the good science-fiction writer does is "the real business of all art forms; go below the surface and see what makes things tick." Or consider the claim: science fiction is didactic—an old form of teaching; it presents solutions to human problems. (Ref. Center for Cassette Studies tapes: "Science Fiction In Our Time" 508; "Science Fiction—Its Future" 30428; and "Science and Fiction" 020/12060.) This sounds as if more than Olaf Stapledon, "a Doctor of Philosophy," were and are concerned with reflection, a disciplined imagination, philosophical ideas and human problems and solutions.

The subdivisions of Philosophy carry such seemingly technical and intimidating names as Epistemology, Metaphysics, Logic, Axiology, and a number of Philosophy of ——————— fields. Simply recasting these terms into what I hope will be more understandable and thereby more meaningful terms may serve two purposes: it may make more apparent the similarity of concerns which science fiction and philosophy have, for probably most devoted readers of SF will be able to think of two or three stories built upon any one of these questions or an answer to one of the problems; and it may serve as the basis for trying to answer the question, "Does this combination of science fiction and philosophy work in the classroom?"

1) Epistemology means the study or theory of knowledge. Here such

ROBERT E. MYERS

questions as the following are posed and alternative answers evaluated: Is knowledge possible? What can be known? How do you know? What level of certainty is possible? Are there different ways of knowing? What are the means of checking, the criteria of, our knowledge claims? 2) Metaphysics is concerned with the basically real status of a number of things. What is the ultimate nature of the universe or of reality? How is the real (or Real) related to appearances or to what seems to be? Or: Is there such a thing as truth? What is the real status of cause and effect? The real nature of being human? 3) Logic is concerned with detecting and distinguishing between accurate and inaccurate reasoning procedures, valid and fallacious arguments. It examines the relation between truth and validity, and those conclusions that follow necessarily from premises (and thus are certain) and those that follow with some degree of probability—deductive and inductive forms. Formal logic concentrates on the *form* or pattern of an argument and attempts to show how to recognize and evaluate that form independent of the specific *content* of the argument. 4) Axiology, the study of value, is usually divided into Aesthetics and Ethics. Aesthetics traditionally explores the nature of the beautiful; it also examines the creative process of the artist, the nature of the art object, the materials of the artist, the value of art, the experience of appreciating art, and illusion. Ethics or moral philosophy is concerned with value as it relates to the "moral" behavior of persons in society. This includes examination of the major ethical systems; the criteria for ethical decision making; the basis of ethical judgments that actions are good/bad, right/wrong, moral-immoral-amoral; and the place of duty, obligation, consequences, freedom and responsibility in moral behavior. 5) In the Philosophy of ——————— areas, the methodology, basic working principles and fundamental concepts upon which the field or particular examples within the field operate are identified, analyzed and evaluated.

III. Does the Combination Work in the Classroom?

For several years I've conducted college courses that involved some mixture of science fiction and philosophy, including a freshman seminar developed out of this blend. However, the Introduction to Philosophy is probably the most appropriate one to mention here briefly, since most of the topics or philosophic subdivisions listed above are "introduced" in this course.

The catalogue description of Philosophy 100 indicates that it is "Intended primarily to involve students in an introductory exploration into the range of problems with which philosophers wrestle. 'Living issues' confront us in such vital areas as the nature of self, man, mind, values, knowing, freedom, philosophic outlooks, religious traditions, and even the nature of philosophy itself." Correlated to each topic is a section of a philosophy textbook, a short film or filmstrip and a set of science-fiction stories.

For example, under the topic of "Reasoning and Communicating (Ways of 'Saying Something' and Analyzing Problems)" we examine the forms of communication, linguistic and nonlinguistic, and enough logic to understand how one begins to evaluate reasoning and argument. Filmstrips from the movies *The Time Machine* and *War of the Worlds* indicate the possibilities of divisions without communication, as well as a bit of Wells's irony. Daniel Keyes's SF story, "Crazy Maro," provides an excellent account of nonlinguistic communication and how attitudes are transmitted through words and behavior—as well as a touching account of Maro, who was called "crazy," struggling to find someone who really trusted him so he could trust another. Isaac Asimov's "Reason" presents Robot QT-1, a created robot who or which uses the same form of "reasoned" argument that humans have used for centuries but with different conclusions; so cogent and insistent is QT-1 that his creators begin to doubt their own "reason"—at least until they "reason" out an explanation, on the basis of analyzing the problem and evaluating the argument of QT. Jack Williamson's story "Breakdown" is an excellent account of what can happen to a society and members of that society when communication breaks down.

Or, as another example, consider the topic, "On Being Human (Self, Machine, Others)": obviously we study Descartes and his mind-body dualism, the self as a thinking substance and the mechanistic interpretation of the body, and other philosophical and psychological theories of self, and of others and relating to others. The film for this section is *Future Shock*. (That some of the material is dated has not produced a problem for students; rather than react in criticism, they tend to begin to marvel over how rapidly things change—which serves as a springboard for going into another topic.) Isaac Asimov's "Evidence" provides a fascinating challenge to try to find out what one could use as a test to prove one is not really a robot—particularly when Dr. Calvin, Robopsychologist, explains that there is really no significant behavioral difference between a sophisticated robot who or which follows the Laws of Robotics and a truly good man who follows the best moral codes human beings have devised. Are we to conclude then that the "self" is not a uniquely human possession? Jack Williamson's "Dead Star Station" gives an excellent account of how we evaluate people, usually others, on the basis of certain characteristics and/or on their "success" or their immediate usefulness. Was Gideon Clew a "person"? Was he treated as a person? Ursula K. LeGuin's "Nine Lives" presents an intriguing account of what is involved in the struggle to relate to, and to come to recognize, the other; the shock of one member of a clone-group (essentially a closed community of basically identical selves—or does one say "self"?) who survives and must make the readjustment to the other, the non-self, grips most Intro. students.

ROBERT E. MYERS

Correlated to other topics in Intro. we've used the following: most of the stories in *The Best of Jack Williamson,* Asimov's "Runaround," Jerome Bixby's "It's A *Good* Life," Arthur C. Clarke's "The Nine Billion Names of God," Rachel Cosgrove Payes's "In His Own Image," Theodore Sturgeon's "Microcosmic God," Lester del Rey's "Helen O'Loy," Tom Godwin's "The Cold Equations"—and others.

The combination of philosophy textbook, films, and science-fiction stories seems to provide complementary approaches for the students in Intro. to develop both an awareness of the significance of basic human problems and to become involved in a critical assessment of the major alternative solutions and their likely consequences. My own impressions, an examination of the work being done, the level of class discussion, student course evaluations, and the creative integration shown in the group term projects—small group term projects, presented in class, have been used instead of the standard final examination; the group has to handle questions from the other members of the class—indicate that this combination is "working" well. It seems clear that a surprising number of Intro. students do acquire philosophic insight through science fiction. My own biases aside, the experience with this combination in the Introduction to Philosophy course seems to confirm the insight that another had years ago: good science fiction is "the philosophic literature."

SOMETHING HAPPENS

BY KATE WILHELM

Science fiction matters to teachers and students of writing, simply because it's still a live literary form. Back in the thirties, there were strong markets for every sort of category fiction: western stories and love stories, war stories and crime stories, slick stories and pulp stories. Even the cheaper magazines were professional schools where the young writer could polish his skills for pay. Most of them died years ago, killed by TV and the comic book. But not SF. Year by year, more and more people are eager to write it, print it, read it.

Earlier in this book, Robin Wilson told how he founded the Clarion Writer's Workshop, where such a startling number of the students really learned to write and sell. His techniques came largely from the Milford Conference, the week-long annual workshop for SF professionals conducted for many years by Damon Knight and Kate Wilhelm, his gifted wife. Here's Kate's report on how it happens, a precious lesson for any writer or writing teacher.

We arrive at Clarion with no set theory, no teaching aids, no formal training in teaching writing, or anything else. The students have had each other for four weeks, have had other visiting lecturers, have had Robin who does have the theory and training. We feel we are the innocents, the neophytes in this situation. Waiting for us is a stack of manuscripts. Some of them were brought from home, most of them written at Clarion. Some of them are in the third version already, with the other two versions also in the stack and no way of telling by looking which came first. Twenty names, all free-floating until a day or two in class when the names settle down on the persons, and the manuscripts seem to adhere to their owners. After the first twenty-four hours you accept this as the way of life. Classes in the morning, reading and talking to the students afternoons and evenings.

The talk goes on most of the time. It doesn't matter where it starts, it comes back to writing. And you realize that probably for the first time for most of these kids they are being treated as peers by those hired to instruct them. And you also realize that successful teaching is a two-way exchange. After several days we begin to schedule individual conferences.

"Why did you put a spaceship in the middle of the town?"

"Nothing was happening. I wanted them to blow it all up."

"Why?"

"I hate it so much."

"*You* hate it. We all have someplace that we hate with that much intensity, and by bringing in the hand of God, so to speak, and letting him do the dirty work you deny us the opportunity of getting rid of that hated place." Silence. "Why does your protagonist hate it, anyway?"

That breaks the silence. Half an hour later: "That's your story. When you started to talk about the town you started with little things, and they built and built. You haven't done anything to ease your feelings about it at all. Having a spaceship come down and wipe it all out won't relieve the anxiety you've aroused. Your protagonist has to be honest about his feelings, and has to be honest in dealing with them, somehow. He can blow the town up, or run away from it, or be conquered by it; but he has to deal with it. Not an eleventh hour spaceship."

And with another student, another kind of story problem: "Saying it's horrible doesn't make it horrible. Rather it dilutes what I conceive of as being horrible. Read that sentence over without any adjectives at all. Now what else do we positively have to know about the castle?"

"I hate that kind of flat writing. I like to read flowery language."

"Flowery. As in a garden? Where each plant is selected for a particular effect? Or as in a weedy patch where seedlings have been allowed to crowd out the hybrids? That's what happens, unwanted and unnecessary words creep in and spoil the overall plan. Like here, ancient, crumbling, mouldering, ruined, shadowy, menacing, and so on. You don't have to beat us over the head with it."

"Why did you circle words here and there?"

"They aren't the right words. It reminds me of an artist who reaches without looking for the colors he wants, and then settles for what he finds on his brush. Often the words are close, sometimes they hit, but quite often they are approximations. Flaunt isn't flout. A bell can peal, not a light."

Again and again the question of words as signs comes up. Symbols rise from the unconscious, quite unbidden; words are conscious attempts to evoke in the reader the same meaning that was in the mind of the writer. Too many descriptive words hide the story just as effectively as too many billboards hide the landscape. If the approach to writing can be classfied at all, I would be tempted to dichotomize: those who start as storytellers, and those who start as wordsmiths, poets. The drive of the story pushes the storyteller into clumsy phrases, purple prose, redundancies, but he has a story complete with beginning, middle, end. Things happen and there is a resolution. The wordsmiths often have collages of beautifully sketched images, and little else.

"This is so well done that I'd like to see you finish it somehow. It isn't a story." And what is a story? I have to ask myself, and realize that there is no one answer. But I know it when I see it.

"How?"

Perverse. Perverse. "There has to be tension between the reader and the story, and through it to the writer. Not surface suspense, no chases or threats, nothing like that. But a recognition that your man is you, that he is me, that when you describe him thoroughly alone in a city of millions, you're really talking about every one of us. The story doesn't do that. He never seems to know that he is that alone and always will be."

"But I've felt exactly like that. Go home and close the door and go to bed because there's nothing else to do."

"Sure. But at some point in your life you made the discovery that that's how it was. That was the crucial point, the thing that's missing from the story. We have no way of knowing if your man has learned that, or if he ever will learn it. If it doesn't matter to him, the story dissolves into a bit of trivia, and we feel cheated because you have aroused our anxieties without defining them or resolving them in some way, even in the negative by saying, that's how it is folks, no use fighting it."

"And what about the story where nothing happens? The slice of life story?"

"There's no such story. If nothing happens on the page, it has to happen to the reader. But something happens, or there's no story. An intimate glimpse into the daily life of a person can satisfy in that it reveals not just the character, but also the author, his attitude toward life, other people, situations. Or perhaps it forces the reader to examine his own attitudes. But something happens. The words bridge the emptiness between the writer's unconscious and that of the reader."

Writing is addictive. At first it is very hard to find the time for it. Life is too demanding; family, friends, school, movies, whatever, they all get in the way and the weeks flow. An hour now and then, a story that you want to finish, and sit up half the night to do, and finally after some time, you know that writing won't work like that. It's painful to be interrupted in the middle of something and find on returning that it no longer is alive. So you try to arrange a schedule, one hour every day, or two hours three days a week, anything that you can live with. And the time comes when if you use your writing hours for anything else you are edgy and unhappy. That's when you know you're hooked. For most people I suspect the primary reward of writing is writing. For a brief time you are in touch with your own unconscious, things you didn't know you knew appear on the paper, you become oblivious to the small nuisances that in the beginning were enough to stop you cold. A minor headache is forgotten. Tomorrow's worries fade out of sight. Yesterday's disappointments dim. And you're writing. After that first sacred draft is completed, then comes the real work.

Successful writing is a happy combination of mixing conscious control with unconscious creation. Neither will produce good fiction. Sometimes you will see the unconscious trying awkwardly to disguise the product of its own outpourings.

"Just tell me what you want the story to mean?"

"Well, this man is a mediocre artist until he gets this statuette, and when he rubs it, occult powers flow into this time period and invade him and turn him into a really great artist . . ."

They know. These children who have never turned out a salable story, who are still smooth-cheeked, they know. Basically the story is about the possession of art, and the jealousy of the girl whose lover is so possessed. And there are occult powers and too many characters and evil spirits doing diabolical things. But underlying it all is the honest, very true story of the artist's struggle with those forces that would make him accept a life of normality, at the cost of his art. So you talk with the young writer, try to find out if he is ready to face the reality behind his fiction. Sometimes they aren't ready yet. One student, who had turned out juvenilia for five weeks, came up with a powerful story questioning the beliefs of his people—honest, true, real, lovely, poignant. When confronted with what he had, he withdrew it. It would hurt his parents too much. He didn't know the answers yet. Back to the juvenilia. In the present case the boy was excited by the story that he finally uncovered after more than an hour of talking. At an early point in that time, he began doing the questioning, and the story as it evolved from the mass of wordage was his story. All there from the start, but buried under such a load of garbage that it never would have been found by anyone not actively searching for something.

Again and again we stress that: it is your story. What do you want it to do? What effect are you trying for? Story as entertainment? Therapy? Surrealist imagery? Communication? What do you want? I try not to influence anyone toward any particular school of writing. I do try to help them find out what they want to do. I want them to deal honestly with their material.

Years ago in high school I wanted to become an organic chemist. The dean of women had me in for an hour-long interview, and the message that I carried away was simply forget it. Unless you want to teach there's no future for women in science.

So I've been on that firing line for a long, long time. When I started to write I debated about what name to use. At that time there were far fewer women in the field of science fiction than there are today, but it didn't occur to me to use initials. I was debating about using my maiden name, Meredith, or Catherine or Kate. Actually, and only incidentally, my real name is Katie, but that would have been silly. I have four brothers, three sons, and a husband. I learned along about the time I was cutting my two-year molars that if you want to compete with males in any field you've got to be as good as, or preferably better than they are. Or don't race.

So I see the initialed manuscripts and ask, "Why?"

"I want to be published."

"I get published. I could reel off the names of a dozen other women who get published, without hiding behind initials."

Silence.

"What I think when I see initials is that *they* have won. *They*'ve made you ashamed of being a woman." I'm certain it isn't so much what I say as what I am—a woman writer with husband and family, getting along, that lets them listen to me. They know what they face. "It won't be easy," I tell them. "The highest compliment many men can pay a woman writer is to say, 'Hey, you write as good as a man.' And your answer, which you should rehearse to achieve just the right shade of sweetness and bite is: 'Oh, no, you're wrong. I write a damn sight better than most men.' If you're good, you'll succeed. And the sweetest success is the hardest to come by, forcing *them* to accept you and recognize your worth on *their* terms."

Invariably there are those who will want to tell you their stories, or hand you the beginning and tell you the rest, to get an opinion before they waste time writing it. Frankly I can only say I don't know yet. A story has a shape, balance, and rhythm, quite aside from its fictional content. You can't assume these qualities until it is a finished thing. Bad writing doesn't necessarily mean a bad story, not from a new writer. If the basic soundness is there, then it can be salvaged in spite of bad writing, sometimes. But, and more important, a piece of fiction has its own energy. A short story has a burst of energy that is dispelled in a relatively short time, usually, while a novel is like a slow charge on a battery. It can be drained off just as slowly without harm. Any generality about writing is as valuable as generalities about anything else. Always regard them with suspicion. However, that warning out of the way, I go back to the position already stated. A writer should not use up the story energy in telling it, discussing it with other people. He should write it. I won't comment on unfinished work unless it is a novel. And that's a whole new game.

I give out personal assignments, too. After reading a few stories from each of the students it is sometimes not too difficult to see where the stumbling block lies. Write a story about someone you really despise, but from a sympathetic viewpoint. (People don't go around shooting each other, you know. Think about your people a bit more. Know them.) Or, write a story set in your own home town, about places and people you know. (One Star Trek story after another. Can he do anything else?) Or, write a story that is plotted first. (His stories all tend to go A . . . B . . . B$_1$ . . . B$_2$ . . . B$_3$ . . . Z. A beginning, something happening again and again and again, an end. No real development.) Or, do a character study showing why a man did something he knew would have unpleasant consequences. (His stories are so full of fights and action that you never know who hit whom or why for all the dust.) Or, a quiet horror story. Or, a story about a man from his viewpoint. (When told she could probably do confession stories with the style she had slipped into, she was furious. Can she change it?) And so on.

What I'm really saying over and over is: Care! Write where you care. Write where it hurts, where you're puzzled, or frightened, or joyous. All you have to give is yourself, and if you hide too far behind your story, I won't be touched by it. I won't read it.

Do we teach writing? I don't know. Something happens. Maybe just having things pointed out that all writers find out eventually telescopes the time it takes from that first purple epic to a published story. Maybe being accepted by writers as potential if not actual writers is enough to get them over the first hurdles. Maybe having lecturers who want them to succeed, who believe in them does it. I don't know. Something happens.

RUSTY PAPERCLIPS AND PERSONALIZED REJECTION SLIPS: OPPORTUNITIES FOR NEW WRITERS

BY VONDA N. McINTYRE

Kids are born creative—see Barry Longyear's essay above. Though the system routinely stifles imagination, that can be revived. A good many SF courses include writing assignments, and students enjoy trying fiction of their own. A few want to turn professional; most would like to know more about the SF marketplace. Here's an honest and useful market report from Vonda N. McIntyre, a gifted young pro whose Dreamsnake *is sweeping up awards.*

Of all fiction, science fiction is probably the hardest to write well. Yet SF short stories are probably the easiest fiction to market. This may be an inexplicable contradiction; but it's also possible that despite the near extinction of other short story markets, SF publications survive simply because SF, when done well, is so rewarding. For some reason, explicable or not, SF magazines are healthy, while general magazines have cut back on their fiction or have disappeared altogether. Theme and overview SF reprint anthologies flourish; mainstream fiction has a small handful of reprint anthologies per year. Mainstream fiction has only the rare counterpart of original SF anthologies such as *Universe, New Dimensions,* or *Chrysalis.*

Information about SF markets is readily available to new writers. The *Bulletin* of the Science Fiction Writers of America publishes market reports; *Locus,* the SF newsletter, is extremely useful, particularly for information about the frequent short-term or one-time-only markets. It regularly reports the types and lengths of stories that magazine editors prefer or need, as well as the opening dates and themes of anthologies. Charles N. Brown, *Locus*'s editor, researches hardcover and paperback novel markets on a regular basis. For mainstream market reports, writers can turn to *Writer's Market* and *Writer's Digest,* but their announcements often conclude "No unsolicited manuscripts," a phrase virtually unheard of in SF.

New writers of SF short stories therefore have a built-in advantage over aspiring writers of realistic fiction: a larger and more open market, part of which—the magazines—must be filled on a relentless monthly or bimonthly schedule.

The field has another quality that, for the beginner, is a definite advantage. It is small enough and insular enough that editors will often do more for talented new writers than (as has happened to me with mainstream submissions) fasten printed reject slips to their manuscripts with rusty paper clips. Despite the press of time, editors sometimes respond personally to a promising writer even if they reject the writer's submission. The late John W. Campbell, of *Analog,* was notorious for his ten-page reject letters. (I'm one of the few people I know of who ever actually got a printed *Analog* rejection—well-deserved, I might add, for a perfectly dreadful early story.) All of the magazine and anthology editors have published a healthy number of first stories. How many of them respond directly to stories they reject I do not know, but my own first-written, first-submitted, first-rejected story came home with an encouraging note attached. I can't help but believe that this kind of reaction is a qualitative difference between SF and mundane magazines, rather than a simple quantitative one related to differences in circulation and slushpile size. I once sent a story to a large-circulation mainstream magazine, a slick; my story was sponsored by a writer they had published. They returned my manuscript with a highly personalized letter: a mimeographed slip altered in red ballpoint from "Dear Contributor" to "Dear Ms. McIntyre."

Until very recently the SF marketplace, though receptive and encouraging, had as a drawback a certain general poor reputation. The phrase, "This can't be science fiction—it's too good!" popped up all too often, and most magazines paid rates that had not risen significantly in decades. This appears to be changing, though it's far too early to tell if the increased attention focussed on SF by media events such as *Star Wars* and *Alien* will have a permanent effect on the field—or even whether the effect will be positive or negative. The same can be said for increased attention by critics and the academic community. Also making its mark—more as a symbol of commercial success than by any adventurousness in the fiction it has published as of this writing—is *Omni.*

Though the markets for short fiction pay better than they did a few years ago, and though most existing publications are robust, the absolute number of stories required at any given time is somewhat smaller than it was a few years ago. This is not necessarily a bad thing, for the pool of SF writers (beginners included) is finite. It can only produce a certain number of decent stories at once, and for a while that number was being seriously surpassed. But the day of the mediocre assembly-line anthology appears to have ended.

The novel market, on the other hand, is expanding rapidly. It remains to be seen if a similar dilution of quality will occur or if we will reach some sort of steady-state condition where unforced output and demand more nearly match. Philosophical questions aside, opportunities for new writers abound in the field of novels. In fact, some people believe it is easier to break into print with a book than with a story. This would be difficult to test, I think; but whether or not it's true, SF editors at publishing houses are just as eager to discover new talent as are the editors of magazines or anthologies. About ninety percent of the novels published by a good paperback house are solicited manuscripts or novels written on contract by established pros. But the other ten percent is unsolicited work: manuscripts discovered in the much-maligned slushpile. This is a *far* higher percentage than any ever encountered in mundane fiction. (There is a story—which I hope is apocryphal but which I fear is true—of an old, well-established hardcover house that only once in its entire history published an unsolicited novel. I don't know quite how to react to that except to feel that working for them as a first reader must be one of the most deadly frustrating jobs available to literate humankind.)

Every editor has a slightly different ideal procedure she or he would like you to follow in submitting your manuscript. But the basic idea is the same in all cases; and since editors are notorious for changing jobs, it would be confusing to list names, publishers, and protocols here. By the time the article appears in print at least some of the information would be outdated. It *is* important to address your manuscript or query letter to a real person, preferably someone who is still at the company you have chosen as ideal for your book. It may cost you a long-distance phone call to the publisher's switchboard to find out who the current SF editor is, but it's worth it. I do not, by the way, recommend calling editors direct to tell them about your book. A phone call demands an immediate answer, and I suspect that replies to phone queries tend toward the negative or at best the grudging positive.

There's some disagreement over whether it is best to send a query letter, or three chapters and an outline, or a completed manuscript. If this is your first novel, forget three chapters and outline. You are very unlikely to sell a novel on that basis, simply because you have no track record of being able to finish a novel. Of the other two possibilities, my general advice is to begin with a query letter. The attitudes toward queries range from "a very good idea" to "can't hurt too much." Though it will often be answered with "Please send the completed manuscript," it can save you time and postage if an editor's publishing schedule is crammed full through 1984. The letter serves as your introduction, so keep it short, simple, and to the point. Don't beg the editor to buy your book because your two-month-old baby and your senile old grandfather are dying of malnutrition. Don't enclose Xeroxes of all the reject slips the work has collected, no matter how

VONDA McINTYRE

complimentary. (I would have thought that advice was self-evident, except that according to several editors it happens all the time.) It is not necessary to mention that you have twenty-three unsold novels in your desk drawer, nor even that your submission is your first novel. Don't approach the editor with a toe-scuffing, "Gee, I'm sure you aren't interested, but . . ." attitude; on the other hand it isn't advisable to come on like a combination of Superman, Tarzan, and The Incredible Hulk, either: there's a difference between self-assertion and aggressive self-promotion. If an established writer suggests that you send a particular manuscript to a particular editor, by all means mention that if the writer gives you permission.

When you have sent out your query, received a favorable reply, sent out your manuscript, and received an offer for your book, every editor I've spoken to said that then was a good time to look for an agent. In fact, several editors said they would put new writers they wanted to publish in touch with agents. Book contracts are complicated beasties, and while it is possible to negotiate one on your own, even with your first book (never sign the publisher's boiler-plate contract!), it is far easier to manage if you have an agent. And while you will find it very difficult to get a good agent before you have any publishing credits, you will find it quite possible when you have a firm offer on a novel. (By the way, standard agent's commission is ten percent. Never get tangled up with an agent who demands a reading fee. Conversely, if publishers tell you they will take good care of you and you don't need an agent, you may wish to consider how publishers can look out for their interests and yours simultaneously.)

Other quick tips include enclosing a self-addressed stamped envelope with your query letter, sufficient return postage with your manuscript, and your phone number under your address on letters and the first page and/or cover page of your manuscript. Last, take the time and trouble to find out proper manuscript preparation, and use the form. There are reasons for all the apparently arbitrary or trivial rules. Discussing them is not the purpose of this chapter, but the appearance of your manuscript will affect its reception. The more professional it looks and the easier it is to read, the better impression it will make.

The theme of this article is opportunities for new writers, but the emphasis on submitting and marketing your work must not be allowed to overshadow the most important first step in any writer's career: *the writing itself.* Your first task—your real work—is to do the best job you can. There is no point in writing if you are going to be satisfied with merely being competent; there is no point in writing science fiction if you are going to be satisfied with imitating what has come before. The attraction of the field is that it is boundless. Don't neglect its potential—or your own.

THREE
SYLLABI

BY DAVE SAMUELSON, GARY GOSHGARIAN,
AND DENNIS LIVINGSTON

The editor of this book, in the course of reading several hundred syllabi for SF courses, found each one different—one exciting appeal of academic SF is its freedom from stifling conformities. Here are three course descriptions of particular interest.

Dave Samuelson is an associate professor of English and Coördinator of Future Studies at California State University, Long Beach. His dissertation has been published as Visions of Tomorrow: Six Journeys from Outer to Inner Space. *Gary Goshgarian is an assistant professor of English at Northeastern University and perhaps the most successful teacher of SF anywhere—something of a showman, he has drawn some 6,000 students through his classes. Dennis Livingston is a futurologist at Marlboro College in Vermont. Though future studies is now another thriving discipline, it was born from SF. As Livingston shows, the two aren't yet entirely separate.*

Science Fiction and Speculative Fantasy
(English 498: Topics in English)
By Dave Samuelson

I teach science fiction as literature, which means both more and less than many people expect. It is not an attempt to prove that SF *is* literature, nor is it limited to aspects of writing we call "literary" because we have no other label for them. Primarily, I try to focus on what happens when a work of literature interacts with memories and patterns that define a reader's individuality. This means class sessions deal with the history of our time, with the wonders and threats of science and technology, with the nature of people and the craft of storytelling, and also with purely idiosyncratic responses (mine and others').

The objectives of my class for Spring 1975 (eighth offering, fourth structure, in six years) read as follows: "to become familiar with a broad range of times and types of science fiction; to sample different ways of reading (science fiction, among other things); to express your perceptions of what goes into the writing and reading of science fiction; to become aware of similarities and differences between science fiction and other kinds of literature; to increase your awareness of the utility of writing and reading 'scenarios' of alternative futures (presents, pasts); to develop a concrete sense of possible images of the future; to gain some awareness of the critical literature on science fiction and of the 'non-fiction' literature of Future Studies which parallels much of science fiction." How these objectives are to be realized, however, differs with each student.

Since responses vary tremendously with a reader's background and sense of perspective, I try to make sure that my students have access to what I know and what their classmates know about science and technology, our industrial (or post-industrial) age, literature in general, and science fiction in particular. I lecture occasionally, I ask them to read the historical and theoretical introductions to science fiction in my *Visions of Tomorrow* (Arno Press, 1975), I point them toward other relevant background materials, and I compile and distribute a Student Directory with names, addresses, phone numbers, academic majors and personal interests in SF. Breaking down artificial classroom barriers, I also try to get them to share ideas in class discussion and through reading each other's journals, making learning a more cooperative and less competitive activity. I try to take advantage of the wide disparity in academic backgrounds students bring to an SF class, enabling all students to feel of value, contributing what they know, and to learn from their peers (not just from me). Through this cross-talk, I hope by the end of the course that they are all acquainted with some idea of literature, literary standards, and critical tools, with arguments for the legitimacy of popular culture and commercial literature, with respect for science and technology, and with a healthy skepticism about conventional social attitudes.

Basic to my format is a large amount of individual freedom and responsibility. Each student chooses what to read, though the choices are limited (too much choice, given a large class, has proved chaotic in the past). For Spring 1975, after setting up some ground rules and reading some short stories in common, they were offered four choices of "historical" material *(Frankenstein* or *20,000 Leagues Under the Sea; The Island of Dr. Moreau* or *The War of the Worlds; Looking Backward* or *We; Last and First Men* or *Star Maker).* The point is not to establish a canon but to illustrate SF parameters of Gothic adventure, utopia, dystopia, and philosophical "myth-making," while exposing them to the "classics." Students also choose one of four groups which will rotate responsibility for class discussion during the rest of the semester. Trade-offs are permitted, and a student can, with a good reason, substitute something not on the official reading list. For that purpose, among others, one of my handouts is a seven-page list, alphabetical by author but cross-indexed by certain topics, of SF books

I feel have some "significance." The official reading list varies with the availability of paperbacks in print, but it balances literary works and adventure stories, "hard" and "soft" science fiction, and utopian and dystopian viewpoints, though it tends to emphasize American authors since World War II.

The Spring 1975 list was as follows: *The Skylark of Space; Beyond this Horizon; The Foundation Trilogy*; The Martian Chronicles; Earth Abides; City; Childhood's End; More than Human; Mission of Gravity; Cities in Flight*; The Sirens of Titan; A Canticle for Leibowitz; The Man in the High Castle; A Clockwork Orange; The Dream Master; The Einstein Intersection; Stand on Zanzibar*; Dune* and *Dune Messiah*; Camp Concentration; Macroscope; The Left Hand of Darkness; Barefoot in the Head; Other Eyes, Other Days; Dying Inside;* and—for everyone—*Solaris.* (The order is chronological, and titles asterisked were given more than one fifty-minute period for discussion.)

Class time usually centers on discussion of a book that only one group has read, and about which others ask questions. A group's job is to describe the book (not just plot—but characters, ideas, design elements, etc.), to place it (in time, and in relation to certain aspects of SF), and to evaluate it (making their criteria explicit). Though I ask that they first set up a framework, so that listeners can understand what they're talking about, these are not panels. Group members have access to each other between presentations; but they are not encouraged to organize set statements, imitating the worst features of their duller instructors. Rather, they are supposed to interact with each other, with the class, and with me, with no fear of a grade hanging over them. Although I may interrupt at times with my own comments or judgments, I try mainly to prod and encourage, acting as a verbal traffic cop. A high compliment I once received was that I didn't seem like the teacher, but more like "the best prepared student in class."

What does get graded is students' written work. A permanent record for each one to keep is his journal, in which he writes down responses to what he reads, sees, hears, and otherwise experiences, which leads toward a better understanding of science fiction. This allows him to develop ideas at more length than in class, but not necessarily in essay form, to give me direct feedback about my performance, and to sketch out plans for a paper. It lets me check on his reading progress (qualitatively as well as quantitatively), to give him direct feedback, and to help out with proposals for papers. Although my preliminary instructions about keeping a journal are deliberately vague and general, so as not to force everyone into any one set mode of writing, rather to enable each person to find one which is comfortable, I try in my comments in a journal to encourage the student to explore things he may have overlooked or ignored, to expand on cryptic notes, and to formulate generalizations based on different observations. Adequate coverage of readings alone merits a C. Cross-comparisons and general fruitful inquiries about the nature of the subject must be added for a B. An A requires also a research or critical paper on such topics as motifs, influences, cross-cultural comparisons, literary exegeses, and surveys of SF in the mass media, which must be thoughtful and well-written (lesser papers can make a B grade out of a C journal, however). Because of the heuristic nature of the journal, turned in at frequent intervals, I rarely have to turn in a grade lower than C.

This kind of class requires instructor responsibility beyond the preparation of lectures and examinations. I must have information at hand, or know where it can be found, in answer to student questions. I have to treat each student as an individual, with unique problems, goals, and assignments against which to evalute his progress, not just the objectives I outlined at the start of the semester. To some extent, I have to efface myself, to get students to look for their own answers, rather than relying entirely on mine. And I have to keep before us reminders that inquiry is never over; if I do my job well, I will by no means cover all the material, rather I will have opened up for my students a lifetime interest in enlightened enjoyment and critical awareness.

A Course through Space and Time
By Gary Goshgarian

[In a recent note, Professor Goshgarian updates the catalog description of English 30.141 Science Fiction. "The first half of this course explores the various debates among SF writers concerning man's love-hate relationships with his technological creations. The second half concentrates on other world visions of man and his universe and investigates some sociological, psychological, philosophical, and religious themes." A three-dollar lab fee goes for feature films, such as *2001, A Clockwork Orange, The Andromeda Strain, Slaughterhouse-Five, Invasion of the Body Snatchers,* etc. The course, he writes, "is still a Frankenstein monster, still drawing the bodies." The average term enrollment is 500. The classes are mostly lecture, but casual enough to let students ask questions and make comments.]

Catalogue descriptions of college courses are about as useful as the index of a botany textbook when shopping for flowers. Five years ago, I entered the following description of my science-fiction course in the Northeastern University catalogue: "30.141 Science Fiction—The myths and rhetorical (scientific and pseudoscientific) strategies of science fiction from Mary Shelley's *Frankenstein* through current authors such as Vonnegut, Bradbury, Heinlein, Clarke, etc." Nobody seems to know what it really means, including me. But I remember trying to suggest that SF had official class, like the way *taraxacum officinale* apologizes for the dandelion.

I also remember that in Fall 1970 when I introduced the course, the objective was not to fill a need, but to create one. The department chairman had sent out a general distress call about the drop in body count in English courses, not to mention our majors. And because I had a background in physics and literature and had read SF by the pound, I was tapped for the job. The above promo drew a horde of thirty-five on the first day, and neither I nor the students knew what the hell to expect. They just kind of stared back at me like catfish in a pond. The challenge was ulcerating on three counts: one, I had to prove to those defiant uninitiates out there that SF wasn't just that gee-whiz kiddie lit that they made into those Warner Brothers beasties; two, I had to make it by those SF junkies who took the course out of a smug predatory impulse to see me screw up, give up or turn their blood into ink; three, how does one teach something that hasn't yet got a good definition? Not to mention my colleagues who thought it was a real prestige to have a department Sci-Fi man—kind of like boasting you have dysentery.

I was prepared less for SF and more for a horror show; and for lack of better design, I decided to approach some general themes chronologically beginning with *Frankenstein,* which was safe since even the junkies hadn't read it. Although I no longer follow the historical approach, I still begin with the Shelley classic because it proved to be a kind of portrait of modern technology as a young man and thus, a precursor of all the machine menace stories in the modern anthologies. It also proved invaluable to examine the moral issues raised in terms of the Creation myth of *Genesis.* The parallels abound. Even my junkies could appreciate intellectualizing on the ambiguities of creator-creation relationships that are hammered to simplicity in most of the movie versions. The novel also makes a crucial distinction between knowledge and the wisdom to use that knowledge which, I think, lies at the heart of technological menace themes, fictional and actual.

The second stage of the course was a logical extension of the man-and-machine opener: utopia-dystopia. Here I integrated various short stories with novels like Vonnegut's *Player Piano,* Van Vogt's *Slan,* Wells's *The Time Machine* and either Ira Levin's *This Perfect Day* or Anthony Burgess's *The Wanting Seed,* when available. In this section, which I now call Man and Man, one can find a plethora of works—several of them good. Discussion on these demonstrated SF's unique consciousness-raising characteristic; it also raised their anger and cynicism. Indeed, a future shock effect, and through fiction!

The final stage explored the alien alternatives (man and gods) particularly the mystical-religious speculations such as Blish's *A Case of Conscience,* Heinlein's *Stranger in a Strange Land* and Clarke's *Childhood's End,* which has polled as the most popular SF novel of the thirty-five I've used to date.

Well, that's a rough idea of what the course looked like five years ago. It hasn't changed much, although I've refined the structure (man-and-machine, -man, -aliens and -gods) and added different works here and there. I also think we've met our original objective since, despite the catalogue description, the course has drawn to date over 4,000 students and has had enrolled at one time as many as 632, or about 65 percent of the total upper class department enrollment. Last year the demand was so great that I had to open a second section. They draw an average of 275 each class per quarter. I'm no longer apologizing for it.

The challenge of teaching an SF course has become compounded by that of teaching one so large. I cannot give an easy assessment of its personality because I cannot separate myself from it. The Boston *Globe,* which did a feature story on the course in its Sunday supplement, said it was a teaching performance that "ranged from whacky to profound" and that despite its size, the class had a "close sitting-around-the-table feeling." I guess that's so. It has something to do with the subject matter and something to do with the entertainment element in the presentation, an element I find as essential to teaching as to literature. The typical class, if there is one, begins as a dramatic monologue that on so-so days is an end in itself, on good days spreads into dialogue and on great days provokes a general free-for-all. That's when consciousness-raising is surpassed by a general hysteria over how badly the future seems to be shaping up. The stories that have turned my class into a Roman arena are those that go for the jugular such as Harlan Ellison's *Dangerous Visions,* Pohl's *Nightmare Age,* or novels like Levin's *This Perfect Day,* John Brunner's *The Sheep Look Up,* or the less vitriolic satire, *The Space Merchants* by Pohl and Kornbluth. And the response is ample reason for continued use. *Mirror of Infinity* and *Science Fiction Hall of Fame* are two other reliables, although their contents are not so shrill as the Ellison collection.

Because of the size of the class and because most students are not English majors or junkies, I have to select novels (usually six) that can each sustain at least three days' discussion. (Our semesters are twelve-week quarters.) That means meaty stories with the right combination of entertainment and content and quality. The task is made more difficult by publishers who have the bad habit of pulling a gem off the shelves for a few years. Burgess's *Wanting Seed* is one of them. Curiously enough, not all the favorites in SF circles make it in a class so large as mine where utilitarian precepts must rule selection. *Babel-17* was a bomb; *Left Hand of Darkness* bored them; *Dune* was fine but too long; *Rite of Passage* was silly and inconsequential; *A Canticle for Leibowitz* was too literary; *Andromeda Strain* wasn't literary enough; *More Than Human* was fifty-fifty; *Pebble in the Sky* was fun but gave them nothing to say after the second day. Thank God it's not a course in Bible Studies. But as I said above, *Childhood's End* has come in first each quarter, because it has it all: visit by benign messianic aliens, a half-mystical yearning for the stars, a glimpse at a one-world utopia, telepathy, Jungian premonitions of the apocalypse, noncorporeal intelligence, and a splendid *götterdämmerung* finale. Any day now I expect it to go out of print.

I give a midterm and a final which are graded by a small team of graduate students. Papers are optional, and they can be either critical or original science fiction. Most choose the fiction option and most are obvious first attempts. Thus a million last-man-in-the-world fantasies, postwar dooms, and the familiar new twists to Frankenstein and his attempts to improve on Nature. But some of the projects are first-rate; several have made it in print; and at least one in one of the big three SF magazines, which is better than their mentor has done.

I cannot hide the fact that the success of my course is personally satisfying. And a good part of it comes from student feedback about what they learned SF was capable of. From the defiant uninitiates, a kind of awkward "Oh-wow That-stuff's-really-heavy" humility; from the junkies, a half-conciliatory, half-perceptible smirky nod of approval that says "Not bad, but why not a Gray Lensman or two?" Finally, my faithful colleagues who still don't believe in SF, who still cringe when they look through the course descriptions, but who are thanking Mary Shelley through Clarke, etc. for paying their salaries.

Science Fiction Taught as Futurology
By Dennis Livingston

Almost invariably, science-fiction courses initiated at the high school or college levels find their academic niche in English departments, where the basic issues for class discussion are likely to be those relevant to literary analysis, e.g., the place of SF in literary history, the aesthetic criteria for judging SF, the mutual influences of SF and mainstream fiction, the merits of SF authors in terms of style, and so on.

There is nothing wrong with this approach; but other issues may be posed as well, equally relevant and perhaps more important. As a social scientist and futurist, my context is to treat SF as an archive of speculative material on alternative possible futures with which it is imperative we be familiar as humankind tries to bring about satisfying national and global futures in the real world. I use the content of SF as a set of images of futures—visions, prophecies, proposals, warnings—which may be studied for the patterns they form, their "feedforward" effects on the present via influence on the popular imagination about futures, their impact on present lifestyles and ways of perceiving the environment, their reflection of current social concerns and value biases, their accuracy in anticipating public policy problems

D. SAMUELSON et al

of the present, their comparison and contrast with nonfiction attempts to predict futures, their role in psychologically preparing people for the future shock era, and their sophistication in analyzing forces of sociotechnic change and in depicting alternative social systems.

In sum, the goal of my SF course—and indeed, any course in which I use SF—is to orient students toward perceiving SF, apart from its entertainment values, as a literature of alternative futures, better or worse, more probable or less probable, but all conceivable paths whose social consequences can first be played out in the laboratory of the imagination that SF represents. The particular array of images a class could explore would depend on the interests of teacher and students. I tend to divide SF futures into three broad categories useful for studying the kinds of issues noted above. These categories, and the kinds of stories that might be used, are as follows:

1) Alternative Lifestyles—the role of women, family systems, work and leisure, professions—all excellent subjects for exploring deep-rooted assumptions and cultural biases in our own society, as reflected in SF works; stories which transcend these biases include Gerald Jonas's "The Shaker Revival"; Pamela Sargent, ed., *Women of Wonder;* Joanna Russ's *The Female Man;* Ursula K. Le Guin's *The Left Hand of Darkness.*

2) Alternative Technologies—interaction of science, technology, and society, policy-making for science and technology, roles of scientists and engineers, fears and hopes about technology; good novels include D.F. Jones's *Colossus;* Fred Hoyle's *The Black Cloud;* David Gerrold's *When Harlie Was One;* Arthur Clarke's *2001;* John Brunner's *Stand on Zanzibar.*

3) Alternative Societies—holistic views of differing social patterns; utopias and dystopias; contemporary works here include Ursula K. Le Guin's *The Dispossessed;* Robert Silverberg's *Son of Man;* Isaac Asimov's *The Caves of Steel;* George Stewart's *Earth Abides.*

Wherever possible, I also play off SF material with futuristic nonfiction to compare or contrast forecasting methods used and to make clear the differences between prediction and anticipation/design. Useful anthologies for this include Dick Allen's *Science Fiction: The Future,* and *Total Effect: Survival Printout.*

In addition to discussing the social options portrayed in the literature, I try to use simulations with SF-type content to get students involved at an "action" level in conceiving of alternative futures. Two such games are *Humanus* (Similie II, 1150 Silverado, La Jolla, California 92037), in which a cassette tape of a "computer" gives a series of instructions to survivors of a world disaster living in a "survival cell"; and *Future Decisions: The IQ Game* (Simulation & Gaming Association, RR #2, Greentree Rd., Lebanon, Ohio 45036), in which students must rank in order the applications of couples, representing a wide variety of lifestyles, who have applied for the use of a new drug that can raise the intelligence level of fetuses *in utero*. The debriefing sessions for games like these are excellent means for getting students to express their personal reactions to the kind of futures these scenarios, and similar SF, portray.

Finally, as a major research project, I ask students to undertake an exercise in "applied science fiction": they are to select a particular present or near-future problem/opportunity in public policy, analyze possible solutions to it offered in relevant SF stories and films, and compare these SF solutions to any speculation and proposals being offered in nonfiction. There is obviously no lack of possible topics here; subjects in which SF has a lot to say include overpopulation, pollution, nuclear war, cybernation and unemployment, anomie in a mass society, crime, energy/resource depletion, etc. In this way, students are encouraged to begin to exercise their own rights as participants in shaping real-time futures for our society.

THE TOOLS

THE TINSEL SCREEN: SCIENCE FICTION AND THE MOVIES

BY JAMES GUNN

In this concluding section we look at special resources for the science-fiction teacher. James Gunn surveys the SF film, shares his experience with film in the classroom—pinpointing hazards to be avoided—and describes the series of films he has produced for the SF course. Bob Barthell tells how he staged an SF minicon in an isolated Wyoming community. The Panshins illustrate the evolution of modern SF with an annotated bibliography of selected titles. Neil Barron discusses library holdings and reference books.

A professor of English at the University of Kansas, Gunn is one of a very few people doing top-flight work as both writers and scholars of SF. His novels include The Listeners, Kampus, *and* The Immortals—*which became a TV series. His* Alternate Worlds *is, perhaps, the best introduction to SF yet written. He teaches an outstanding SF course and a fine summer seminar for SF teachers. His new three-volume paperback series,* The Road to Science Fiction *(Mentor), is a highly recommended classroom text.*

Motion pictures are popular with students. They are entertaining, exciting, and effortless—the ideal medium for education. Well, maybe. Surely this is true of science-fiction films. Well, yes and no.

Films have their drawbacks. They are expensive. Divided among an audience of any size, the expense, it is true, is no greater than providing an equal number of books; but institutions have evolved acceptable mechanisms for buying books: not so with films. Then, too, because films are entertaining, exciting, and effortless, students seldom exert themselves to consider the ideas or the medium critically. Most important of all when it comes to the student of science fiction, there are virtually no good films that also are good science fiction.

That is a harsh judgment—and hardly appropriate for an article devoted to the use of the science-fiction film. But perhaps cautions about science-fiction films are more useful than encomiums. Let me try to document my position and, in the process, suggest how science-fiction films may and may not be used successfully in connection with science-fiction classes. As sort of an appendix to this discussion, I will describe a personal experiment in the use of film for teaching science-fiction that has made available a body of films about science fiction.

Let me begin with a confession: I have sponsored four series of science-fiction feature films in connection with my science-fiction classes at the University of Kansas. I had two major reasons: I thought students should be familiar with the classics of science-fiction film, such as they are; and I wanted to show some teaching films in the evening program and save class time for other things. I had a couple of less important and less admirable reasons: I planned to use some of the profits from the film series (they can be profitable) to bring visiting lecturers to the campus, and I thought the films would enhance the enjoyment of the class. I did bring some lecturers to the campus who were appreciated, but I had fewer compliments on the films than complaints from students who had seen a number of the films or who could not attend them because of conflicts.

I have given up the series, for the present anyway. The problems were greater than the rewards. I started with the feeling that I could count the films that were good science fiction on the fingers of three hands—just enough for a thirteen- or fourteen-week series. But I discovered that in any one semester only about half the films I wanted were available: some were temporarily out of circulation and some weren't available at all, and some films that were promised never showed up.

Moreover, to help provide the profits I mentioned above as well as spread the delight farther, I opened the films to other students; this meant that I couldn't keep showing the same films again and again. The science-fiction film historian and collector, Forrest J Ackerman, has seen *Metropolis* twenty-five times; once is enough for most viewers, although *King Kong* and a few other films might be exceptions. Television, which can be an asset (more of this later), can be a competitor—sometimes showing the same film on television within weeks of the campus scheduling.

Since I was teaching a science-fiction class and not a film class, I discovered that students had little to say about the films as science fiction and most of what they had to say was critical. As a matter of fact, I discovered that I had little to say beyond a brief description of the film's theme, sometimes a comment on the book that inspired it, and occasionally a description of the circumstances or problems of production. These objections were most serious and finally led to giving up the whole idea.

The problem with the science-fiction film is that it adds nothing to science fiction except concreteness of image—and this may be more of a drawback than an asset.

John Baxter, in one of the better books about science-fiction movies, *Science Fiction in the Cinema,* says that science-fiction literature and science-fiction film come from different origins and provide different views of the world. "Science fiction," he says, "supports logic and order, SF film illogic and chaos. Its roots lie not in the visionary literature of the nineteenth century, to which science fiction owes most of its origins, but in older forms and attitudes, the medieval fantasy world, the era of the masque, the morality play, and the Grand Guignol."

I like the distinctions but I find curiously lacking from Baxter a defense of them. Why doesn't (or can't) the science-fiction film reflect written science fiction? Why doesn't (or can't) it support logic and order? Why isn't it (or can't it be) a medium of ideas? Baxter accepts the situation as a given, much as I have heard science-fiction filmmakers surrender to the Hollywood sickness with a shrug and a "you've got to work within the system."

I would say, first of all, that Baxter's distinctions do not always hold up; on my list of good science-fiction films are several that reflect the values of written science fiction, *Things to Come,* say, or *2001: A Space Odyssey.* Where a science-fiction writer has had a major influence on the development of the film, the result has been better science fiction and a superior film; you can beat the system if you are able to persuade the system of the truth of that statement.

But Baxter is right about most science-fiction films. The people who made them knew nothing about science fiction. When they bought science-fiction stories, they didn't know what they bought; they threw away the best parts and kept the worst, and didn't know the difference. They set out to make what they understood—monster movies, usually, with lots of special effects, but keep the budget low, and if you have to skimp do it on story and acting because nobody will notice.

Take a familiar case in point: John W. Campbell's classic novelette "Who Goes There?"—a suspenseful story about an alien monster discovered frozen in the Antarctic ice by a group of scientists; they thaw it out and it gets loose in their winter camp; it has imitated one or more of the animals and one or more of the men down to their cells and memories; it must be discovered by some scientific test which will distinguish man from monster. . . . Hollywood turned it into *The Thing,* about a plant creature from Mars discovered after a flying saucer plunges into Arctic ice.

Why must science-fiction films deal only with simple images? Why must filmmakers suffer a failure of imagination when they come to science fiction? These are the questions which bedevil the science-fiction reader. The filmmaker seems content with his ingenious models, his trick photography, his gruesome monsters, and his tabletop destruction.

Most science-fiction films if translated into written form would be unpublishable because of lack of logic or originality. I stand behind that statement even in the face of the success of the novelized versions of a variety of recent SF films, including *Star Wars* and its sequels.

The ideas in a film such as *THX 1138*, much praised for its visual impact and filmic images, were old in 1949 when George Orwell wove them into a sophisticated novel of ideas, *Nineteen Eighty-four*. Another visually interesting recent film, *Silent Running*, has almost no logic at all: why put parks into space? who visits them? what is saved by destroying them?

If a class cannot discuss the ideas of a science-fiction film, it can only discuss the images or the special effects, which makes the class at best a course in film appreciation. I can forgive Susan Sontag for her statement (in "The Imagination of Disaster") that science-fiction films are concerned with the aesthetics of disaster; she is talking about monster and worldwide destruction movies, not written science fiction, though she might have pointed out the difference. But I would argue with her conclusion that dealing with disaster in an imaginative way becomes "itself a somewhat questionable act from a moral point of view," by normalizing "what is psychologically unbearable, thereby inuring us to it." If applicable to science-fiction films, why not to written science fiction? Here, it seems to me, the fallacy becomes more apparent. The alternative is not to deal fictionally with disaster, perhaps not even to think about it. Ms. Sontag, perhaps, would have us nourish an unspecific horror of things which concern "identity, volition, power, knowledge, happiness, social consensus, guilt, responsibility . . ."

There is not much difference, as far as inuring goes, in visualizing a horror and writing about it, and I cannot believe that Orwell, to take one example, inured us to the horror of the all-intrusive state by writing *Nineteen Eighty-four*, or that the film, though clearly inferior to the book, made us more likely to accept the conditions it depicts. The difficulty with Ms. Sontag's position is that most persons do not think about consequences until they are faced with them in terms of people's lives. Some—no, all—disasters should be thought through, analyzed, weighed, considered. Some disasters may be inevitable; they must be prepared for. Others are avoidable and must be prevented. Still others offer a choice of alternatives from which one must be chosen as superior to the other. Some are not disasters at all but only seem like disasters. Some may be short-term disasters and long-term boons. Some may be individual disasters and racial necessities.

The basic problem with the science-fiction disaster film is that it imagines disaster but seldom considers alternatives; it stirs our stomachs but seldom our heads. The film critics, accepting what is for what must be, say it can do no other.

We run into this kind of nonsense from film critics. I can forgive Bernard Beck (in "The Overdeveloped Society: THX 1138") for describing science fiction as "often nothing more than a language structure for describing events which are concretely unimaginable or meaningless in ordinary terms," but I cannot forgive him for equating that language structure to "the production, the creation of a concrete image of the impossible out of available techniques" in the science-fiction film. Overcoming the technical difficulties of making science-fiction images concrete on film is not the same as the difficulties of making a science-fiction situation believable. Fiction responds to difficulties; the ideas which lie within the science-fictional situations are most dramatically expressed when the difficulties are surmounted. Beck would have us believe that the film's creation of the concrete image is enough to delight us. It had better be.

The only place where greater caution with the film critic should be exercised by the science-fiction teacher is the point at which the critic begins to refer to "a synthesis of insightful visual imagination" and "an interpenetration of fantasy and reality." Phrases like those suggest that the logic of the film won't bear inspection.

If the science-fiction film actually makes images concrete, it may be the concreteness of the image which ultimately turns us off. Science fiction, like fantasy, is a literature of the imagination; it requires vigorous participation on the part of the reader, a willing suspension of disbelief—although science fiction, in contrast to fantasy, gives him reasons for believing. This reader participation allows the science-fiction writer to span parsecs believably, to cross centuries credibly; to suggest the most sensational of cities, the most creative of creatures, the most startling of social systems, the most incredible variations upon a theme. And if the writer has done it persuasively, the reader constructs for himself, out of his own imagination, what he longs for or dreads.

As John W. Campbell pointed out in 1947 (in an essay called "The Science of Science Fiction Writing"), "the trick is to describe the horrified, not the horror; the love-struck, not the lady-love." But the science-fiction film, at great expense and difficulty, applies a face to the horror, and it seems prosaic or laughable; the film is stuck with its images, and in them the viewer does not participate. Often the film image cannot live up to the reader's expectations; that is why books seldom make good movies, even though we want to see the impossible achieved. This is particularly true of science-fiction books. Moreover, when the effort to make the image concrete represents the major accomplishment of a film, the substance becomes incidental. Where science fiction is specific about ideas and suggestive about images, the science-fiction film is specific about images and allusive—elusive as well—about meaning. The difference is all the difference in this world—or another.

Stan Freberg, the satirist turned adman, once created a radio commercial about the advantages of radio advertising over television; it began with an announcer turning Lake Michigan into a gigantic bowl of Jello, covering it with whipped cream, and towing into position overhead a cherry the size of an island; and it ended with the announcer challenging a television executive to create a similar commercial.

The same thing might be said about science fiction and fantasy on radio; radio brought out the best in science fiction: the sound effects were relatively easy and much more effective than visual images in suggesting scope, changing scenes, creating moods, and eliciting listener imagination. If the science-fiction teacher must use teaching aids—and it does seem particularly appropriate—let them be recordings. The famous 1938 Mercury Theater production of *The War of the Worlds* is available on tape and record and is still remarkably effective in creating a mood in the classroom, although its length—one hour—creates problems for our fifty-minute academic units. Half-hour recordings and tapes of the old *X Minus One, Dimension X,* and other dramatic radio programs are available from collectors and can be effective with classes. Many of them are well done. And there are a veritable hurricane of recordings issued in the past few years, dramatic readings by the author or actors, talks, interviews. . . .

If, in spite of all the drawbacks of films, the science-fiction teacher persists in a masochistic desire to show science-fiction movies, where can help be found? I suggest that the teacher stay away from film critics unless the course is about film; most critics talk nonsense about the obvious, and they will only confuse the teacher about science fiction, and the students, too, if their influence gets that far. They insist, for instance, on referring to science fiction as "Sci-Fi," which immediately alienates the science fiction reader; he knows that the only legitimate abbreviation is "SF," although some modern writers insist that "SF" also can stand for "speculative fiction."

The best book about science-fiction films I have found is William Johnson's *Focus on the Science Fiction Film,* which presents both sides of most issues and includes comments by writers as well as critics and filmmakers. John Baxter's *Science Fiction in the Cinema* is thorough; Denis Gifford's *Science Fiction Film* lists more titles than any other book but says less about each. Ralph J. Amelio's *Hal in the Classroom: Science Fiction Films* contains some provocative but often misguided essays; among them are Susan Sontag's and Bernard Beck's. All the books listed above have useful bibliographies and filmographies. A different kind of book, *Cinema of the Fantastic* by Chris Steinbrunner and Burt Goldblatt, has many hard-to-find photographs, and chapters on fifteen movies from Meliés's *A Trip to the Moon* to *Forbidden Planet.* The May 1979 issue of the SFRA *Newsletter* recommends a new study, John Brosnan's *Future Tense: The Cinema of Science Fiction.*

If a teacher wished to offer a history of the science-fiction film, the obvious starting point is Meliés's *A Trip to the Moon,* a brief bit of whimsy filmed in 1902 and patterned after Jules Verne's *From the Earth to the Moon* with influences from H.G. Wells's *The First Men in the Moon.* Meliés had a couple of earlier efforts, *An Astronomer's Dream* and a version of *She.*

After a number of other curiosities that are available and probably not worth seeing for anything more than antiquarian purposes (with the exception of the 1925 film of A. Conan Doyle's *The Lost World* with Wallace Beery as Professor Challenger and some effective, early, animated dinosaurs), the German director Fritz Lang produced *Metropolis* in 1926 and *Woman in the Moon* in 1929. Both are historically important, particularly for special effects, and both are melodramatic and overacted; student audiences usually find them funny. An American film of 1930, *Just Imagine,* is supposed to be funny but is only ridiculous; it does include some impressive futuristic shots of a 1980 metropolis.

The meaningful history of filmed science fiction (as opposed to science-fiction film) begins in 1931 with *Frankenstein,* the Boris Karloff version that inspired a thousand parodies, including the most recent, Mel Brooks's *Young Frankenstein.* Yet the original film still has the power to move audiences. So does the more cultish film *King Kong,* epic in scope and special effects, and even interesting thematically. The remake has little to recommend it but color. The teacher who wants to focus on the science fiction can do worse than begin with two films in my list of thirteen or fourteen good SF films, *Frankenstein* and *King Kong.* Another on my list, *The Invisible Man,* came along the same year as *King Kong.* Although it perpetuated the persistent medieval themes "he meddled in God's domain" and "he ventured into areas man was meant to leave alone," the film does better than most at considering more than one side of a question, in this case the drawbacks as well as the advantages of invisibility, and the special effects are well done. About the same time came a film that doesn't quite make my list but is nevertheless a reasonably effective adaptation of Wells's *The Island of Dr. Moreau,* namely *The Island of Lost Souls* (1932) with Charles Laughton. Again, the recent remake is poorer.

I once thought that the British *Things to Come* (1936) was the only good science-fiction film ever made; it was based on H.G. Wells's 1933 book *The Shape of Things to Come;* and it had a scenario and frequent memoranda to the participants by Wells, leading to my later conclusion that the really good science-fiction movies had someone intimately associated with the production who knew a great deal about written science fiction. Since *Things to Come* other films have come along, and the virtues of *Things to Come* have not survived the intervening years undiminished. The early war scenes are cheaply executed and betray their simple pacifism. But the final sequences, projected into the year 2036, still have the power to captivate; and Raymond Massey's final statement of man's destiny still sounds the clear, pure call of main-current science fiction. I have been surprised at the number of science-fiction authors of my generation, such as Isaac Asimov and Fred Pohl, who have expressed the same reactions to this film.

The Flash Gordon and Buck Rogers serials produced between 1936 and 1940, along with such lesser works as *The Phantom Empire* (1935) and *The Undersea Kingdom* (1936), are high camp today with their comic-strip villains and heroes, their cardboard robots, their firework rocketships, and their absurd and sometimes cheating cliffhangers. But I have usually included them in my film series as a kind of reliving of the old thirties Saturday matinee experience, and students have found them good fun.

Destination Moon (1950) was George Pal's first science-fiction production, and the first film adapted from the work of a magazine science-fiction writer, Robert Heinlein; he also worked on the script, which was based on his Scribner's juvenile, *Rocketship Galileo*. The film is marred by melodramatics and some ridiculous comic relief, but the space sequences and the lunar episodes (the moonscapes were painted by astronomical and sometime science-fiction artist Chesley Bonestell) are remarkable bits of prophecy. I have found it useful to point out to students how the visual predictions of space and the moon surface were realized during the Apollo trips, and the experience of *déjà vu* that many of us experienced when we saw the actual, televised landing.

George Pal, as producer and later director, would have much to do with later adaptations of science-fiction classics such as Balmer and Wylie's *When Worlds Collide* (1951), Wells's *The War of the Worlds* (1953), and *The Time Machine* (1960). All are worth including as adaptations of written science fiction, although all fall short in one way or another, the first two more than the last.

Of the some two thousand or so remaining films, I would include in my series: *Forbidden Planet* (1956), which has Robbie the Robot, comic relief, and an idiotic love story (all modeled, to be sure, on *The Tempest*), but also the marvelous idea of the Id monster and scenes of the lost civilization which produced it; *The Invasion of the Body Snatchers* (1956), about the replacement of people by pod duplicates, which is nicely and soberly done, and liked by many critics more than I do (the remake has produced mixed reactions); *The Village of the Damned* (1960), a relatively faithful adaptation of the Wyndham novel (the 1963 *Day of the Triffids* is not as faithful and a lesser film); *Barbarella* (1967), which has a bit of nudity for the students and also lovely scenes and a delightful satire on a number of science-fiction themes; and, of course, the incomparable *2001: A Space Odyssey*, which in spite of some quarrels with its obscure ending and the unexplained murderousness of HAL is the most completely realized vision of the future yet achieved on film and an excellent motion picture.

The recent *Star Wars* (1977) and *Close Encounters of the Third Kind* (1977) are more important for what they have accomplished at the boxoffice than what they have achieved artistically. *Star Wars* is an appealing fairy tale and can be enjoyed effortlessly at that level, along with the lived-in quality of its scenes and costumes and the scope and

JAMES GUNN

effectiveness of its special effects. *Close Encounters* has a magnificent final epiphany in the appearance of the alien spaceship, but it seems to me that the first two-thirds of the film is irrelevant and the two UFO fanatics who have fought their way to the scene end up as spectators little more relevant to what goes on there than the rest of the audience. The most important aspect of the two films, however, is their refutation of the frequent excuse against making first-class science-fiction films, that SF films never make money. *Battlestar Galactica* has demonstrated, however, that special effects do not an SF movie make, though it will be cited as a reason not to do SF on television.

All of these can be shown effectively, along with films that have a similar appeal but are not sufficiently distanced from the present to qualify as science fiction: such as *Lost Horizon* (1937), *The Man in the White Suit* (1951), and *Dr. Strangelove* (1964).

Many science-fiction films have been produced since *Destination Moon*, but if I haven't listed them above I find them seriously flawed or completely hopeless. Some film critics, for instance, like *The Day the Earth Stood Still* or *The Thing*, both released in 1951; but any reader who recalls the science-fiction novelettes "Farewell to the Master" by Harry Bates and "Who Goes There?" by John W. Campbell must reject the films based on them if only for tossing away a good story and making a lesser one.

The Verne adaptations, *Journey to the Center of the Earth* (1959), *From the Earth to the Moon* (1964), *Twenty Thousand Leagues Under the Sea* (1965), and others generally are performed as period pieces; students find them amusing but don't take them seriously as science fiction. Neither do I; they are flawed and unfaithful. My favorite of this type is a Czech film, *The Wonderful Invention* (1958), sometimes called *The Fabulous World of Jules Verne*, but I've never been able to rent it. Godard's science-fiction film *Alphaville* (1965) is frequently admired, but I find it obscure and unconvincing.

Other films have been marred by mindless antiscientism, such as *The Incredible Shrinking Man* (1957) or *The Power* (1967); or by illogical elements, as in *Fahrenheit 451* (1966), *Planet of the Apes* (1968) and its many sequels, *Charly* (1968), or *Colossus: The Forbin Project* (1970); or by no logic at all, as in *The Andromeda Strain* (1971), *Silent Running* (1972), *Westworld* (1973), or *Soylent Green* (1973). It is interesting to note that the resolution that *Soylent Green* presents as the ultimate in horror could make a satisfying science-fiction story—if the problem were how to convince the public that its prejudice against eating a product made from human flesh was irrational and unreasonable. *A Clockwork Orange*, on the other hand, justifies, if it does not actually glorify, violence; I find this more repugnant than the small, neat crackers of *Soylent Green*.

In spite of their flaws, the films listed above are the best of their kind, and all of them may find their place in a science-fiction series with the reservations noted. Their kind simply is not a high art.

Science fiction on television is even worse. Its only value—in the way *Amazing Stories* was once considered by John W. Campbell as a primer for the more demanding science fiction published in *Astounding*—is to provide an introduction for students willing to move on to the written word. Series have even more flaws than science-fiction films and demand larger audiences (thus requiring a reduction to lowest-common-denominator approach) for survival. Nevertheless, a familiarity with the better-known series, *Star Trek* certainly and perhaps *The Twilight Zone* and *Night Gallery* among others, can be helpful in communicating with students. And, although schedules are seldom known far enough in advance to have programs incorporated into a course, teachers can set up a kind of haphazard series by calling students' attention to the weekly appearances of films on television and follow the viewing with analysis and criticism.

After criticizing what film and television have done to science fiction, my own series of lecture films about science fiction may seem like self-contradiction.

The series began in 1969 when I was approached by Continuing Education at the University of Kansas to prepare a high school module on science fiction. I didn't have the time, but I did provide a lecture on book publishing for a taped series. Shortly after that I attended the World Science Fiction Convention in St. Louis and became involved in talking to radio and television interviewers. I realized their interest, the growing public awareness of science fiction, and the increasing academic interest in science fiction. When I put all of those factors together with the lack of qualified teachers of science fiction, I proposed a series of films which eventually might form a course. I was encouraged by Continuing Education and by such stalwarts of science fiction and of the Science Fiction Writers of America as Damon Knight, Gordon Dickson, Robert Silverberg, and Isaac Asimov.

We had several choices of direction in which to develop the series, but we had neither the experience nor the funds for a professionally produced course; we decided to film the writers themselves talking about different aspects of science fiction. It seemed to me then, and it still seems right, that students would benefit the most from hearing from the people who were actually creating science fiction as writers and editors; in addition we would be making a valuable film record of a genre at its high point. Moreover, we could preserve on film science-fiction people who might soon be lost; already it was too late to film Hugo Gernsback and Tony Boucher and their opinions about science fiction, but it was not too late, quite, to film John Campbell; and one of the precious moments on film is my interview with John Campbell just three months before his death, and the luncheon discussion with Harry Harrison and Gordon Dickson that resulted in their *Analog* serial *Lifeboat*, retitled *Lifeship* in its book version.

So it began, slowly, with the twin difficulties of inexperience and inadequate funds. But we persevered and we learned, and today we have a catalog of twelve films—enough for a short course in science fiction or a liberal choice of auxiliary materials for a regular course. Eleven of the films were conceived and produced at the University of Kansas or wherever we had to go to film the person we wanted. We tried to film them in their own locations talking about topics that they wanted to discuss and were particularly qualified to discuss.

The list of films is below. They should be ordered, well in advance (they are booked solidly as soon as the semester begins), from the Audio-Visual Center, the University of Kansas, Lawrence, Kansas 66045. Students can be helped to get the most from the films by information about what to expect, what to look for. Some biographical information about the writers is useful, as well as the advance reading of their stories.

The films are 16mm, color, sound.

Films

STRANGER THAN SCIENCE FICTION
A CBS 21st Century News Production narrated by Walter Cronkite compares yesterday's science fiction with today's reality.

Time: 27 min.
Daily rental: $ 14
Five-day rental: 21
(for purchase, contact McGraw-Hill films)

THE EARLY HISTORY OF SCIENCE FICTION
Damon Knight describes the development of science fiction from Lucian of Samosata through the magazines of the thirties.

Time: 25 min.
Daily rental: $ 14
Five-day rental: 21
Purchase price: 325

THE HISTORY OF SCIENCE FICTION:
FROM 1938 TO THE PRESENT
Isaac Asimov describes the development of science fiction from the time John Campbell became editor of *Astounding* to the present.

Time: 32 min.
Daily rental: $ 16
Five-day rental: 24
Purchase price: 420

PLOT IN SCIENCE FICTION
Poul Anderson describes how plot interrelates with theme and character, and how ideas develop into stories.

Time: 25 min.
Daily rental:$ 14
Five-day rental: 21
Purchase price: 325

SCIENCE FICTION FILMS:
Forrest J. Ackerman, a collector and
historian of SF and SF film, discusses
the history of SF films in his museum of
a home.

Time: 30 min.
   Daily rental: $ 16
   Five-day rental: 24
   Purchase price: 390

LUNCH WITH JOHN CAMPBELL
Harry Harrison and Gordon Dickson
discuss an idea for a story with John
Campbell over a luncheon table—which
turns into the novel *Lifeboat*.

Time: 28 min.
   Daily rental: $ 16
   Five-day rental: 24
   Purchase price: 365

IDEAS IN SCIENCE FICTION
Frederik Pohl describes the ideas
science fiction has used over the
years—and their influence on science
fiction.

Time: 40 min.
   Daily rental: $ 20
   Five-day rental: 30
   Purchase price: 520

SCIENCE FICTION AND THE
MAINSTREAM
John Brunner, English science-fiction
author, talks about science fiction's
relations with the rest of literature,
with examples from his own work.

Time: 19 min.
   Daily rental: $ 12
   Five-day rental: 18
   Purchase price: 250

THE EARLY DAYS OF THE SCIENCE
FICTION MAGAZINES: An Interview
with Jack Williamson. James Gunn
talks with Jack Williamson about the
early magazines and their editors.

Time: 21 min.
   Daily rental: $ 12
   Five-day rental: 18
   Purchase price: 275

THEME IN SCIENCE FICTION
James Gunn and Gordon Dickson
discuss the major themes in which
science fiction has expressed itself.

Time: 32 min.
   Daily rental: $ 16
   Five-day rental: 24
   Purchase price: 420

A CAREER IN SCIENCE FICTION:
An Interview with Clifford Simak.
James Gunn interviews Clifford Simak
about his work and his feelings about
being a science-fiction writer.

Time: 20 min.
   Daily rental: $ 12
   Five-day rental: 18
   Purchase price: 260

NEW DIRECTIONS IN SCIENCE
FICTION
Harlan Ellison conducts a seminar on
where he thinks science fiction is going

Time: 25 min.
   Daily rental: $ 14
   Five-day rental: 21
   Purchase price: 325

and the new directions set forth in his
Dangerous Visions.

Important Productions in the History of the Science-Fiction Film

1898 An Astronomer's Dream (Meliés)
1899 She (Meliés)
1902 A Trip to the Moon (Meliés)
1906 The ? Motorist (Booth)
1909 A Trip to Jupiter (French Pathé)
1910 A Trip to Mars (Edison)
1919 The First Men in the Moon (Abbas)
1924 Aelita (Russian)
1925 The Lost World (Hoyt)
1926 Metropolis (Lang)
1930 Just Imagine (Butler)
1931 Frankenstein (Whale)
1932 The Island of Lost Souls (Kenton)
1933 King Kong (Cooper)
     The Invisible Man (Whale)
     Deluge (Feist)
1934 Transatlantic Tunnel (Elvey)
1936 Things to Come (Menzies)
1936-40 Flash Gordon and Buck Rogers
     serials
1937 Lost Horizon (Capra)
1950 Destination Moon (Pal)
1951 When Worlds Collide (Pal)
     The Thing from Another World (Hawks)
     The Day the Earth Stood Still (Wise)
     The Man in the White Suit (Macken-
     drick)
1953 The War of the Worlds (Pal)
1954 1984 (Anderson)
1955 20,000 Leagues Under the Sea
     (Fleischer)
1956 Forbidden Planet (Wilcox)
     The Invasion of the Body Snatchers
     (Siegel)
1957 The Incredible Shrinking Man (Ar-
     nold)
1958 The Wonderful Invention (Zeman)
1960 The Time Machine (Pal)
     Village of the Damned (Rilla)
1963 The Day of the Triffids (Sekeley)
1964 From the Earth to the Moon (Haskin)
     Dr. Strangelove (Kubrick)

1965 The Tenth Victim (Petri)
     Alphaville (Godard)
1966 Fahrenheit 451 (Truffaut)
     Fantastic Voyage (Fleischer)
1967 Barbarella (Vadim)
1968 2001: A Space Odyssey (Kubrick)
     Planet of the Apes (Schaffner)
     Charly (Nelson)
1970 Colossus: The Forbin Project (Sar-
     gent)
1971 A Clockwork Orange (Kubrick)
     The Andromeda Strain (Wise)
     THX 1138 (Lucas)
1972 Silent Running (Trumbull)
1973 Westworld (Crichton)
     Soylent Green (Fleischer)
1974 Young Frankenstein (Brooks)
     Zardoz (Boorman)
1975 A Boy and His Dog (Jones)
     The Land that Time Forgot (Connor)
     Rollerball (Jewison)
     The Stepford Wives (Forbes)
1976 The Food of the Gods (Gordon)
     Futureworld (Heffron)
     Logan's Run (Anderson)
     The Man Who Fell to Earth (Roeg)
1977 Close Encounters of the Third
     Kind (Spielberg)
     Demon Seed (Cammell)
     The Island of Dr. Moreau (Taylor)
     The People that Time Forgot (Connor)
     Star Wars (Lucas)
     Wizards (Bakshi)
1978 The Invasion of the Body
     Snatchers (Kaufman)
     Lord of the Rings (Bakshi)
     Superman (Donner)
     Watership Down (Rosen)
1979 Alien (Scott)
     Star Trek: The Motion Picture (Wise)

Bibliography of Books about Science Fiction Film

Amelio, Ralph J., editor. *Hal in the Classroom: Science Fiction Films.*
Pflaum, 1974.

Baxter, John. *Science Fiction in the Cinema.* Paperback Library, 1970.

Brosnan, John. *Future Tense: The Cinema of Science Fiction.* St. Martin's, 1979.

Gifford, Denis. *Science Fiction Film.* Studio Vista/Dutton Pictureback, 1971.

Johnson, William, editor. *Focus on the Science Fiction Film.* Prentice-Hall, 1972.

Steinbrunner, Chris, and Goldblatt, Burt. *Cinema of the Fantastic.* Saturday Review Press, 1972.

STAGING
A MINICON

BY ROBERT BARTHELL

The convention has a big place in the folkways of fandom. The far-scattered members of the SF microculture may try to keep in touch through fanzines and letters, but it's the cons that allow the fen to meet, speak their own slanguage, swap books and tattered mags, maybe even get the autograph of a pro. There are world cons, regional cons, scores of minicons. Devout instructors here and there have begun to stage minicons as class activites. The one Bill Lomax put on at Benjamin Franklin High School in Los Angeles, with Gene Roddenberry, Ray Bradbury, and the editor as guests, was no longer very mini—it drew 700 people!

Robert Barthell writes about Wyocon One, the minicon he staged in the spring of 1974 at Northwest Community College at Powell, Wyoming, an isolated town in the Big Horn Basin. He teaches science fiction and popular culture courses there, and was editor of Cthulhu Calls, *an SF quarterly published at the college. He is now gathering SF materials for the Wyoming Popular Culture Center, to be distributed to high school teachers for use in classes. His highly successful minicon deserves imitation.*

Probably the most overlooked form of community and school art festival is the science-fiction convention. Although generally limited to large population centers, it actually offers more to the resident of the isolated, rural community than to his city cousin. Fans of science-fiction literature and art can be found everywhere, and the small "minicon" is one form of popular culture which can be made welcome in the small community. The conventions began as a way for fans to get together to discuss science, science fiction, and writers in the field. During the thirties and forties fans were few and widely scattered around the country, but they found the time and finances to get together for local, regional, and national meetings. Writers, if they lived close by, were glad to meet with their readers to discuss and promote their work. In time the conventions acquired a format and traditions.

Generally speaking, a science-fiction convention offers an art show, writing contest, panels on various topics, films, huckster room, masquerade contest, auction, and various games. It also features a guest of honor who is a professional writer or an active fan. The writing and art contests are often judged by the guest of honor. Prizes for the various events are given out at a banquet. Anyone interested in putting on a "con" should, if possible, attend a regional or national convention to get a firsthand look at the world of fandom.

With more and more schools teaching SF and the general readership expanding, the SF convention seems likely to move toward the school. In the isolated rural community, especially, it can be enjoyed by the teacher, the student, and the general public.

In 1974 the first science-fiction convention in Wyoming was held. What follows is a description of the planning and rationale for Wyocon One and a discussion of what Wyocon's application might be in similar regions of the country. Wyoming is a large state with a small population, roughly 360,000 people, who live in ranching/farming communities. These communities are small, isolated, and at great driving distances from one another. Throughout the winter months, travel is difficult; and most people find their activities and recreation tied to the local school. The local high school or junior college tends to provide the activities which would normally be handled in large cities by the library, theater, museum, or university. In a sense the schools "belong" to the people more than they would in an urban area.

Northwest Community College, the site of Wyocon One, is located in Powell, a town of 5,000, at the center of cultural and artistic programs in the Big Horn Basin which covers approximately 15,000 square miles with a population density of three people per square mile. The local college or high school in such a locale can sponsor events which attract residents of the area and involve local people in their planning and promotion.

Under these conditions, it would be impossible—or at best difficult—to put on an SF convention in Wyoming without working through the local schools. Prior to Wyocon there had been several programs which familiarized residents of the Big Horn Basin with SF. These programs were also sponsored by local schools.

In 1971 Frank Herbert appeared on the campus of Northwest Community College as a guest speaker. His appearance was arranged by the college student senate. Since there was a good turnout for Herbert's lecture, the college applied for a grant from the Wyoming Committee for the Humanities to do a lecture/film series on horror–science-fiction film, The Committee for the Humanities and Northwest Community College jointly funded the film series for a year and gave active support to its initial planning and development. The film series, titled "Skeletons in Our Closet: The Horror-Science Fiction Film in American Life," consisted of nine films presented once a month during each month of the school year. The films were shown in three communities in the Basin. Each film was preceded by a thirty-minute lecture relating the film to some phase of national policy such as racism, violence,

ROBERT BARTHELL

or biological research.

In addition to the films, three guest lecturers appeared in the program: actors John Carradine and Vincent Price, and science-fiction writer Ed Bryant. Each of the artists spoke on some aspect of horror–science fiction in a special evening program held on a separate date from the film lectures. Attendance for the year's program (nine films and three lectures) reached a total of 3,095 people in the Big Horn Basin, another indication of a rather wide interest in SF.

Following the film series, in the school year 1972–73, a new publication, *Cthulhu Calls,* was started at the college. This was a quarterly review of SF, fantasy, and horror literature. It had a twofold purpose: to provide an outlet for amateur writers in the Wyoming-Montana region, and to give out information for area teachers who were beginning to use science fiction in their classrooms. The magazine as a resource for teachers was especially important, because there are few cities in Wyoming that can support bookstores, and most of the teachers have little contact with SF publishers or writers.

The regional response to the film series and the magazine was excellent; more important, these two programs introduced SF into several communities as community projects, and these in turn formed a base for Wyocon One.

Since Wyocon was to be the first SF convention in the state, we anticipated problems, but these turned out to be less severe than expected. Our first concern, of course, was funding. We had conceived a program that was almost grandiose by Wyoming standards but felt that, since this was to be the state's first SF convention, we should show as many sides of SF as possible. We also had to consider the fact that many people could come for one day only and many of the events would have to be duplicated for the two days the convention ran. Wyocon had been planned for a weekend so people living on outlying farms and ranches could combine a visit to the convention with their weekend shopping.

What we had in mind was to introduce as many people as possible to a sampling of all the traditional events. Even with a one-day stop at the convention, a person could leave with a somewhat rounded sense of what a SF convention was like. This would require a variety of activities—and the money to fund them.

Wyocon was to be funded in three ways: cash donations by the college, a grant from the Wyoming Council on the Arts, and fees paid by persons attending the convention. The budget was rather large, but we did learn that future conventions could be put on for less money. The key to keeping expenses down lay in developing a coöperative effort in which high schools and the various college departments could participate.

A major cost item was tied to the fact that we brought in three guests of honor, but we felt it would be easier to finance more modest programs in the future if this first convention was a success. The success would depend on the visiting writers because the public would be familiar with their names even if they were not familiar with SF conventions. Consequently, we asked the Wyoming Council on the Arts to provide money for the guest artists.

An item which is more important than money is the support of the faculty and administration of the school. In our case, the president and trustees of the college gave money and opened the school facilities to Wyocon. They also worked with the convention committees in setting up the equipment borrowed for displays. The college let us use the college print shop and public relations office to print and mail out promotional material on Wyocon. This kept us from buying ads on the local radio and in regional newspapers. The local press coverage was extensive and effective, an advantage the small town "minicon" has over the large city convention.

The number of school and community people involved in a minicon is also important. These should be volunteers. Unwilling participants will turn a minicon into another required school activity. Wyocon committees solicited help from the faculty and students at the college and in area high schools. They ended up with more than an adequate number of volunteers. This reduced the work load on committees and permitted release time so volunteers could attend various events. Using the volunteer approach produced a bonus in the form of a concert. The college music department offered their wind ensemble for the concert and asked to be given an active part in the convention. The rehearsal time, lighting, and stage decorations were all donated and would not have been forthcoming if an administrative fiat had been issued to force participation.

At this point we should perhaps discuss the schedule of events. Wyocon ran on a Saturday and Sunday, and offered a varied program. On Saturday we ran five of the ten feature films, radio tapes, slides, and the space documentary films. We also scheduled an art seminar by the visiting artist and a panel discussion by the two guest writers on "Teaching Science Fiction." All film and slide/tape programs were shut down during the seminars. Outside of the seminar periods the films and multimedia events were run continuously throughout the day for the benefit of those people who could only attend one day of the convention. The masquerade contest was held Saturday evening, and the day's programming closed with films and slides.

Sunday's program began with films and multimedia shows that ran until the banquet began at noon, and the prizes for the various events were given out at the banquet with Ed Bryant and Jack Williamson acting as toastmasters. After the banquet there was a seminar on "Science Fiction and Society" which lasted until the concert at three o'clock. The Sunday activities closed at ten o'clock with films and slide shows. As on the previous day, the other events were closed down

ROBERT BARTHELL

during the seminar and concert. Because of a special appeal to towns-people, the art exhibit was kept open both days and during the seminars.

Since the main event of the convention would be the appearance of two writers and an artist, I ought to comment on our choice of these guests. We wanted to recognize both the early SF writers and the newer, emerging authors. Jack Williamson was the obvious first choice because of his background in the early pulp magazines and his ties to the academic world. Teachers had an important role in organizing Wyocon and would be interested in the academic side of science fiction. They would appreciate Jack's scholarly work, degrees, and position in various professional organizations. He was a member of the Science Fiction Research Association, taught at a university, and could discuss the scholarly side of science fiction with authority. We were trying to reach classroom teachers who were generally not as far advanced in reading SF as their students and who might also need some scholarly rationales for offering SF classes in their schools. Jack was also willing to judge the writing contest, a real attraction in getting people to enter the competition.

Ed Bryant was our choice for a new writer. He had worked with the college before on the film program and was familiar with the state. He is a former Wyoming resident and a graduate of the University of Wyoming. Since he would be considered part of the New Wave in SF, we felt that he could present the newer developments in the field.

The guest artist was Morris Scott Dollens. Morris has been doing SF painting and illustrations for many years and goes back to the thirties in his fan and professional interests. The art show and seminars were important to us because we felt that SF art has long been overlooked by college and high school art departments. We felt that Morris's work with astronomical subjects would interest fans and academics, and would have an appeal to the general public who might not be interested in SF art, but who might be attracted to his realistic astronomical representations. More than the two writers, Dollens would be dealing with an art form new to area residents and teachers.

The guest writers and artist were involved in writing and art contests which began two months before the convention. Entry forms for the contests were sent out to people who responded to notices in area newspapers and to art and English departments in schools throughout the state. People on the mailing list for *Cthulhu Calls* were also contacted, and many inquiries came in from those who had heard about the contests indirectly. In all, a total of sixty entries registered for the art contest and sixty-five for the writing competition. The entries came from all over the state and were not restricted to the Big Horn Basin.

The writers were competing for the first three places in two categories: poetry and short story writing. The art entries could be in any medium but were limited to three entries per person. For the art contest we gave first-place awards in three categories: horror, fantasy, and science fiction. The writing entries were mailed to Jack Williamson as they came in. The art entries were placed in the school art gallery and would be judged by Morris Dollens and two NWCC art instructors. The instructors made all the arrangements for the art show and carried on the necessary correspondence concerning the contest. Trophies for placing in the art and writing contests were awarded at the Sunday banquet. In addition to receiving trophies, the winners of the writing contest had their stories and poems printed in a special issue of *Cthulhu Calls*.

The convention also had a number of multimedia presentations which consisted of old radio shows on tape cassettes, slide shows, films and documentaries on various aspects of space exploration. The radio shows were samples of *Lights Out, Inner Sanctum, X Minus One,* and other science-fiction–horror programs popular during the thirties through the fifties. We also showed slides of Dollens's astronomical art in the lounge of the student union during program breaks. We had a number of astronomical slides that we purchased from the Hale Observatories. These were pictures of nebulae, comets, planets, and galaxies taken through the various large telescopes of the observatory system. They have remained a popular item on loan from the college long after the convention was over.

During the two days of Wyocon we showed ten feature films. We wanted to cover the history of SF films from the twenties to the sixties. The committee tried to get films that were representative of a time period, but which were also not seen regularly in the local theaters or on television. Film selections ran from the silent classic *Metropolis* to *Flash Gordon* serials and *The Three Stooges in Space*. In addition to the feature films we ran a number of space documentaries and films on SF literature. They were cheap rentals, some of them free from various corporations, and they covered everything from films of Goddard's early rocket experiments to the latest space shots from NASA.

The writers' seminars were set up to cover the teaching of SF and its relationship to society. The appeal, we hoped, would be to both teachers and the general public. The art show was tied into the art seminars and art contest. The show ran both days of the convention and was open to the public without charge. The concert was also open to the public because we wanted to get local people interested in SF through something they would view as a traditional cultural program. We found that the art exhibit tended to draw people interested in art, but who were not interested in SF as literature. The seminars were conducted by Dollens. They consisted of five sessions covering the history of SF art, the art of Morris Dollens, amateur fan art, and the techniques used by Dollens in his work.

The art show and seminars were an unexpected success. Some of the seminars had up to eighty participants, and Dollens spent his time between lectures meeting with the local people and fans to discuss his work. Several hundred people filed through the art exhibit during its two-day tenure, and we received many inquiries about the possibility of continuing the art show as an annual event. For many of the viewers, this was their first exposure to science-fiction art.

The concert on Sunday afternoon was also open to the public without charge, and it provided a sort of tongue-in-cheek, fun activity. The college wind ensemble played a medley of American popular songs, presenting them as records of a vanished civilization. The stage was set up with special lighting, and slides of science-fiction art were shown on screens fixed to the sides of the stage. Model spaceships hung over the musicians, who wore makeup and antennae to give an alien appearance. The director of the wind ensemble, a long-time SF fan, conducted in makeup and disappeared at the end of the program in a cloud of smoke. It was an inexpensive and popular event which could be expanded or altered for any size musical group. Music still remains one of the more neglected elements at SF conventions, but one which can be used effectively.

There was some doubt that we would get anyone to sign up for the masquerade contest, but fifteen people showed up, and it turned out to be one of the more interesting, lively events. Traditionally the masquerade contest consists of people made up as characters in SF stories who are readily identifiable to the fans in the audience. Contestants can give a short dialogue from the story or novel or simply appear in costume. The cost of such a program is minimal because the participants make their own costumes. This is an event that drama students can enjoy and one which has enough spectacle in it to draw the attention of the public.

We actually hadn't planned to have an auction. This is another traditional part of a convention program which owes its origin to the need to raise money to meet convention expenses. It is based on the collector instinct which seems to exist in all SF fans. Items such as badges, artwork, books, and old magazines are donated to the auction and the proceeds turned over to the convention committee. The Denver Area Science Fiction Association fans who came to Wyocon wanted to hold one. The auction was initiated and planned by Doris Beetem of DASFA who assembled the necessary items, acted as cashier, and persuaded Ed Bryant to act as auctioneer. Funds from the auction were turned over to DASFA to set up a travel fund for a fan to attend the annual Denver Milehicon. The auction attracted a crowd and was a fun event that everyone enjoyed.

Another activity born out of convention financial needs and fan collectors is the huckster room where collectors and sellers offer their wares and active trading can take place. A fee is charged for the use of the room and can be turned over to offset convention costs. We did not set up an area for a huckster room until after the convention was under way. This was poor planning on our part, and the little huckstering that went on did not seem to have any attraction for people unfamiliar with SF conventions. They did not have the interest in collecting and were not familiar with the items for sale. I think the huckster room should be included in a minicon because students and the public seem to be more aware of collecting in recent years.

The banquet is usually a sort of wrapup of the SF convention. Wyocon used the school cafeteria and the college food service provided the meals at reasonable cost. Outsiders could buy a ticket for the meal only, and for the price could eat, watch the awards given out, and hear short talks by the guest artists. The prizes given out at the banquet were trophies purchased for the different events. However, the prizes could also be made or take the form of books, posters, and donated art works.

A final assessment of Wyocon showed that just over three hundred people attended from places as far away as Denver and central Montana. At least one-quarter of the attendants were involved in some aspect of the minicon: planning, decorations, art show, concert, or registration and programming. We found that other schools would be interested in contributing to the cost of bringing in a guest of honor if they had been informed in time to include it in their yearly budgets. Schools planning a convention should remember that there are state and federal agencies which can fund such activities. The best thing about a minicon is that it can fit several school budgets: drama, art, and English departments. It can be an all-school activity that will certainly cost less than a football or basketball team and will have a wide public appeal. However, you have to show the administration that the interest is there, and this is why community involvement helps. It gives the administration some sign that people off campus would be interested in attending. The schools have one way of saving a convention money: they can provide free or low cost building use.

SF fans have demonstrated through the years that an interested group of people can put on an interesting, fun-filled convention and make it pay. They do it because they are interested in science fiction and the world of fandom. There is no reason why that kind of enthusiasm cannot take root in the schools and small communities.

Notes

Something about the history of fandom and the format of the SF convention can be found in Harry Warner's *All Our Yesterdays* and Sam Moskowitz's *The Immortal Storm*. Many fan magazines carry information on upcoming cons and reports on cons that readers have attended. I would recommend a subscription to *Locus,* put out by Charles N. Brown, a fan and industry trade publication covering the market news for writers and carrying reports on films and upcoming conventions.

Bibliography

Books
Moskowitz, Sam. *The Immortal Storm*. Hyperion Press, 45 Riverside Ave., Westport, Connecticut 06880.
Warner, Harry, Jr. *All Our Yesterdays*. Advent: Publishers, Inc., P.O. Box 9228, Chicago, Illinois 60690.

Film Sources
Black Hawk Films Bulletin, Eastin-Phelan Distributing Corp., Davenport, Iowa 52808. Low cost 8mm films of early SF films and documentaries. Also carry a wide range of slides on technical topics and many NASA photos.
Budget Films, 4590 Santa Monica Blvd., Los Angeles, California 92060. Write for catalog. Films are cheap and include many science-fiction classics.
Director, Independent Study, Continuing Education Building. The University of Kansas, Lawrence, Kansas 66045. (See chapter by James Gunn.) Film series. Major writers and editors discuss SF. A good source of classroom material.
University of Utah, Education Media Center, Milton Bennion Hall 207, Salt Lake City, Utah 84410. Write for the *Mountain Plains Educational Media Council Film Catalog*. This catalog carries a number of films available on loan from schools in the Mountain States. Listings.include rentals, free films, documentaries, and feature films.

Funding
National Endowment for the Humanities, 806 15th Street, N.W., Washington, D.C. 20506. Write to NEH and ask for information on state level funding and a description of the programs offered.

Slides and Tapes
Director, Palomar Observatory, Palomar Mountain, California 92060. Write for slide catalog.
Dollens, Morris Scott, P.O. Box 692, Gateway Station, Culver City, California 90230. Write for tape and slide catalog. Dollens carries a number of slides on different SF and fantasy artists.

A BIBLIOGRAPHY OF TWENTIETH-CENTURY SCIENCE FICTION AND FANTASY

BY ALEXEI AND CORY PANSHIN

In Chapter 6, Alexei and Cory Panshin presented a survey of the writers of modern SF. The following historical and critical bibliography of twentieth century science fiction and fantasy, is a companion piece. It is not exhaustive, but rather a first overview of the field, limited to fewer than one hundred titles. At the end of each entry, cross-references are given in parentheses to other works in the bibliography that compare interestingly.

A. 1900–1938

Respectable British literary scientific romance. Disreputable American pulp romance. Satire. Dystopia. Fantasy. The new American science fiction.

A1. Asimov, Isaac, ed. *Before the Golden Age.* Doubleday, 1974.
Asimov's autobiography, ages 11–18, in terms of the magazine science-fiction stories that impressed him, 1931–38. 30,000 words of autobiography. Twenty-five long stories. Limited by Asimov's teen-age tastes, this book nonetheless affords a unique look at the rapid development of American science fiction during the thirties.
(Compare early stories to A2, A10; later stories to B11.)
A2. Burroughs, Edgar Rice. *A Princess of Mars.* McClurg, 1917.
This romance, the first of Edgar Rice Burroughs's many SF stories, was serialized in the general pulp magazine *All-Story* in 1912. John Carter on Mars. Burroughs is more lively and colorful than more respectable writers of the same period like Doyle and Wells.
(B3; B4; "A Rose for Ecclesiastes" by Zelazny in B16 or D29.)
A3. Campbell, John W. *The Best of John W. Campbell.* Ballantine, 1976.
In these short stories, all but one originally published under the

name Don A. Stuart, Campbell explored mood, idea and method. The influence of these stories, and of Campbell's extension of their implications as the paramount editor of SF, post-1937, is visible throughout modern science fiction.

(A11; A16; B11; C11.)

A4. Čapek, Karel. *War with the Newts* (1936). Putnam, 1939.

A Czech author who died in 1938, Čapek wrote the play, *R.U.R.* (1921), which gave us the word "robot." This book is a satire about a strange new species of animal which we eat, set to labor for us, and then are overwhelmed by.

(A19; A8; C7.)

A5. Doyle, Arthur Conan. *The Lost World*. Doran, 1912.

Doyle wrote scientific romances as well as Sherlock Holmes stories and historical novels. Here Professor Challenger discovers a prehistoric world preserved on a plateau in the South American jungle. British.

(A2; A10; A16, particularly *The Island of Dr. Moreau*.)

A6. Eddison, E.R. *The Worm Ouroboros*. Cape, 1922.

An ornate chivalric fantasy, nominally set on Mercury. A war between Witches and Demons. Declamatory. Rich. Old-fashioned. British.

(B22; C23; D30.)

A7. Huxley, Aldous. *Brave New World*. Doubleday, 1932.

This dystopia about a scientifically controlled future belongs to a British literary tradition of nay-saying reaction to the utopian visions of H.G. Wells. One part fashionable despair; one part prescience.

(E.M. Forster's "The Machine Stops" in C8B; B15; D5.)

A8. Lewis, C.S. *Out of the Silent Planet*. Lane, 1938.

A voyage to Mars where Christianly-intelligible marvels occur. Traditional religious concerns in science-fiction dress, by a close friend of Tolkien. The first book of three. British.

(H.G. Wells's *First Men in the Moon* in A16; A14; B9; C7.)

A9. Lindsay, David. *A Voyage to Arcturus*. Methuen, 1920.

Grotesque and beautiful ethical fantasy. Hallucinatory. To some degree derived from occultist metaphysics. A special taste. British.

(A18; A8; A13; D25.)

A10. Merritt, A. *The Moon Pool*. Putnam, 1919.

Originally appeared in *All-Story*, the general pulp magazine. A lost race novel set in Polynesia. Color is the long suit of this romance.

(A2; A6; S.P. Meek's "Submicroscopic" and "Awlo of Ulm" in A1.)

A11. Moore, C.L. *The Best of C.L. Moore*. Ballantine, 1975.

Six stories from the thirties, four from the forties. In a period when SF writers, science- and machine-oriented, were almost exclusively male, Moore held a place as a major writer on the strength of these stories, rich in color, mood and ambience.

(A10; B14; D8; D29.)

A12. Shiel, M.P. *The Purple Cloud.* Chatto and Windus, 1901.

Classic British post-catastrophe last man-last woman novel.

(*The War of the Worlds* in A16; B19; Alfred Bester's "Adam and No Eve" in B11.)

A13. Smith, E.E. *The Skylark of Space.* Buffalo, 1946.

Serialized in *Amazing Stories* in 1928—previously considered unpublishable. A pivotal book: the first starships. This novel is at the same time a late scientific romance and an early example of the vigorous American genre literature, science fiction.

(A2; B18; Heinlein's *Methuselah's Children* in B13; C3.)

A14. Stapledon, Olaf. *Last and First Men, and Star Maker.* Dover, 1968.

Two strange visionary fictions by a British philosopher, originally published in 1930 and 1937. Successively larger overviews of the future progress of man and the universe. Ponderous. Overwhelming.

(A18; B17; B13; C11.)

A15. Weinbaum, Stanley G. *The Best of Stanley G. Weinbaum.* Ballantine, 1974.

Stories of strange inventions and bright romps with alien playfellows on the planets of the solar system. These stories were highly influential in original magazine appearance.

(A1; B18; C12; C1.)

A16. Wells, H.G. *Seven Famous Novels.* Knopf, 1934.

Wells has completely dominated British literary science fiction since his own time. His influence on American genre science fiction is only slightly less marked. Seven science-fiction novels, 1895–1906, including *The Time Machine* and *The War of the Worlds.*

(C10; C26; D1.)

A17. Williamson, Jack. *The Legion of Space.* Fantasy Press, 1947.

The most popular science-fiction novel of the thirties, serialized in *Astounding* in 1934. A stew of romance elements, the Three Musketeers, and Falstaff.

(A10; A13; C20.)

A18. Wright, S. Fowler. *The World Below.* Longmans Green, 1930.

A British vision of the far future of humanity.

(H.G. Wells's *The Time Machine* in A16 or C8A; "Twilight" by Campbell in A3, B16 or D28; C11; D1.)

A19. Zamyatin, Eugene. *We.* Dutton, 1924.

The joys of unfreedom in a regimented culture, by a Russian writer influenced by Wells. Never published in Russia.

(E.M. Forster's "The Machine Stops" in C8B; A7; B15.)

B. 1939–1950

The basic works of modern science fiction. Contemporary rational fantasy. Questions about reality. The future of man.

B1. Asimov, Isaac. *The Foundation Trilogy*. Doubleday Science Fiction Book Club, not dated.

These stories, originally published in *Astounding*, 1942–50, later appeared as three separate volumes: *Foundation, Foundation and Empire*, and *Second Foundation*. Five hundred years of the fall of a future Galactic Empire.

(A14; B13; B18; C4.)

B2. Blish, James. *Jack of Eagles*. Greenberg, 1952.

A short version, under the title "Let the Finder Beware," appeared in *Thrilling Wonder* in 1949. Author set aside his skepticism to write this novel of psionic wrestling for power.

(B21; B6; C5.)

B3. Brackett, Leigh. *The Sword of Rhiannon*. Ace, 1953.

Originally "Sea-Kings of Mars" in a 1949 issue of *Thrilling Wonder*. A space opera largely set in the remote past of Mars. A romance of a sort not printed in *Astounding,* the dominant science-fiction magazine of the period.

(A11; B22; "The Martian Way" by Asimov in C8B; "A Rose for Ecclesiastes" by Zelazny in B16 or D29.)

B4. Bradbury, Ray. *The Martian Chronicles*. Doubleday, 1950.

Connected short stories set on a Mars of Bradbury's imagination, reflecting Midwestern American childhood. Emotional, antimaterialistic fantasies. These stories, unique in SF, were originally published in peripheral magazines like *Planet Stories*. In book form, won wide general popularity.

(C9; "The Green Hills of Earth" by Robert Heinlein in B13; C25.)

B5. Brown, Fredric. *The Best of Fredric Brown*. Ballantine, 1977.

Brown's stories, more than any others in SF, smell of the pulps. Not surprising, since Brown was a successful writer of pulp detective stories. Here are joybuzzers, biters-bit, alcoholic nightmares, fireworks, and entertainments, along with many of Brown's nifty short-shorts.

(B6; A15; C17.)

B6. Brown, Fredric. *What Mad Universe*. Dutton, 1949.

In *Startling Stories,* 1948. Science-fiction magazine editor thrown by catastrophe into a bewildering and dangerous alternate universe. In part, satire on late forties pulp SF magazines. In part, reality-trip. Like much of Brown's work, simultaneously funny-cute and frightening.

(B14; B10; C20.)

B7. de Camp, L. Sprague, and Fletcher Pratt. *The Compleat Enchanter*. Ballantine, 1975.

Two 1940 novellas and a 1941 novel from *Unknown,* fantasy companion magazine of *Astounding,* also edited by John W. Campbell. A mathematical psychologist transfers himself into the worlds of Norse

myth, Spenser's *Faerie Queene,* and Ariosto's *Orlando Furioso.*
(B8; B6; C2.)

B8. de Camp, L. Sprague. *Lest Darkness Fall.* Holt, 1941.

An inadvertent time traveller tries to prevent the fall of Rome by introducing modern technology. Published in *Unknown,* 1939.

(A2; "The Sands of Time" and "As Never Was" by P. Schuyler Miller; "Time Locker" by Lewis Padgett (Kuttner and Moore); and "By His Bootstraps" by Robert Heinlein—all in B11.)

B9. Graves, Robert. *Watch the North Wind Rise.* Creative Age, 1949.

A poet spends a week in an imperfect future utopia. Strange, static, pedantic, poetic. British.

(A7; C16; D16.)

B10. Harness, Charles L. *Flight Into Yesterday.* Bouregy and Curl, 1953.

In *Startling Stories,* 1949. An example of pulp SF at its most bizarre, complex and didactic. Space travel; time travel; metamorphosis; apotheosis.

(B21; B6; C6; D10.)

B11. Healy, Raymond J., and J. Francis McComas, eds. *Adventures in Time and Space.* Random House, 1946.

Mammoth early science-fiction anthology, largely consisting of stories from *Astounding* under the early (1938–45) editorship of John W. Campbell. Still available as quality paperback, and as Modern Library Giant under the title *Famous Science Fiction Stories.* Highly recommended.

(A1; B1; B13.)

B12. Heinlein, Robert A. *Beyond This Horizon.* Fantasy Press, 1948.

Literally completed on the eve of World War II, published in *Astounding* in 1942. Unhappiness in utopia, and the search for the meaning of life. Rich book, but misshapen.

(A7; B9; C5.)

B13. Heinlein, Robert A. *The Past Through Tomorrow.* Putnam, 1967.

A collection of Heinlein's Future History stories, originally published in *Astounding* 1939–41 and elsewhere after World War II. Collected previously as *The Man Who Sold the Moon, The Green Hills of Earth, Revolt in 2100* and *Methuselah's Children.* As Asimov imagined space given political structure, Heinlein imagined future time given historical structure.

("Universe" by Robert Heinlein in C8A; B17; D4; D2.)

B14. Kuttner, Henry. *The Best of Henry Kuttner.* Ballantine, 1975.

Clever short stories from a writer whose impact was diluted by his many pseudonyms. Much of his work done in collaboration with his wife, C.L. Moore. Chief pseudonyms include Lewis Padgett and Lawrence O'Donnell.

(See Kuttner stories in B11 and B16; B20; B5; B23.)

B15. Orwell, George. *Nineteen Eighty-four.* Harcourt, 1949.

This novel of a totalitarian near-future by a dying author partly reflects his personal circumstances, partly reflects the bleakness of postwar Britain. Powerful. Haunting.

(E.M. Forster's "The Machine Stops" in C8B; A7; D4.)

B16. Silverberg, Robert, ed. *The Science Fiction Hall of Fame, Volume One.* Doubleday, 1970.

Twenty-six short stories—three from the thirties, eleven from the forties, eleven from the fifties, one from the sixties—chosen by vote of the membership of the Science Fiction Writers of America. Printed in chronological order. Good collection.

(C8A and C8B; A1; D28.)

B17. Simak, Clifford D. *City.* Gnome Press, 1952.

In these stories, all but one originating in *Astounding* 1944–47, intelligent dogs tell of the times when there were men. International Fantasy Award, 1953.

("World of the Red Sun" by Simak in A1; "The Big Front Yard" by Simak in C8B or D3; B14; D1.)

B18. Smith, E.E. *Gray Lensman.* Fantasy Press, 1951.

Serialized in *Astounding,* 1939. Grand galaxy-shaking. Crude, but with immense scope and vitality. For his series of Lensman novels and for his earlier Skylark stories, Smith was considered the dominant SF writer of the thirties.

(A13; A14; D14; D7.)

B19. Stewart, George R. *Earth Abides.* Random House, 1949.

Stewart has always found his own unusual subjects. This, his one venture into science fiction, is about survival after worldwide disaster. International Fantasy Award, 1951.

(See stories by Merril, Matheson, Leiber, Boucher, and Bixby in B16.)

B20. van Vogt, A.E. *Slan.* Arkham House, 1946.

Van Vogt's first novel, serialized in *Astounding* in 1940. The story of a persecuted boy superman. Van Vogt was one of the three most influential writers of SF of the past thirty-five years, along with Asimov and Heinlein, also early John W. Campbell discoveries.

(See van Vogt stories in B11 and D28; B21; " 'If This Goes On—' " by Robert Heinlein in B13; C10.)

B21. van Vogt, A.E. *The World of Null-A.* Simon & Schuster, 1948.

Serialized in *Astounding,* 1945. Van Vogt offers complex plots, relentless action, boundless concepts and mental funk. This novel is about a superman with identity problems, involved in galactic huggermugger. The plot does not bear examination. Nonetheless, strangely powerful.

(B10; C6; D10.)

B22. Vance, Jack. *The Dying Earth.* Hillman Books, 1950.

Stories set in the final, magical, decadent days of Earth. Early Vance. Cool. Richly romantic. A strange masterpiece.

(Vance stories in C8B and D3; A9; A10.)

B23. Williamson, Jack. *The Humanoids.* Simon & Schuster, 1949.

Scientist versus robots following directive to "serve and obey and guard man from harm." Serialized in *Astounding,* 1948.

(Williamson's "With Folded Hands" in C8A; A4; C4.)

C. 1951–1960

Social science fiction. Mapping time and space. Tales of engineers and admen. Holocausts and infernos. Intimations of a new humanity.

C1. Anderson, Poul, and Gordon R. Dickson. *Earthman's Burden.* Gnome Press, 1957.

Stories of the Hokas—teddy bear-like aliens so struck by humanity that they do impressions of our games. Wild West Hoka. Pirate Hoka. Foreign Legion Hoka. Sherlock Holmes Hoka.

(A13; "First Contact" by Murray Leinster in B16; "The Dragon Masters" by Jack Vance in D3.)

C2. Anderson, Poul. *Three Hearts and Three Lions.* Doubleday, 1961.

Serialized in *Fantasy and Science Fiction* in 1953. Rationalized other-world fantasy in the tradition of *Unknown* (1939–43). Order versus Chaos. Carolingian hero Holger Danske must remember himself. Author's nerve fails at the conclusion.

(B7; "Sidewise in Time" by Murray Leinster in A1; A6; A11.)

C3. Anderson, Poul. *The Man Who Counts.* Ace, 1978.

Serialized in *Astounding,* 1958. Stranded Earthmen must educate aliens in order to be saved. Falstaffian Dutchman Nicholas van Rijn demonstrates ideal character in action.

(Anderson stories in C8A and D3; C7; D17.)

C4. Asimov, Isaac. *The Caves of Steel.* Doubleday, 1954.

Extrapolative SF novel, serialized in *Galaxy,* 1953. A human and a robot detective attempt to solve a murder in a New York City of the future, monolithic and closed in upon itself.

(Asimov's "The Martian Way" and Pohl's "The Midas Plague" in C8B; Kornbluth's "The Marching Morons" in C8A or D28; A19; C5.)

C5. Bester, Alfred. *The Demolished Man.* Shasta, 1953.

Serialized in *Galaxy,* 1952. Murder in a telepathic society. Intense and flamboyant. Pop amalgam of *Les Miserables* and *Crime and Punishment.* Hugo Award, 1953.

(B20; B2; D22.)

C6. Bester, Alfred. *The Stars My Destination.* Signet, 1957.

Serialized in *Galaxy,* 1956. All color and raw emotion. Bester's *Count of Monte Cristo:* revenge in a teleporting society. Jazzy. The novel lacks a middle.

(Bester's "Adam and No Eve" in B11; Bester's "Fondly Fahrenheit" in B16; Bester's "5,271,009" in D28; C5; C7.)

C7. Blish, James. *A Case of Conscience.* Ballantine, 1958.

A short version of this 1959 Hugo Award winner appeared in *If* in 1953. Theological argument cast as science-fiction drama. A Jesuit priest-biologist and a planet he believes to be a trap created by the Devil. Intellectual case.

(Boucher's "The Quest for Saint Aquin" in B16; C18; D15.)

C8A and **C8B.** Bova, Ben, ed. *The Science Fiction Hall of Fame, Volumes Two A and Two B.* Doubleday, 1973.

Twenty-two long stories, one from the turn of the century, one from the twenties, one from the thirties, seven from the forties, nine from the fifties, and three from the sixties. Chosen by vote of the membership of the Science Fiction Writers of America. A generous sampling of good science fiction.

(A1; B11; D3.)

C9. Bradbury, Ray. *Fahrenheit 451.* Ballantine, 1953.

This short novel is Bradbury's longest science-fiction story. Future where books are burned. Short version as "The Fireman" in *Galaxy,* 1951. Pessimistic protest literature.

(B4; Kornbluth's "The Marching Morons" in C8A or D28; C15.)

C10. Clarke, Arthur C. *Childhood's End.* Houghton Mifflin, 1953.

The coming transformation of humanity. A portion appeared in *Famous Fantastic Mysteries* in 1950 under the title "Guardian Angel." Since the early fifties, Clarke has been Britain's most successful writer of science fiction.

(Wells's "The Time Machine" in A16 or C8A; A14; D15; Zelazny's "For a Breath I Tarry" in D28.)

C11. Clarke, Arthur C. *The City and the Stars.* Harcourt, 1956.

Begun in 1937. Early version in *Startling,* 1948, as "Against the Fall of Night." The last men in a sand-surrounded city, a billion years from now.

(A17; B22; "The Last Castle" by Vance and "Nightwings" by Silverberg in D3.)

C12. Clement, Hal. *Mission of Gravity.* Doubleday, 1954.

The adventures of an alien ship crew sailing the seas of a high-gravity planet in search of a human rocket crashed at its south pole. Serialized in *Astounding,* 1953. Meticulously created alien environment.

(C3; C13; D2; D19.)

C13. Heinlein, Robert A. *Have Space Suit—Will Travel.* Scribners, 1958.

From 1947 to 1959, Heinlein published a juvenile science-fiction novel every year. A deliberately conceived science-fiction education in widening horizons. This charming, wayward SF fairy tale, serialized in *Fantasy and Science Fiction* in 1958, is Heinlein at his most winning. Solid.

(Williamson's "The Moon Era" in A1; A17; "By His Bootstraps" by Anson MacDonald (Heinlein) in B11; Schmitz' "The Witches of Karres" in C8B; D21.)

C14. Herbert, Frank. *The Dragon in the Sea.* Doubleday, 1956.

Serialized as *Under Pressure* in *Astounding,* 1955. Republished as *21st Century Sub.* Submarine stealing oil reserves off enemy coast in future war. Freudian questions, Freudian answers.

(C5; D5; D18.)

C15. Knight, Damon. *Hell's Pavement.* Lion, 1955.

Conditioned consumers in inverted future where economic conglomerates rule. Melodrama of underground resistance. Original paperback blurb: "A Madcap Blonde and Her Reckless Lover Challenge a World of Rollicking Chaos." Portions appeared in *Astounding* in 1952 and *Thrilling Wonder* in 1953.

(Knight stories in B16 and D28; A19; Pohl's "The Midas Plague" in C8B; C17.)

C16. Kornbluth, C.M. *The Syndic.* Doubleday, 1953.

Serialized in *Science Fiction Adventures,* 1953. Eccentric utopian future where gangsters govern. The life and death of societies. Pessimistic melodrama. Novel typical of socially oriented early fifties SF.

(C9; C15; C19.)

C17. Leiber, Fritz. *The Best of Fritz Leiber.* Ballantine, 1974.

Twenty-two short stories, three from the forties, fourteen from the fifties, five from the sixties and seventies. Alien presences, devastated landscapes, and hallucinatory beauties. Darkly romantic, often kinky.

(A6; A11; C16; D5.)

C18. Miller, Walter M., Jr. *A Canticle for Leibowitz.* Lippincott, 1959.

The struggle to survive and rebuild civilization after an atomic war, reflected in the trials of a monastic order over a period of 1,800 years. Roman Catholic postures. Hugo Award, 1961.

(A12; B8; "Nerves" by Lester del Rey in C8A; "In Hiding" by Wilmar H. Shiras in C8B; C26.)

C19. Pohl, Frederik, and C.M. Kornbluth. *The Space Merchants.* Ballantine, 1953.

Inverted future in which ad agencies control. Serialized in *Galaxy* as *Gravy Planet,* 1952. First and best example of a school of SF social satire centered in *Galaxy* in the early fifties.

(Kornbluth's "The Marching Morons" in C8A or D28; A7; Heinlein's " 'If This Goes On—' " in B13; D10.)

C20. Pohl, Frederik, and C.M. Kornbluth. *Wolfbane.* Ballantine, 1959.

Late fifties desperation; an ad hoc inverted future so strange that it becomes a reality-trip. Expansion from short serial version in *Galaxy,* 1957, was Kornbluth's last major work before his early death. May be this collaboration's best book.

(C19; C22; D12.)

C21. Russell, Eric Frank. *Wasp.* Avalon, 1957.

Saboteur on enemy planet in interstellar war. Like many of Russell's stories in the fifties, antirational, anti-authoritarian. Impudent. British.

(Russell stories in B11 (one under the name Maurice A. Hugi) and C8A; A3; B18; B1.)

C22. Sturgeon, Theodore. *More Than Human.* Ballantine, 1953.

Six people together form a higher whole. International Fantasy Award, 1954. Portion in *Galaxy,* 1952, as "Baby Is Three", reprinted C8A.

(Sturgeon story in D28; C10; C26; D11.)

C23. Tolkien, J.R.R. *The Lord of the Rings: The Fellowship of the Ring; The Two Towers; The Return of the King.* Houghton Mifflin, 1954, 1955, 1956.

The modern epic fantasy. Old-fashioned. Highly detailed secondary universe. Begun prior to World War II, many years in writing. British. International Fantasy Award, 1957.

(A6; A8; C2.)

C24. Vonnegut, Kurt, Jr. *Player Piano.* Scribner's, 1952.

Satirical view of failure of revolution against automation. Vonnegut's first and most conventional science-fiction novel.

(Forster's "The Machine Stops" in C8B; C15; C19.)

C25. Vonnegut, Kurt, Jr. *The Sirens of Titan.* Dell, 1959.

Jazzy, impudent black humor. Satire disclaiming the meaning of history. In spirit, anti-science fiction.

(C24; C18; D18.)

C26. Wyndham, John. *Re-Birth.* Ballantine, 1955.

Gentle novel about our mutant offspring after an atomic war. British.

(A12; B19; C10; D20.)

D. 1961–1974

Reactions against classic science fiction. Other worlds, exceptional worlds, and alternate realities. Rebels against the system. Seekers of truth. Pitfalls. Dead ends. Heavy changes.

D1. Aldiss, Brian. *The Long Afternoon of Earth.* Signet, 1962.

The devolution of man in a future day when the Earth no longer rotates and spider webs reach to the Moon. These connected short stories appeared in *Fantasy and Science Fiction* in 1961. Hugo Award, 1962. British. Alternate title: *Hothouse.*

(A9; A18; B22; C11.)

D2. Asimov, Isaac. *The Gods Themselves.* Doubleday, 1972.

Interplay between us in our universe and alien life forms in another universe. Asimov's first original SF novel in fifteen years. Serialized in *Galaxy* and *If,* 1972. Hugo and Nebula Awards, 1973.

("The Moon Era" by Williamson, "Old Faithful" by Gallun, "The Brain Stealers of Mars" by Campbell in A1; "Nightfall" by Asimov in B11, B16, or D28; B13; C7.)

D3. Asimov, Isaac, ed. *The Hugo Winners, Volumes One and Two.* Doubleday Science Fiction Book Club, not dated.

Contains Hugo-winning short fiction. Volume One (1962) with nine stories 1955–61. And, of particular interest, Volume Two (1971) with fourteen stories 1963–70. Chronological order. Good representative sampling.

(B16; C8A and C8B; D28.)

D4. Brunner, John. *Stand on Zanzibar.* Doubleday, 1968.

This massive novel is a portrait of an overpopulated near-future. Combines Dos Passos technique with sixties sensibility. British, but working within American SF tradition like Eric Frank Russell, Arthur C. Clarke, and Brian Aldiss. Hugo Award, 1969.

(C19; D5; D13; D11.)

D5. Burgess, Anthony. *A Clockwork Orange.* Heinemann, 1962.

Stylistically inventive vision of nasty and violent near-future. Perhaps influenced by American SF, but not written from within the modern science-fiction tradition. British.

(B15; C9; D4.)

D6. Clarke, Arthur C. *Rendezvous with Rama.* Harcourt Brace, 1973.

Except for the book connected with *2001,* the first Clarke novel in ten years. Humans investigate strange aloof ship invading our solar system. Serialized in *Galaxy,* 1973. Nebula and Hugo Awards, 1974.

(C10; Clarke stories in B16, D3 and D28; D2.)

D7. Delany, Samuel R. *Babel-17.* Ace, 1966.

Black American science-fiction writer's attempt to raise pulp space opera to literature. Concerned with language. Nebula Award, 1967.

(B18; B21; B10; D30.)

D8. Delany, Samuel R. *Driftglass.* Doubleday Science Fiction Book Club, 1971.

Ten short stories, 1967–70, including two Nebula Award winners. Like many SF works of the later sixties and early seventies, literarily ambitious. Along with Zelazny, Delany was a major new influence during the sixties.

(D7; D22; D29.)

D9. Dick, Philip K. *The Man in the High Castle.* Putnam, 1962.

Dick's theme is the nature of reality. The *I Ching* was used to write this novel of a United States that lost World War II: In the Rocky Mountain States of America, a novelist writes a book in which Germany and Japan lost World War II, using the answers of the *I Ching* to guide his writing. Hugo Award, 1963.

("By His Bootstraps" by Anson MacDonald (Heinlein) in B11; B6; B14.)

D10. Dick, Philip K. *The Three Stigmata of Palmer Eldritch.* Double-

day, 1965.
Drugs and shifting realities in an unpleasant future. This book is strange enough to scare you.
(Dick's "Faith of Our Fathers" in D28; D9; C25; D23.)

D11. Disch, Thomas M. *Camp Concentration.* Hart-Davis 1968.
Drug derived from syphilis used on protesters. Raises intelligence. Eventually deadly. This novel by an American writer with literary ambitions was serialized in the British SF magazine *New Worlds,* 1967. Ending is over-convenient.
("Descending" by Disch, "Pleasure Garden of Felipe Sagittarius" by Moorcock, and "No Direction Home" by Spinrad in D28; "Time Considered as a Helix of Semi-Precious Stones" by Delany in D3 or D8; D27.)

D12. Farmer, Philip José. *To Your Scattered Bodies Go.* Putnam, 1971.
Sir Richard Burton, the Victorian explorer, is reborn—along with all other dead humanity—in some strange otherworld. The "Riverworld" stories saw first publication in *Worlds of Tomorrow* in the mid-sixties. Hugo Award, 1972.
(Farmer's "Riders of the Purple Wage" in D3 and "Don't Wash the Carats" in D28; "Arena" by Brown in B16 or B5; "A Matter of Size" by Bates in B11.)

D13. Heinlein, Robert A. *Stranger in a Strange Land.* Putnam, 1961.
Heinlein's best-known work. A human raised on Mars returns to Earth with upsetting effect. Hugo Award, 1962.
(B12; C7; D22.)

D14. Herbert, Frank. *Dune.* Chilton, 1965.
Galactic intrigue and planetary ecology. This enormous book was serialized as two novels in *Analog,* formerly *Astounding,* in 1963–64 and 1965. Hugo and Nebula Awards, 1966.
(A2; C14; D13; D16.)

D15. Lafferty, R.A. *Fourth Mansions.* Ace, 1969.
Lafferty is unique. This strange, hyperbolic, monster-haunted Irish Catholic lie has been described as "a psychedelic morality play" by Roger Zelazny. Approach with caution, read with respect. One of the Ace Science Fiction Specials edited by Terry Carr.
(B21; B2; C22.)

D16. Le Guin, Ursula K. *The Dispossessed.* Harper & Row, 1974.
Subtitled "An Ambiguous Utopia." Subtle, bleak, pellucid novel of anarchist society. Like Lafferty, Le Guin seems ready to be discovered by a larger reading public. Hugo and Nebula Awards, 1975.
(D17; B12; D24.)

D17. Le Guin, Ursula K. *The Left Hand of Darkness.* Ace, 1969.
Taoist-influenced novel of hermaphroditic human society. Slow, clear, chilly. An Ace Science Fiction Special. Hugo and Nebula Awards, 1970.
(Le Guin story in D28; D15; D21; D22.)

D18. Malzberg, Barry N. *Beyond Apollo*. Random House, 1972.

Anti-science fiction. Two astronauts on first trip to Venus. Only one returns and he is mad. What happened? Highly reflective of its time. (A1; B4; C25; D4.)

D19. Niven, Larry. *Ringworld*. Ballantine, 1970.

The culminating novel of a young writer's Future History series. Adventure on a unique artificial world. Nebula and Hugo Awards, 1971.

("Neutron Star" by Niven in D3; A3; D6; D12.)

D20. Pangborn, Edgar. *Davy*. St. Martin's, 1964.

A young man's adventures in the countries of North America 300 years after the atomic war that destroys our civilization. Portions appeared in *Fantasy and Science Fiction* in 1962 under the titles "The Golden Horn" and "A War of No Consequence." Gentle and bittersweet. (B19; C26; C18.)

D21. Panshin, Alexei. *Rite of Passage*. Ace, 1968.

Concerned with questions of maturity. A young girl coming of age in a spaceship society. A portion appeared in *If,* 1963, as "Down to the Worlds of Men." An Ace Science Fiction Special. Nebula Award, 1969. ("Universe" by Heinlein in C8A; C4; D19; D16.)

D22. Russ, Joanna. *And Chaos Died*. Ace, 1970.

A spacewrecked castaway encounters strange human beings, and with their aid develops psi powers. A strange, demanding, ambitious and occasionally obscure novel. An Ace Science Fiction Special. (A8; B20; "The Witches of Karres" by Schmitz in C8B; C7.)

D23. Sheckley, Robert. *Mindswap*. Delacorte, 1966.

A human swaps bodies with a Martian. To get his own body back again becomes a chase through many worlds and bodies. Bizarre, humorous and satirical reality-trip. (D10; B6; C20.)

D24. Silverberg, Robert. *A Time of Changes*. Signet, 1971.

The effects of a drug on a man and his society. Reflects the impact of psychedelic drugs on America during the sixties. Serialized in *Galaxy,* 1971. Nebula Award, 1972. (Silverberg stories in D3 and D28; D21; D11.)

D25. Smith, Cordwainer. *The Best of Cordwainer Smith*. Ballantine, 1975.

Selection of short stories—cool, eccentric, legendary, remotely interconnected—by a military psychologist, Paul Linebarger, writing under a pseudonym. Unusual. Not a taste for every reader. (C11; Vance's "The Moon Moth" in C8B; D14.)

D26. Smith, Cordwainer. *Norstrilia*. Ballantine, 1975.

Like other Cordwainer Smith, this bizarre, murky and fascinating novel is about the appearance of cracks in a fossilized and ritualistic society. Written in 1960. Portion in *Galaxy,* 1964, as "The Boy Who Bought Old Earth." Portion in *If,* 1964, as "The Store of Heart's Desire."

Published as two books: *The Planet Buyer* (1964) and *The Underpeople* (1968). Now for the first time in one volume.

(D25; B12; B1.)

D27. Spinrad, Norman. *Bug Jack Barron*. Avon, 1969.

Sex, race, politics, media power and immortality in the near future. Very Now—especially if your Now is 1968. Unrestrained language. Serialized in *New Worlds,* the British SF magazine, in 1968, but very American.

(*Methuselah's Children* by Heinlein in B13; C17; stories by Ellison in D3; D4.)

D28. Spinrad, Norman, ed. *Modern Science Fiction*. Anchor, 1974.

Twenty-one stories, ten from 1934–57, eleven from 1960–71. A solid collection, with emphasis on experimental New Wave works from the sixties and on the evocative and emotional, rather than the scientific and intellectual, aspects of earlier SF.

(A1; B11; D3.)

D29. Zelazny, Roger. *Four for Tomorrow*. Ace, 1967.

Four novelettes, including a Nebula winner. Zelazny made the strongest impact of any new SF writer to appear since the early sixties. These stories demonstrate why.

(D28; D30; D8.)

D30. Zelazny, Roger. *Lord of Light*. Doubleday, 1967.

Humans playing at being Hindu gods. Charming and colorful. Portions appeared in *Fantasy and Science Fiction* in 1967 under the titles "Dawn" and "Death and the Executioner." Hugo Award, 1968.

(A10; B3; C1; D7.)

LIBRARY
AND REFERENCE
RESOURCES

BY NEIL BARRON

An active fan in the 1948–53 period, Neil Barron has retained a scholarly interest in the field. The critical guide to SF he edited, Anatomy of Wonder *(see C1 following), was widely reviewed in both general and specialty magazines and is a recognized standard. He now edits* Science Fiction & Fantasy Book Review *from his Vista, California, home.*

The library user of science fiction has always faced difficulties. Few libraries have significant holdings; few even attempt systematic collection. Of the 239 new hardcover SF titles published in the U.S. in 1978 (*Locus's* figure), few libraries acquired even ten percent, and those were probably selected on the basis of the author's name or inadequate reviews or both. Still suspect as "serious" literature, older titles are routinely discarded.

The problems begin with the selection sources. Except for books by such better-known authors as Heinlein, Clarke, or Vonnegut, few SF titles are reviewed in general or library magazines; and the reviews which do appear are brief and usually superficial. The standard selection tool for much fiction by most libraries is the *Library Journal,* which in 1979 was reviewing five to eight SF titles every other issue, or sixty to a hundred titles per year, a small fraction of the total. Paperback originals are generally ignored, and even when bought are often not catalogued because of cost. Though large libraries employ subject specialists in book selection, such expertise is not common in SF, and the choices are predictably erratic.

Standard card catalogs and indexes are likely to prove of limited value to the researcher. Science fiction as a subject heading came into use only about 1950, and library usage still varies widely. The Library of Congress, whose subject headings are widely used by academic and larger public libraries, uses the term only for anthologies or nonfiction, identifying single-author collections or novels only as "Fiction in English," a singularly unhelpful heading.

As academic acceptance of SF has grown, a number of libraries have acquired large collections. The following libraries hold relatively large collections of SF and often fantasy. They are listed alphabetically by state, Canada at the end. Fuller details regarding these collections are included in my *Anatomy of Wonder* (C1). The *National Union Catalog,* owned by large libraries, lists the reported holdings of over 700 North American libraries and may help locate specific titles, which may usually be borrowed on interlibrary loan.

University of Arizona, Tucson
California State University, Fullerton
San Francisco Public Library
University of California, Los Angeles
University of California, Riverside
University of California, Santa Cruz
University of Colorado, Ft. Collins (future wars)
University of Georgia, Athens
Northern Illinois University, DeKalb
Southern Illinois University, Carbondale
University of Illinois, Urbana (H.G. Wells)
Indiana University, Bloomington
Iowa Commission for the Blind Library, Des Moines (braille
    & recordings)
University of Kentucky, Lexington
Tulane University, New Orleans
University of Maryland, Baltimore
Boston University
Harvard University
MIT SF Society Library
Michigan State University, East Lansing
University of Michigan, Ann Arbor (imaginary voyages)
University of Minnesota, Minneapolis
Eastern New Mexico University, Portales
University of New Mexico, Albuquerque
Syracuse University, Syracuse, New York
Duke University, Dunram (utopia collection)
East Carolina State University, Greenville, North Carolina
Bowling Green University, Bowling Green, Ohio
Case Western Reserve University, Cleveland
Ohio State University, Columbus
Penn. State University, State College, Pennsylvania
Temple University, Philadelphia
Brown University, Providence (Lovecraft)
University of Tennessee, Nashville
Texas A & M University, College Station
Sam Houston State College, Huntsville, Texas
Brigham Young University, Salt Lake City
University of Virginia, Charlottesville (Cabell)

Virginia Commonwealth University, Richmond (Cabell)
University of Wisconsin, Milwaukee
Wisconsin State University, La Crosse
University of Wyoming, Laramie
Queen's University, Kingston, Ontario
Toronto Public Library, Spaced Out Library
University of British Columbia, Vancouver
University of New Brunswick, Ward Chipman Library, St. John
University of Winnepeg, Manitoba
North East London Polytechnic Library, London

Many instructors will find several paperbacks and/or one of the text/anthologies (see section F) enough for the undergraduate or high school course, with minimal library demands. College bookstores can usually acquire mass market or trade paperbacks, but these are often easiest to obtain from specialist dealers such as the F&SF Book Co., Box 415, Staten Island, New York 10302, whose catalogues list both paperback and hardcover SF, although usually excluding titles specifically aimed at the classroom or library market.

A decade ago the instructor had relatively few reference sources to which he or she could turn. The change in the past few years has been dramatic, and a large number of valuable and sometimes indispensable tools are now available for both instructors and students. Annotated below are works which instructors should at least be familiar with. The ones I judged most valuable for direct support of instruction and research are starred. Most are in print, some in moderately priced paperback editions. A few works, too important to ignore, were scheduled for publication in late Summer or Fall 1979 and are so noted.

A. History & Criticism

★1) Aldiss, Brian W. *Billion Year Spree: The True History of Science Fiction*. Doubleday, 1973. Written by a distinguished writer and critic, this is the best single critical history of SF and is essential background reading. Aldiss sees *Frankenstein* as the seminal work in the field but does not ignore earlier writings such as fantastic voyages and utopias, although he rejects the idea of a distinct continuity between such writings and more modern works. Perceptive and balanced, though the post-1950 period is treated somewhat sketchily.

★2) Amis, Kingsley. *New Maps of Hell*. Harcourt, 1960. Instrumental in gaining SF a wider and more thoughtful critical acceptance, this was one of the best of the earlier critical studies. Amis sees social criticism and satire as SF's major virtues, adventure and action as artifacts from the pulp era. The easy conversational tone and wit make it an especially enjoyable work.

★3) Ash, Brian, ed. *The Visual Encyclopedia of Science Fiction*. Harmony, 1977. A moderately detailed chronology from 1805 to 1976 in tabular form gives a synoptic overview of key books, stories, films, TV serials, and fan events. Nineteen chapters by well-known writers show how various themes have been used in SF, which will help teachers using a thematic approach. Not an encyclopedia in a true sense but still a useful and colorful survey.

4) Ashley, Mike. *The History of the Science Fiction Magazines,* volumes 1–4. New English Library, 1974–78. A valuable if largely uncritical history of English and foreign language SF magazines, each volume treating a decade beginning with 1926–35. A representative story from each year in the decade is included with bibliographies of the featured authors, notes on editors, etc. Volume 5 is awaiting a publisher.

5) Bailey, J.O. *Pilgrims Through Space and Time; Trends and Patterns in Scientific and Utopian Fiction*. Argus Books, 1947. The first scholarly and comprehensive study of what were then called scientific romances, derived from a 1934 doctoral thesis. Although the emphasis is on pre-World War I works, enough attention is paid to subsequent works to show the continuities in themes and methods.

6) Berger, Harold L. *Science Fiction and the New Dark Age*. Bowling Green University Popular Press, 1976. This groups roughly 300 works in twelve thematic categories to show the variety of treatments of dystopian themes. More inclusive than any other survey, but less analytic than Hillegas (A16) or Walsh (A32).

★7) Bretnor, Reginald, ed. *Science Fiction, Today and Tomorrow*. Harper & Row, 1974. A valuable survey of the field by fifteen writers, editors, critics and academics, twenty-one years after the editor's *Modern Science Fiction: Its Meaning and Future* appeared.

★8) Carter, Paul A. *The Creation of Tomorrow: Fifty Years of Magazine Science Fiction*. Columbia University Press, 1977. Unlike the typical fan history, which is long on plot summaries and short on critical detachment, this gracefully written and very readable account blends enthusiasm with unobtrusive scholarship to relate the thematic concerns of American magazine SF to the wider world.

★9) Cawelti, John G. *Adventure, Mystery, and Romance; Formula Stories as Art and Popular Culture*. University of Chicago Press, 1976. Especially well written, this study provides great insight into the nature of mysteries, westerns and melodramatic fiction. Cawelti's remarks are often applicable to SF and fantasy, and the book would be an excellent choice for an instructor teaching a course in popular literature.

10) Clareson, Thomas D., ed. *Many Futures, Many Worlds: Theme and Form in Science Fiction*. Kent State University Press, 1977. An

excellent selection of essays, mostly original or revised, many of them of interest to the nonspecialist.

★11) Clareson, Thomas D., ed. *SF: the Other Side of Realism; Essays on Modern Fantasy and Science Fiction.* Bowling Green University Popular Press, 1972. A balanced collection of modern criticism from academic, popular and specialist sources. Individual works and authors are discussed as well as the meaning and significance of SF in various media. Compare A19.

12) Clareson, Thomas D., ed. *Voices for the Future: Essays on Major Science Fiction Writers,* volumes 1 and 2. Bowling Green University Popular Press, 1977, 1979. The first two volumes of a series contain original critical essays about both genre and so-called mainstream writers, e.g., Vonnegut, C.L. Moore, Simak, Sturgeon, and Bradbury.

13) Clarke, I.F. *The Pattern of Expectation: 1644–2001.* Basic Books, 1979. The author of the valuable annotated bibliography, *The Tale of the Future* (C5) here provides a detailed, wide-ranging, and fascinating history of fictional speculation about the future, from the earliest works to recent SF.

★14) Franklin, Howard Bruce. *Future Perfect: American Science Fiction of the Nineteenth Century.* Oxford University Press, 1966. Revised edition, 1978. An anthology of writings by both well- and less-known nineteenth century writers (Poe, Melville, Bierce, Bellamy, Hawthorne, etc.) with excellent notes and commentary. The revisions in the 1978 edition are relatively minor, and either edition is satisfactory.

★15) Gunn, James. *Alternate Worlds: The Illustrated History of Science Fiction.* Prentice-Hall, 1975. A thorough history of the field and how it was shaped by scientific, social, and philosophical influences. Hundreds of illustrations, many in color, including several hundred photographs of SF and fantasy authors. Not a critical study like Aldiss (A1), but usefully complements him.

★16) Hillegas, Mark Robert. *The Future as Nightmare: H.G. Wells and the Anti-Utopians.* Oxford University Press, 1967. A perceptive study of Wells and his influence on writers such as Zamyatin, Capek, Forster, Huxley, Orwell, and others, including some of the better-known SF writers like Bradbury, Clarke, and Vonnegut. Compare A6 and A32.

17) Holdstock, Robert, ed. *Encyclopedia of Science Fiction.* Octopus Books, 1978. Colorfully illustrated essays by British contributors dealing with major themes of SF, films, art, magazines, etc. Somewhat similar are the books by David Kyle, *A Pictorial History of Science Fiction* (Hamlyn, 1976) and *The Illustrated Book of Science Fiction Ideas & Dreams* (Hamlyn, 1977).

★18) Kateb, George. *Utopia and Its Enemies.* Free Press, 1963. A carefully reasoned analysis of utopian thought which would be of great value in a course on utopias and which also gives insight into recurrent themes in SF, as in the works of Bellamy, Wells, and Skinner.

19. Knight, Damon, ed. *Turning Poings: Essays on the Art of Science Fiction.* Harper & Row, 1977. The twenty-three essays here were written over a 30-year period by genre authors, academics, and writers better known for their non-SF writings, such as Kingsley Amis. Similar to but not quite equal to A11.

*20) Le Guin, Ursula K. *The Language of the Night: Essays on Fantasy and Science Fiction.* Putnam, 1979. A superior collection of essays by one of the field's most distinguished writers. A number of the sixteen essays and introductions are reprinted from earlier appearances. A valuable checklist by Susan Wood of Le Guin's writings is a bonus.

21) Lundwall, Sam. *Science Fiction: An Illustrated History.* Grosset & Dunlap, 1978. An informal account from a European perspective which usefully challenges some of the conventional wisdom of works like Gunn (A15). The illustrations are often from European sources, and the multilingual bibliography will help the scholar. Lundwall wrote a similar account sans illustrations in *Science Fiction: What It's All About* (Ace, 1971).

22) Magill, Frank N., ed. *Survey of Science Fiction Literature.* Five volumes. Salem Press, 1979 (forthcoming). Patterned after *Masterplots,* this library tool contains more than 500 essay-reviews of novels, plays, and short fiction, including many works not yet translated into English. Bibliographies of criticism and reviews follow the essays.

23) Moskowitz, Sam. *Explorers of the Infinite: Shapers of Science Fiction.* World, 1963. A largely uncritical history of early SF through writers from the seventeenth century to selected writers of the thirties, with little attempt to place their work in a broader literary perspective.

24) Moskowitz, Sam. *Seekers of Tomorrow: Masters of Modern Science Fiction.* World, 1966. This sequel discussed twenty-one writers from the forties through 1965, virtually all from the pulps.

*25) Nicholls, Peter, ed. *Science Fiction at Large.* Harper & Row, 1977. Most of these eleven pieces were delivered as lectures in London to a nonspecialist audience and are of a consistently high level. The speakers included Le Guin, Brunner, Disch, Harrison, Sheckley, and Dick.

*26) Nicholls, Peter & John Clute, eds. *The Science Fiction Encyclopedia.* Doubleday, 1979 (forthcoming). The first true encyclopedia, compiled by about thirty contributors. The alphabetically arranged entries will include authors, editors, critics, illustrators, magazines, SF in various countries, etc. Instructors should find particularly valuable the 171 essays which trace through stories various recurrent themes in SF, such as mutants, aliens, time travel, etc.

27) Riley, Dick, ed. *Critical Encounters: Writers and Themes in Science Fiction.* Ungar, 1979. Nine original essays of interest to both the general reader and the specialist, they treat topics such as Herbert's

Dune, Asimov's robots and Heinlein's *Stranger in a Strange Land.* A volume in the Ungar Recognitions series.

28) Rottensteiner, Franz. *The Science Fiction Book: An Illustrated History.* Seabury, 1975. A predecessor of Lundwall (A21) and somewhat similar, although the illustrations somewhat overwhelm the text. The author wrote a useful companion work, *The Fantasy Book: An Illustrated History from Dracula to Tolkien* (Collier Books, 1978). Gunn (A15) is preferable.

*29) Scholes, Robert. *Structural Fabulation: An Essay on Fiction of the Future.* University of Notre Dame Press, 1975. Revised from four lectures, Scholes extols the potentials of SF. The first half is relatively theoretical but clear and is followed by discussions of works such as *Flowers for Algernon* and *Star Maker.* Le Guin rates a chapter.

*30) Scholes, Robert & Eric Rabkin. *Science Fiction: History, Science, Vision.* Oxford University Press, 1977. An excellent choice for an introductory text. The succinct history provides a valuable overview for the novice reader. The sciences of SF are intelligently explained using stories as examples. Vision deals with forms and themes. Ten representative novels from *Frankenstein* to Brunner's *Shockwave Rider* are the subjects of short essays.

31) Suvin, Darko. *Metamorphoses of Science Fiction; On the Poetics and History of a Literary Genre.* Yale University Press, 1979. A densely written scholarly study by the co-editor of *Science-Fiction Studies* (see G9), this is a valuable study for the specialist.

32) Walsh, Chad. *From Utopia to Nightmare.* Harper, 1962. A short survey especially valuable for its analysis of the shift from utopian to dystopian visions. More analytical than A6 but dealing with far fewer works.

B. Biography/Autobiography/Individual Author Studies

As the field ages and hopefully matures, some of the more prominent figures are writing memoirs and are the subject of essays and monographs. Excluded here are writers whose work is not published as SF, such as Vonnegut, who has been the subject of many books and articles. Two of the seminal figures in the field are mentioned, however, in this highly selective listing.

1) Aldiss, Brian W. & Harry Harrison, eds. *Hell's Cartographers: Some Personal Histories of Science Fiction Writers.* Harper & Row, 1976. Fascinating if uneven autobiographical essays by Silverberg, Bester, Knight, Pohl, and the editors. Some of these appeared earlier in *Foundation* (G6).

2) Asimov, Isaac. *In Memory Yet Green: The Autobiography of Isaac*

Asimov, 1920–1954. Doubleday, 1979. Asimov has never been modest (he would argue that he has little to be modest about), but 700-plus pages on his first thirty-four years does seem a bit much, and only diehard Asimov fans and historians will find this helpful.

3) Ash, Brian. *Who's Who in Science Fiction.* Taplinger, 1976. An unsatisfactory bio-bibliography of roughly 400 writers. Tuck (C17) and Reginald (C12) are far more thorough, but this very selective short directory might suffice for brief reference.

4) Costello, Peter. *Jules Verne: Inventor of Science Fiction.* Using primary sources, Costello presents Verne in relation to the science technology, and geographical discoveries of his time. Usefully complements the valuable biography by his grandson, Jean Jules-Verne, *Jules Verne* (1973; translation, Taplinger, 1976).

5) De Bolt, Joe, ed. *The Happening Worlds of John Brunner.* Kennikat, 1976. A valuable study of an important British writer, the subject of eight essays by specialists from different disciplines. The editor's career biography is also valuable, as is Brunner's response.

★6) De Bolt, Joe, ed. *Ursula K. Le Guin: Voyager to Inner Lands and to Outer Space.* Kennikat, 1979. A multifaceted study of the most honored writer to emerge in recent years, this includes a detailed biography and a bibliography of her works and of criticism. Compare A20.

7) Pohl, Frederik. *The Way the Future Was; a Memoir.* Del Rey/Ballantine, 1978. An influential editor as well as an excellent writer and winner of many awards, his account tells us as much about the field as about its subject. An index would have helped. Much more narrowly focussed and of interest more to the historian is Damon Knight's *The Futurians* (John Day, 1977), about a group of which Pohl was a member in the thirties.

★8) MacKenzie, Norman I. & Jean. *H.G. Wells: A Biography.* Simon & Schuster, 1973. The literature on Wells is voluminous and growing rapidly. This is probably the most satisfactory biography. Other useful studies include Bernard Bergonzi, *The Early H.G. Wells: A Study of the Scientific Romances,* University of Toronto, 1961, and Jack Williamson, *H.G. Wells: Critic of Progress,* Mirage, 1973.

Several publisher series have begun which devote individual volumes to established authors. The lengthiest series is that of the Borgo Press (Box 2845, San Bernardino, California 92406). The Milford Series: Popular Writers of Today are 64-page monographs with brief biographies and bibliographies. Featured to date have been Heinlein, Le Guin, Bradbury, Ellison, Vonnegut, Clarke, Aldiss, Delany, Lovecraft, William Morris, Tolkien, Robert E. Howard, Poul Anderson, Anthony Burgess, Frank Herbert, and Isaac Asimov. The Starmont Reader's Guides are edited by Roger Schlobin and issued by FAX Collector's Editions (Box E, West Linn, Oregon 97068). The series began in Spring, 1979 with Eric Rabkin's study of Clarke. Each of these 80-page, $3.95 paperbacks will have a biography, critical introduction, chronology, discussion of the major novels and short fiction, an annotated bibliography, and subject, name, and title indexes. The core analyses are about the same length as the Borgo series. Taplinger's Writers of the 21st Century series are full-length books similar to those of De Bolt (B5, B6). Edited by Joseph Olander and Martin Harry Greenberg, volumes devoted to Clarke, Asimov, Heinlein, and Le Guin have already appeared, with Bradbury and Dick scheduled for publication. The reference book publisher, G.K. Hall, Boston, is planning a Masters of Modern Science Fiction and Fantasy series edited by L.W. Currey. Essays and articles as well as books about individual authors are indexed in Tymn and Schlobin (C21).

C. Bibliographies and Indexes

★1) Barron, Neil, ed. *Anatomy of Wonder: Science Fiction.* Bowker, 1976. A critical guide to the field for libraries, fans, and any interested reader. Narrative historical essays precede each annotated bibliography. About 1,000 adult, 100 juvenile and 150 works of nonfiction are annotated with first purchase recommendations starred. A variety of reference aids are included. This chapter necessarily drew on the guide for 1975 or earlier works.

2) Bleiler, Everett F. *The Checklist of Science-Fiction and Supernatural Fiction.* Firebell Books (P.O. Box 804, Glen Rock, New Jersey 07452), 1978. This revision of the 1948 checklist deleted improper titles and added others. Approximately 5,600 titles in English from 1764 through 1948 are included. Primarily of interest to the collector or historian. Largely superseded by Reginald (C12).

3) Briney, Robert E. & Edward Wood. *SF Bibliographies.* Advent, 1972. The majority of the items listed were fan-produced and are unavailable today. Many are badly dated or obsolete. For the specialist only.

★4) Clareson, Thomas D., ed. *Science Fiction Criticism: An Annotated Checklist.* Kent State University Press, 1972. A listing of over 800 items from academic and popular sources, excluding fanzines, and an essential retrospective guide. Continued by C21.

5) Clarke, I.F. *The Tale of the Future from the Beginning to the Present Day: An Annotated Bibliography.* Second edition. Library Association (London), 1972. The annotations are very brief in this list of about 1,200 utopian, political, and scientific romances published in Britain from 1644 to 1970. Clarke's narrative history (A12) is far more readable and is derived from this bibliography.

★6) Contento, William. *Index to Science Fiction Anthologies and*

Collections. G.K. Hall, 1978. Almost 12,000 English language stories by 2,500 authors in almost 2,000 books are indexed by author, editor, story title, and book title. The original source in a magazine or original anthology is also shown. Particularly valuable for the instructor attempting to locate a source for a specific story.

7) Currey, L.W. *Science Fiction and Fantasy Authors: A Bibliography of First Printings of their Fiction and Selected Non-Fiction.* G.K. Hall, 1979 (forthcoming). An antiquarian bookman thoroughly familiar with enumerative bibliography has produced an invaluable work listing about 6,200 printings and editions of more than 215 authors, noting the points essential to identify them. Scrupulously accurate (98 percent of the books were personally examined), the coverage extends through 1977, and the work will become a standard for the collector. Although having a somewhat different purpose, it heavily overlaps Reginald (C12) and Bleiler (C2).

8) Franson, Donald & Howard DeVore. *A History of the Hugo, Nebula, and International Fantasy Awards.* Misfit Press (4705 Weddel St., Dearborn, Michigan 48125), 1978. This November, 1978, revision of the standard awards list includes an author/editor index. Awards given through 1975 are listed in C1.

9) Hall, H.W., comp. *Science Fiction Book Review Index, 1923–1973.* Gale Research, 1975. Almost 14,000 book reviews of 6,900 books appearing in SF magazines since 1923 and in general reviewing media since 1970 are indexed in this important tool. A useful appendix records full details for all SF magazines for the fifty years. The first four of the compiler's continuing annuals are included in this cumulation. The annuals are available from the compiler, 3608 Meadow Oaks Lane, Bryan, Texas 77801.

★10) Inge, M. Thomas, ed. *Handbook of American Popular Culture.* Volume 1. Greenwood, 1979. A fascinating compilation of synoptic overviews on such topics as automobiles, children's literature, comic art, popular music, the pulps, TV, etc. The chapter on SF is by Marshall Tymn and provides a historic outline, bibliographic essays on reference works, research collections, histories, and criticism, concluding with a bibliography. An important handbook for anyone interested in popular culture.

11) Negley, Glenn. *Utopian Literature; A Bibliography, With A Supplementary Listing of Works Influential in Utopian Thought.* Regents Press of Kansas, 1978. Annotated listing of 1,232 entries. Largely omitted are SF works of the past fifteen years. Of some use for the scholar, but Sargent (C14) is much preferable.

12) Reginald, Robert, comp. *Science Fiction and Fantasy Literature and Contemporary Science Fiction Authors II.* Two volumes. Gale Research, 1979 (forthcoming). A major bibliography of almost 16,000 English language books from 1700 through 1974 and a biographical directory of 1,443 modern SF and fantasy writers, replacing the au-

thor's *Stella Nova* (1970), reprinted as *Contemporary Science Fiction Authors* (Arno, 1974). This will largely replace C1 and heavily overlaps C7 and C13.

13) Rock, James A., comp. *Who Goes There.* Author (Box 1431, Bloomington, Indiana 47402), 1979. A specialized bibliography of over 10,000 books and 2,000 magazine stories by authors who have published at least some of their work pseudonymously. Listed by author, then chronologically under each name used. Heavily overlaps C7, C12 and C23.

14) Sargent, Lyman Tower. *British and American Utopian Literature 1516–1975: An Annotated Bibliography.* G.K. Hall, 1979. A major bibliography of approximately 1,600 entries, including short fiction (mostly SF), each annotated and with a library holding code. Equally valuable are the unannotated entries for about 600 books and 1,600 articles in various languages. Much preferable to Negley (C11).

15) Schlobin, Roger C. *The Literature of Fantasy: A Comprehensive, Annotated Bibliography of Modern Fantasy Fiction.* Garland, 1979 (forthcoming). Since the related genre of fantasy is often studied in conjunction with SF, this work should prove most helpful. The 1,248 descriptively annotated entries include over 800 authors and editors, 244 collections, 100 anthologies, with about 3,600 short stories mentioned but not annotated. Comprehensive author and title indexes. Compare Tymn (C18).

16) Suvin, Darko. *Russian Science Fiction 1956–1974: A Bibliography.* Dragon Press, 1976. A valuable English language checklist for the specialist, including an annotated checklist of criticism in Russian and English books and periodicals.

17) Tuck, Donald H., comp. *The Encyclopedia of Science Fiction and Fantasy Through 1968.* Volumes 1 & 2. Advent, 1964, 1968. The first two volumes are a who's who, with a title index in Volume 2. Brief biographical details are followed by detailed bibliographies, showing contents of collections and anthologies, foreign language editions, pseudonyms, etc. Long a standard, it is inevitably getting dated and now has competitors (see especially C7, C12, C13 and C23). Volume 3 is in preparation.

18) Tymn, Marshall, comp. *Fantasy Literature: A Core Collection.* Bowker, 1979 (forthcoming). Designed partly as a companion to C1, this guide annotates 240 titles from the nineteenth century to date, adult and juvenile (C15 generally omits juveniles). Extensive series of reference aids. Compare C15 and C22.

19) ————, Martin H. Greenberg, L.W. Currey & Joseph D. Olander. *Index to Stories in Thematic Anthologies of Science Fiction.* G.K. Hall, 1978. Indexes 181 anthologies under fifty subject headings (anthropology, history, etc.), of which 167 are in C6. If you use fiction to teach a subject discipline (other than literature), this should prove helpful, as many anthologies are now published for such disciplines.

★20) —————, Roger C. Schlobin & L.W. Currey, comps. *A Research Guide to Science Fiction Studies; An Annotated Checklist of Primary and Secondary Sources for Fantasy and Science Fiction.* Garland, 1977. Annotates over 400 works, from the very general to the very specialized, published through 1976 in the U.S. and England. Subject bibliographies, anthology and magazine indexes, histories, critical studies are among the types of works annotated, including many of the works in this chapter. Over 400 doctoral dissertations are listed but not annotated, many of them far removed from SF. A subject index would have improved this guide.

★21) ————— & Roger C. Schlobin. *The Year's Scholarship in Science Fiction and Fantasy: 1972–1975.* Kent State University Press, 1979. A revised and updated cumulation of four bibliographies which appeared in *Extrapolation* (G1). The entries are grouped into general studies, bibliography and reference, author studies and bibliographies, and teaching aids. Coverage is limited to American and British journals and selected fanzines as well as books, doctoral and selected master's theses, and A/V materials, the last especially valuable for instructors. An invaluable supplement to C4. Appears annually in *Extrapolation;* future cumulations are planned.

★22) Waggoner, Diana. *The Hills of Faraway; A Guide to Fantasy.* Atheneum, 1978. Although the discussion of SF is limited, this provides a useful companion guide to fantasy. The book's core is the annotated bibliography of 996 entries, listing novels, collections, and some short stories and articles. Many works are juveniles having adult appeal as well. Compare C15 and C18.

23) Wells, Stuart W. III, comp. *The Science Fiction and Heroic Fantasy Author Index.* Purple Unicorn Books (4532 London Rd., Duluth, Minnesota 55804), 1978. Useful for quick reference, this lists roughly 5,000 titles published in the U.S. from 1945 through mid-1978. Anthologies and juveniles are excluded. Useful series information. Its currency is its major merit. Compare C7, C12 and C17.

D. SF Illustration

The content and nature of cover art and interior illustrations of SF books and magazines is dictated more by commercial considerations (newsstand sales) and convention (spaceships, rayguns, alien monsters—the usual iconography) than by the traditions of fine art. An opaque overhead projector can be very effectively used to display SF illustrations. Many picture books have appeared in recent years, each heavily overlapping one another. In addition to those few annotated below, many other works are extensively illustrated and may easily suffice for most instructors. These include A3, A15, A17, A21, A28.

★1) Aldiss, Brian W. *Science Fiction Art*. Crown, 1975. An oversize paperback which includes the work of thirty American and British illustrators from the twenties through the early seventies, showing, describing, and contrasting their individual techniques and strengths. The covers of seventy-nine magazine titles are shown. The commentary is informed and often witty.

2) Frewin, Anthony. *One Hundred Years of SF Illustration, 1840–1940*. Pyramid, 1975. A useful historical survey emphasizing the twenties and thirties, with over forty covers reproduced in color, some full-size. Succinct, intelligent text which relates SF illustration to its historical context.

3) Summers, Ian, ed. *Tomorrow and Beyond: Masterpieces of Science Fiction Art*. Workman, 1978. Ignoring the hyperbole of the subtitle, this assembles over 300 color illustrations from sixty-seven primarily American artists whose works appeared on mass-market paperbacks of the seventies, LP jackets, in articles, etc. Unforgivably lacks any biographical information about the artists, and the text is meager.

E. SF Film & TV

Given the nature of cinema, the emphasis in almost all SF film or TV programs has been on the visually dramatic, and few of the subtleties of the printed text have been apparent on the screen. Awards are usually given for special effects, not for acting, although *Charly* (based on Keyes' *Flowers for Algernon*) brought its lead actor an Oscar. Most books have been as thin as the films, picture books with vacuous text. The serious student should find the books annotated below of help as well as the specialized quarterly journal, *Cinefantastique* (1970-plus, ed. by Frederick S. Clarke, Box 270, Oak Park, Illinois 60303).

1) Baxter, John. *Science Fiction in the Cinema*. Barnes, 1970. A helpful British survey of the field, including SF for TV. Bibliography and filmography, plus many stills. The author thinks SF is inherently unsuited for the cinema.

2) Gerani, Gary & Paul H. Schulman. *Fantastic Television*. Harmony, 1977. All types of fantastic programs on American TV are discussed from the forties to 1976. Informed and judicious, with many illustrations, and well-indexed and organized.

3) Johnson, William, ed. *Focus on the Science Fiction Film*. Prentice-Hall, 1972. The essays span the 1895–1970 period and represent American, British, and European viewpoints about the origin and development of the SF film, its relation to other kinds of film and to SF writing, and its aesthetic values. Filmography, bibliography.

4) Strick, Philip. *Science Fiction Movies*. Octopus (London), 1976. The best primarily pictorial survey by a knowledgeable British critic

NEIL BARRON

who discusses 400-plus films. The thematic approach usefully contrasts with that taken by Brosnan (E5).

★5) Brosnan, John. *Future Tense: The Cinema of Science Fiction.* St. Martin's, 1979. The British seem to have monopolized the writing of intelligent criticism on SF films, and this is the best book of its sort, judicious, informed, and often very witty. Although there are some small black-and-white illustrations, this is engaging history and analysis and should become the standard for some years.

F. Teaching Aids/Writer Guides

The number of books and A/V aids designed for direct classroom use is growing rapidly, and no survey can begin to be comprehensive. The structure and content of the course will heavily dictate the type of materials used. Very helpful for background reading is A30, perhaps supplemented by A1 or A15. Because libraries usually have very inadequate SF holdings, assigned readings present a problem, and asking a student to buy a dozen novels (assuming they are in print) is a questionable and expensive strategy. The most common approach is to assign either a text/anthology designed for classroom use, or select an anthology of outstanding stories for discussion and analysis. Theme anthologies are increasingly common as SF is used in various subject disciplines in addition to literature (see C19). My *Anatomy of Wonder* annotates some of the better efforts in this area, some of which I've repeated below.

1) Allen, Dick, ed. *Science Fiction: the Future.* Harcourt, 1971. *Looking Ahead: The Vision of Science Fiction.* Harcourt, 1975. Designed mainly for freshman or introductory courses, the selection is broad, eclectic, and includes poetry and articles as well as fiction.

2) Allen, L. David. *Science Fiction Reader's Guide.* Centennial Press, 1974. Originally issued in 1973 as *Science Fiction: An Introduction* in the Cliff's Notes series. A later, similar book is Allen's *The Ballantine Teacher's Guide to Science Fiction: A Practical Creative Approach to Science Fiction in the Classroom* (Ballantine, 1975). All include typologies, lists of recommended books and more extended analyses of selected works (the Ballantine guide discusses only Ballantine paperbacks, but the books are quality titles anyway).

3) Calkins, Elizabeth & Barry McGhan. *Teaching Tomorrow: A Handbook of Science Fiction for Teachers.* Pflaum/Standard, 1972. The high school teacher should find this short paperback useful for its basic background information, study guides, case studies, and annotated lists of critical works and novels.

★4) Clareson, Thomas D., ed. *A Spectrum of Worlds.* Doubleday,

1972. Each of the stories, which represent the history and development of the field, is paired with a critical essay about it.

5) Gunn, James E., ed. *The Road to Science Fiction.* Mentor Books, 1977 & 1979. A three-volume chronological text/anthology by a knowledgeable professor of English at Kansas. Volume 1 runs from Gilgamesh to Wells, Volume 2 from Wells to Heinlein, Volume 3 to the present.

6) Lawler, Donald L., ed. *Approaches to Science Fiction.* Houghton Mifflin, 1978. An oversize paperback text/anthology with a perceptive introduction, useful headnotes, questions, etc. A balanced selection representing many of the most common themes.

★7) Spinrad, Norman, ed. *Modern Science Fiction.* Anchor, 1974. Twenty-one stories interspersed with commentary, often trenchant.

8) *Science Fiction: Jules Verne to Ray Bradbury.* Center for the Humanities, 2 Holland Ave., White Plains, New York 10603. One of the better A/V introductions, the LPs and cassettes are supplemented by three carousels containing 240 slides. The voice narration was written by Dick Allen, who wrote the accompanying teacher's guide. For additional citations to the many A/V materials, see C21.

Workshops and courses dealing with the writing of SF have become common in recent years. A number of writer guides have been published, and these can be used both in creative writing courses as well as supplements in courses emphasizing history and criticism.

★9) Bretnor, Reginald, ed. *The Craft of Science Fiction,* Harper & Row, 1976. A valuable series of essays by SF veterans on how SF is written as distinct from how to write it.

10) de Camp, L. Sprague & Catherine C. *Science Fiction Handbook Revised.* Owlswick Press, 1975 (hardcover). McGraw-Hill, 1977 (paper). A sensible, no-nonsense approach to writing and selling SF, particularly of the traditional sort.

11) *Intersections: The Elements of Fiction in Science Fiction.* Bowling Green University Popular Press, 1978. The ten chapters treat topics such as plot, character, setting, point of view, etc., using SF stories as examples. Compare F12.

12) Wilson, Robin Scott. *Those Who Can: A Science Fiction Reader.* Mentor, 1973. Twelve writers accompany their short stories with essays on plot, character, setting, theme, point of view, and style.

G. Magazines

The original pulps from which so much was reprinted after World War II are increasingly scarce and very expensive. Some microform reprints are available from Greenwood Press, University Microfilms and Oxford Microforms Ltd., and a few hardcover reprints have been issued. Industrious fans have thoroughly indexed the SF and fantasy magazines, although few libraries contain back files. The principal indexes include:

1) Day, Donald B. *Index to the Science Fiction Magazines, 1926–1950.* Perri Press, 1950. The pioneering and still standard work, long out of print.
2) Metcalf, Norman, *The Index of Science Fiction Magazines, 1951–1965.* J. Ben Stark, Berkeley, California, 1968.
3) Strauss, Erwin S., comp. *The MIT Science Fiction Society's Index to the S-F Magazines, 1951-1965.* MIT SF Society, 1966.
4) New England Science Fiction Association. *The NESFA Index to the Science Fiction Magazines and Original Anthologies.* 1976 and 1977 indexes available; cumulative index for 1966–75 in preparation Summer, 1979. Box G, MIT Branch PO, Cambridge, Massachusetts 02139.

See also Contento (C6), who relied on the above indexes and who thus provides a periodical index for reprinted stories. A4 and A8 also provide useful historical background on magazine science fiction.

Excluding the so-called prozines (those which publish most of the magazine fiction) and the more ephemeral fanzines, there are several magazines which the instructor should be familiar with:

★5) *Extrapolation,* ed. by Thomas D. Clareson, 1959-plus. Quarterly. $15/year (libraries), $10 (individuals). Kent State University Press, Kent, Ohio 44242. The first academic journal devoted to the field, it went from semi-annual to quarterly publication in Spring, 1979. Articles, bibliographies, and reviews, mostly by academics.
6) *Foundation; the Review of Science Fiction,* ed. by Malcolm Edwards. 1972-plus. Three issues yearly. $7.50/year. North East London Polytechnic, Longbridge Rd., Dagenham, Essex RM8 2AS, England; checks payable to Science Fiction Foundation. The leading British journal, containing excellent articles, reviews and letters, well-edited and lively. G.K. Hall reprinted issues 1–8, 1972–75, in one volume.
★7) *Locus,* ed. by Charles N. Brown. 1968-plus. Monthly. $12/year (individuals). Box 3938, San Francisco, California 94119. Subtitled *The Newspaper of the Science Fiction Field,* this is a valuable primary source for information about publishing, writers, markets, books, and films. The monthly book listings in recent years provide relatively comprehensive coverage of SF and fantasy books distributed in the U.S. Gregg Press reprinted the 1968–77 issues in two volumes. A recent competitor, a spinoff from *Starship* (G10), is *Science Fiction Chronicle,* ed. by Andrew Porter. Monthly. $12/year (individuals). *Starship* Magazine, Box 4175, New York, New York 10017.

★8) *Science Fiction & Fantasy Book Review*, ed. by Neil Barron. February, 1979-plus. Monthly. $12/year (individuals). Borgo Press, Box 2845, San Bernardino, California 92406. With the demise of the *SF Booklog, Science Fiction Review Monthly* and *Delap's F&SF Review*, the field needed a comprehensive review. Each 16-page issue features seventy-eighty succinct reviews, the length based on the work's importance. Reviewed are originals and reprints, adult and juvenile, hardcover and paperback, including selected foreign language titles not yet translated. Occasional short articles complement the reviews. Since no other magazine publishes more than 150 reviews annually, this should prove useful to a variety of audiences. Annual index in December issue, and indexed by Hall (C9).

9) *Science-Fiction Studies*, ed. by Darko Suvin & Robert Philmus. 1973-plus. Three times yearly. $8/year (individuals). English Dept., Loyola Campus, Concordia University, Montreal, Quebec H4B 1R6. A valuable journal for the specialist which includes a number of translated articles and provides an international perspective. Gregg Press reprinted selected articles from 1973–75 and 1976–77 issues.

10) *Starship; The Magazine About Science Fiction*, ed. by Andrew W. Porter. 1963-plus. Quarterly. $8/year (individuals). P.O. Box 4175, New York, New York 10017. The title changed from *Algol* in Spring, 1979. A thoroughly professional and well-designed magazine which includes articles, interviews, columns, letters, commentary, and considerable advertising in an interesting blend aimed primarily at fans but of value to the scholar. A good choice for an undergraduate collection.

INDEX

Harness, Charles L., 60, 232
Harrison, Harry, 248
Herbert, Frank, 60, 132-133, 140-141, 236, 239
Heinlein, Robert A., 56, 134-135, 232, 235-236
High School, 82-96
Hillegas, Mark R., 97-101, 246
Hogan, James, 133, 135
Holdstock, Robert, 246
Howard, Robert E., 53
Huxley, Aldous, 229

Inge, Thomas M., 251
Intelligence, artificial, 132-133

Jenkins, William Fitzgerald, 53

Kateb, George, 246-247
Klass, Philip, 56
Knight, Damon, 56, 236, 247
Kornbluth, C.M., 56-57, 236
Kuttner, Henry, 57, 232

Lafferty, R.A., 63, 239
Le Guin, Ursula K., 21-25, 63, 239-240, 247
Leiber, Fritz, 57, 134, 236
Leinster, Murray (William Fitzgerald Jenkins), 53
Levin, Ira, 127
Lewis, C.S., 229
Libraries, 243-244
Lindsay, David, 229
Linebarger, Paul, 61-62, 240-241
Livingston, Dennis, 200-202
Logic, 181
Longyear, Barry B., 75-81
Lovecraft, H.P., 53
Lundwall, Sam, 247

MacKenzie, Norman I. & Jean, 249
Magill, Frank N., 247
Magazines, 256-258
Masquerade, 225
McGhan, Barry, 82-96
McIntyre, Vonda, 190-193
Malzberg, Barry N., 240
Miller, Walter M., 60-61, 236
Merritt, A., 53, 229
Metaphysics, 181

Minicon, 219-227
Moskowitz, Sam, 247
Monroe Community College, 104-105
Moore, C.L., 53, 229
Multimedia, 224
Myers, Robert E., 177-183
Myth, 98-99

Nichols, Peter, 247
Niven, Larry, 63, 240
Norton, Andre (Alice Mary Norton), 61

Orwell, George, 162-164

Pangborn, Edgar, 61, 240
Panshin, Alexei, 63, 240
Panshin, Alexei and Cory, 52-64, 228-241
Philosophy, 177-183
Plank, Robert, 157-167
Poe, Edgar Allan, 49
Poetry, 5, 16-17
Pohl, Frederik, 57, 147, 236, 249
Political science, 145-156
Popular culture, 17
Pratt, Fletcher, 231-232
Primary school, 75-81
Psychology, 157-167
Pulps, 35

Rabkin, Eric, 248
Reading lists, 16, 86, 196
Religion, 168-176
Realism, 10, 46, 159
Riley, Dick, 247-248
Robots, 4, 125-126, 128-130
Rottensteiner, Franz, 248
Russ, Joanna, 63-64, 240
Russell, Eric Frank, 57, 237
Russian science fiction, 17

Sagan, Carl, 1-8
Samuelson, Dave, 194-196
Schlobin, Roger, 253
Schmidt, Stanley, 110-120
Schmitz, James H., 61
Scholes, Robert, 248
Science, 110-120
Science Fiction Research Association, 18, 21
Science Fiction Writers of America, 18
Sheckley, Robert, 61